THE
CHRISTIAN
TRAVELERS GUIDE TO

GREAT
BRITAIN

D0803064

IRVING HEXHAM, GENERAL EDITOR
written by IRVING HEXHAM

ZondervanPublishingHouse
Grand Rapids, Michigan

A Division of HarperCollins*Publishers*

This series of books is an unintended consequence of serious academic research financed by both the University of Calgary and the Social Sciences and Humanities Research Council of Canada. Both institutions need to be thanked for the support they gave to the original academic research that allowed some of the authors to visit many of the places discussed in these books. Professor David Martin deserves special thanks for his suggestions about London and Oxford.

The Christian Travelers Guide to Great Britain
Copyright © 2001 by Irving Hexham

Requests for information should be addressed to:

▨ ZondervanPublishingHouse
Grand Rapids, Michigan 49530

Library of Congress Cataloging-in-Publication Data
Hexham, Irving, 1957-.
    The christian travelers guide to Great Britain / Irving Hexham, general editor.
        p.   cm.
    ISBN: 0-310-22552-3 (softcover)
    1. Great Britain—Guidebooks. 2. Christians—Travel—Great Britain—
Guidebooks. 3. Christian antiquities—Great Britain—Guidebooks. 4. Great
Britain—Church history. I. Hexham, Irving.
DA650.C55 2001
263'.04241—dc21
                                      00-051263
                                          CIP

Interior design by Todd Sprague

Printed in the United States of America

01 02 03 04 05 /❖ DC/ 10 9 8 7 6 5 4 3 2 1

About the Writer

Irving Hexham is professor of religious studies at the University of Calgary, Alberta, Canada. He obtained his Ph.D. in history from the University of Bristol and is the author of seven books, including two written with his wife, Karla Poewe.

http://www.christian-travelers-guides.com

Visit our Web site for even more information. You'll find:

- Links to many of the cities and sites listed in our guidebooks
- Information about Christian hotels and bed and breakfasts
- Lists of English-speaking churches so you can plan where to worship
- Information about evangelical organizations in each country
- Diagrams comparing different architectural styles
- Examples of Christian art
- Brief essays on topics of interest to Christian scholars and travelers
- Readings from key historical texts
- Suggested readings for daily devotions as you travel around Europe

Plan your next trip with
http://www.christian-travelers-guides.com

"In an era that often overlooks the significance of the past as such, and certainly the Christian past, Professor Hexham's well-crafted guides for heritage tourists truly fill a gap. Don't leave home without one!"

> **J. I. Packer**
> **professor, Regent College, Vancouver,**
> **author of *Knowing God***

"Using vacations to discover the riches of the Christian tradition is a great idea that's long overdue."

> **Bruce Waltke**
> **professor, Regent College, Reformed Theological Seminary,**
> **and a member of the *NIV* translation team**

"At last! A guidebook which treats churches as windows onto the living faith of Christianity and not just as museums or graveyards. These books bring church history alive."

> **David V. Day**
> **principal, St. John's College, University of Durham**
> **and frequent broadcaster on the BBC**

"Excellent...we can all learn from these books."

> **Terry Muck**
> **professor, former editor-in-chief of *Christianity Today***

Contents

Preface

Remember how the LORD your God led you.

Deuteronomy 8:2

The task of history . . . is to establish the truth of this world.
Karl Marx (1955:42)

Memories of paintings, sculptures, museums, churches last a lifetime.
Edith Schaeffer—*The Tapestry*

Our series of books is designed to awaken an awareness of Europe's Christian heritage among Protestant, particularly evangelical Christians, although we hope all Christians and others who are simply interested in Christianity will also find them helpful. Anyone visiting a large bookstore will quickly discover that it is possible to buy travel guides with titles like *Pagan Europe, Occult France, Magical Britain,* and *The Traveler's Guide to Jewish Germany,* alongside more traditional travel guides which attempt to take in everything worth seeing. Yet even books like the *Frommer's, Fodor's,* and *Rough* guides, although they mention Christian places and events, tend to underplay the Christian contribution to Western Civilization through neglect or a negative tone. Therefore, our guides have

been written to correct what we see as a major oversight in existing works.

Our series is concerned with people and events of historical significance through their association with particular places. Thus we attempt to locate the development of ideas which have changed the world through their relationship with people and places. Consequently, we suggest visits to particular places, because by visiting them you can gain a better understanding of the times when important events took place.

The central theme of these books is the contribution of Christianity to Europe and the world. But not everyone discussed in these books was Christian. Indeed, many of the people we mention were strongly anti-Christian. Such people are included because it is impossible to understand our own times without

7

appreciating the destructive forces that have attempted to replace Christianity by secularism and neopagan religions.

HISTORY AND MEMORY

Christianity is rooted in history. The New Testament begins with a genealogical table that most modern readers find almost incomprehensible (Matthew 1:1–17). The purpose of this genealogy is to locate the birth of Jesus in space and time according to the standards of Jewish history. The appeal to "the first eye-witnesses," in the prologue to the gospel of Luke, is also clearly intended to engage the skepticism of Greco-Roman readers by providing specific historical data against which ancient readers could weigh the writer's claims (Luke 3:1–2). The Gospels contain many references to historical data and specific geographic locations. So important is historical truth that its denial becomes a mark of heresy for New Testament authors (1 Corinthians 15:1–8; 1 John 4:1–3).

Clearly, the Bible is steeped in history and the remembrance of history. Both the Old and New Testaments constantly reminded their readers about particular historical events (cf. Deuteronomy 4:9–14; Acts 7). Thus, parents are commanded to teach their children the significance of history (Deuteronomy 6:4–25) both by retelling the story and through commemorations which enact the central acts of salvation (Exodus

13:3–16; 1 Corinthians 11:23–26). Further, an appeal is frequently made to visible memorials that remind people of God's wonderful deeds (Acts 2:29–36). We also find both Jews and early Christians visiting historic sites as acts of devotion (Luke 2:21–41; Acts 21:17–27).

The importance of history, and the way in which we remember past events, is recognized by many influential opponents of Christianity. Karl Marx, for example, argued that the ability to control history, or rather the interpretation of history, was an essential step in the abolition of religion. Almost a century later, Adolf Hitler made a similar appeal to history and historical necessity. Both Marx and Hitler, following in the footsteps of Enlightenment skeptics like Tom Paine, sought to establish the truth of their revolutions by denying the validity of Christian history.

Our books are, we hope, a small contribution to the reestablishment of a sense of history and cultural pride among Christians. Following the biblical model, we believe that visiting places and seeing where great events took place help people remember and understand the present as well as the past (Joshua 4:1–7). It is our hope that these books will bring history alive, and with a sense of history a growing awareness of the realities of faith in our world. As Francis Schaeffer loved to point out, there is a flow to history because Christian faith is rooted in space and time. To forget our history is the first step to the abandonment of our faith, the triumph of secularism, the ascendancy of New Age spirituality, and the rebirth of paganism.

SEEKING SPIRITUAL ROOTS

The great truth of the New Testament is that Christians are children of God by adoption. Today many people have forgotten that the New Testament preaches the revolutionary doctrine that our relationship to God is not through physical descent, but by adoption (Romans 8:23; Galatians 4:5; Ephesians 1:5).

The implications of this doctrine are profound. All Christians are united by bonds of faith and love, not physical relationships (Ephesians 2). Thus, Christianity is not a tribal religion rooted in local communities bound by kinship bonds. Rather, it is a world faith that unites all believers.

Repeatedly, both the Old and New Testaments point to examples of faith which we are encouraged to follow and remember (Joshua 4; Luke 11:29–32; Acts 7; Hebrews 12). Remembering acts of courage and obedience to God strengthens our own faith. This fact was long recognized by the leaders of the church. Throughout history, Christians have told and retold stories of courage and faith. Yet today these stories are all but forgotten. Lives of the saints which were once standard texts for every educated person and pious believer are now rarely read, and books like *Foxe's Book of Martyrs* (1563) are almost completely forgotten.

Today, Christians are quickly forgetting their rich spiritual heritage as Christian biographies are replaced in popular culture by secular gossip. Popular magazines, radio, and television are full of "lives." But they are the lives of pop singers, film stars, television personalities, and secular politicians. Instead of teaching spiritual lessons, they repeat trivia and revel in scandal. Something has been lost. And it is this something that can be recaptured by Christians who begin to search for their spiritual roots.

Visiting Great Britain to learn about great acts of faith can be a rewarding experience, and it is something all Christians, regardless of race or nationality, can find profitable. This spiritual quest helps us see our own lives in perspective and understand our times against a much greater backdrop than tonight's television news. That is the quest that this book encourages you to begin.

Part I

BRITISH HISTORY

AN OVERVIEW OF BRITISH HISTORY

Archaeologists have found evidence of human settlement in London that date back to around 250,000 B.C., but these remains are fragmentary and isolated. Not until about 40,000 B.C. does fairly extensive evidence of human activity appear, showing that there were cave dwellers as far apart as Derbyshire, Kent, and Somerset. It is reasonable to assume, however, that most of these early communities died out as a result of the last Ice Age that began 17,000 years ago. Later, around 6000 B.C., the British isles as we know them today were created as a result of the gradual melting of the icecaps and glaciers, causing a steep rise in sea level.

About 5000 B.C. various nomadic groups crossed over from continental Europe to occupy Britain, bringing with them domestic animals and an elementary technology. They cleared land, built villages with defensive palisades, and operated shallow mines and at times large quarries for flint and other types of stone. The construction of Stonehenge and other monuments began around 2500 B.C., with the growth of an extensive trade and organizational network. Burial mounds such as those found at Avebury, Wiltshire, Mase Howe, and the Orkneys were also built during this period.

The so-called "Beaker people," named after their distinctive pottery traditions, who seem to have originated in Spain, arrived around 700 B.C. bringing with them more advanced mining techniques. They also seem to have continued the tradition of building stone circles and were responsible for the final phase of Stonehenge. Their language forms the basis of English due to its Indo-European roots that contained words like *mother* and *father*.

The Celts began to arrive in Britain shortly after the Beaker people and are thought to have come from Ireland. Their language was significantly different from that of the Beaker people as was their more advanced technology that included chariots and the use of iron weapons. With the Celts came the Druids.

Although a lot has been written about the Druids and many guidebooks talk about their sophisticated religious beliefs and practices, we actually know very little about them apart from what was recorded by Roman writers. According to the Romans, they were a cruel, evil, hierarchical priesthood that practiced human sacrifice and other atrocities. Today, many people dismiss these reports, claiming that they are simply Roman propaganda written to justify their occupation of Celtic lands. This is not an entirely convincing argument, because the Romans had no qualms about occupying the lands of people they saw as a military threat and do not make similar comments about the religious practices of other nations they conquered.

Julius Caesar (100–44 B.C.) briefly explored parts of southern Britain in 55 B.C. It was not until A.D. 43 that a major invasion force landed under the Emperor Claudius, leading to the conquest of most of what is now England. Two things motivated the Romans to invade Britain. First, they believed that the islands were rich in precious metals. Second, and more importantly, there was always the danger of a major revolt

against Roman rule by the Celtic tribes of France as long as their kinsmen in Britain remained free. After the initial invasion, the Romans made treaties with British kings and built several garrison towns to establish their control over southern England and most of Wales. Then, in A.D. 61, the Iceni, a Celtic tribe led by their Queen Boadicea (d. 62), revolted after almost 20 years of peace. They slaughtered Roman garrisons and sacked towns under Roman control. This led to a swift and brutal reaction that caused the Romans to consolidate their hold on Britain by establishing more garrison towns and military outposts.

It was not until around A.D. 80 however that the whole of Wales and the north were firmly under Roman control. Governor Gneaus Julius Agricola (37–93) built a ditch and defensive wall across the north of what is now Scotland between the river Clyde and the Firth of Forth. The north of Scotland was sparsely inhabited, bleak, and without mineral or other riches; therefore the Romans decided against a full-scale invasion. Forty years later the Emperor Hadrian decided to withdraw Roman forces from what are now the lowlands of Scotland and built a second defensive wall linking the North Sea and Solway Firth between what are today Newcastle and Carlisle. Under Roman rule Britain prospered, with cities like London, Chester, York, and Carlisle becoming the centers of rich Roman culture. The height of Roman influence in Britain was reached in the 3rd century.

Later in the 4th century, seaborne raiders from northern Europe and the Baltic lands began to disturb the Roman peace. At the same time, Rome's defenses were under attack along a long land frontier. At first the Romans employed Saxon and other auxiliary troops to defend outposts of the Empire, like Britain. Then, in 410, the Romans made the fateful decision to withdraw their legions for the defense of Rome itself and Roman areas in continental Europe.

Following the withdrawal of the legions, Saxon raids increased, and Saxon settlers began to arrive in Britain. Not long ago this period of British history was almost a complete fog. But intense archaeological work over the past 30 years has begun to reveal a fascinating and complex picture. Earlier writers believed that as the Saxons raided and then settled in Britain all vestiges of Roman life and culture were destroyed. Now it is generally agreed that the process of settlement was much more complex. In some areas, such as around Carlisle in Cumbria, Roman influence continued to be strong for centuries, with Saxon settlers quickly adapting to Romanised British ways, possibly because some of them first arrived as auxiliary troops when the Romans still ruled Britain.

Whatever the exact nature of the Saxon invasion, it is clear that in some areas new settlers met bitter resistance from local people, who in some cases may themselves have had Saxon origins. Fifty years ago most historians said that the legendary King Arthur was an entirely fictitious figure invented in the Middle Ages. Today, it is generally agreed that he was a real person who emerged as a British warlord, or even king, sometime after the departure of the legions. Whatever Arthur did to impede the advance of invading Saxons came to naught at the Battle of Dyrham, near modern Bath, in 577, when four British kings were killed and the native army annihilated. From that time on, the Saxons controlled most of Britain except a few parts of Wales and Cumbria, until they too were displaced by the Normans in 1066.

During the 6th century, several Saxon kingdoms emerged to dominate different parts of Britain, including what are now the lowlands of Scotland, and within a relatively short time all became Christian. The most important of these kingdoms were Northumbria, in the northeast, Mercia in central England, East Anglia in the southeast, and Wessex in the southwest. In the northern parts of Scotland and parts of Wales, remnants of pre-Roman and Romanised Celtic culture survived in isolated pockets. By the 8th century, the kingdom of Mercia had become the most important Saxon realm, but following the death of its able King Offa (d. 796), Wessex emerged as the main Saxon kingdom. In

825 Egbert, the king of Wessex, was able to demand allegiance from all other kings and kingdoms, making him the first real king of England.

Disaster struck Saxon England in 793 when without warning pagan Viking raiders destroyed the monastery of Lindesfarne in Northumbria, signaling the beginning of almost 300 years of destructive raids and gradual Viking settlement. In 865 a large Danish invasion force landed in East Anglia and began to subdue Saxon England. It met with fierce resistance from the Christian king of Wessex, Alfred the Great (849–99), who combined military skill with pragmatic diplomacy and an enlightened policy aimed at the education of his people.

After Alfred's death the situation deteriorated, but in 973 the king of Mercia, Edgar, was able to gain control over all the other kingdoms and was the first person to be crowned king of England. Following his death, the situation deteriorated again until the Saxon parliament, the Witan, invited the Danish king, Canute (995–1035), to become ruler. His sons succeeded him only to be replaced by a Saxon, Edward the Confessor (d. 1066). Edward was succeeded by the unfortunate Harold (d. 1066), who was immediately challenged by a Danish invasion in the north and a Norman invasion in the south of his realm. Harold marched north and defeated the Danes near York. He then made a remarkable march south and met the

Normans at Hastings, where he was killed and his army scattered.

William I (1027–87), duke of Normandy, an illegitimate who was called both William the Bastard and, more deferentially, William the Conqueror, then imposed his brutal rule on Saxon England, creating a French-speaking ruling class that dominated the towns and countryside from strong castles. Initially, the Normans used prefabricated wooden fortresses that were quickly erected to control key areas. These were replaced by stone keeps and later castles, as time permitted. Norman rule was accompanied by a deliberate policy of obliterating Saxon culture through the destruction of churches and sacred shrines and their replacement with Norman buildings and shrines. In most cases, the abbots and higher clergy of local monasteries, churches, and cathedrals were replaced by Normans. Peasants were driven off the land to create vast hunting areas like the New Forest, while draconian laws were enforced to prevent Saxons from hunting for deer and other wildlife.

Initially there was strong resistance from many Saxons as exemplified by the long struggle of Herward the Wake (d. 1071) and the later legends of Robin Hood. Nevertheless, within three generations considerable intermarriage appears to have taken place, and slowly the Norman overlords and their retainers blended into a greater English society. By the early 13th century it is no longer possible to talk about a "Norman yoke." Rather, England had become English.

Wales, which was never conquered by William I, managed to retain considerable independence for almost 400 years until it was merged with England by Henry VIII's Act of Union. Initially isolated from England by the establishment of a strong frontier area, Wales was brutally conquered by Edward I (1239–1307), who first built a chain of strong fortresses around the coast to control key ports and then gradually extended his rule inland through roads, forts, and strong points. Edward met with strong resistance from Prince Llywelyn (d. 1282), who was eventually defeated and executed before the Treaty of Rhuyddlan was imposed on Wales.

A rebellion broke out in 1294 in reaction to the harsh conditions and arrogance of English rule. It was led by Madog ap Llywelyn (d. 1294) and quickly crushed, leading to even harsher English rule. This led to yet another revolt, this time led by Owain Glyndwr (1354–1416), who proclaimed himself prince of Wales. He succeeded in winning a series of victories against the English when his followers slaughtered English lords and peasants alike along a broad border area. Although he was initially successful and gained the recognition of France and Scotland, he was eventually defeated in 1408, and the independence of Wales was once again brutally crushed.

Scotland fared far better than Wales in escaping the clutches of Norman rule. In 1057 Malcolm III (d. 1093), known as Canmore, which means "bighead," who had spent 17 years in exile at the Saxon court in England, defeated his enemy Macbeth, about whom Shakespeare wrote his famous play, and established himself as king. He introduced the notion of a hereditary kingship and feudal rights to Scottish society and secured his throne by confiscating the land of Macbeth's supporters and giving it to loyal Norman and French knights who had assisted him in his bid for power. After the death of his first wife, he married Margaret, the sister of the Saxon King Harold, who fled to Scotland after her brother's death. She began a series of reforms that finally brought the Scottish Church in line with Rome, thus ending its long association with Celtic Christianity. By establishing an effective administrative system and founding numerous churches and monasteries, Margaret transformed Scottish religious life. She also led the resistance to English rule and died while commanding the defense of Edinburgh Castle. Other secular reforms led to the founding of a series of new towns and the encouragement of trade, which effectively broke the power of the clans.

In 1286 the Scottish king, Alexander III (1241–86), died, leading to a dispute about his succession. This gave Edward I of England the opportunity he had longed for, and he helped John de Balliol

(1249–1315) gain the throne as his vassal. Discontent followed, leading Balliol to forge an alliance with France and renounce his allegiance to Edward. Edward, in turn, invaded Scotland, defeated Balliol, and ruthlessly dealt with all opposition. His tyrannical rule led to a revolt by William Wallace, who created a major problem for the English occupation army. Eventually, however, he was betrayed, dragged off to London, and cruelly executed in 1305. Now Robert the Bruce saw his chance and had himself proclaimed king in 1306. Fortunately for him, Edward died the following year to be succeeded by his much weaker son, Edward II. In 1314 Bruce decisively defeated the English army at the Battle of Bannockburn, and Scotland asserted its full independence from England with the Arbroath Declaration in 1320.

Civil wars in England, the Hundred Years' War with France that began in 1337, and the Black Death in 1349 secured Scottish independence and dominated English history until 1381, when the Peasants' Revolt saw the first major revolt by English peasants against their rulers. Initially successful, the revolt was soon suppressed with great slaughter and brutality. Another major peasants' revolt, known as Jack Cade's Rebellion, broke out in 1450, followed by a series of civil wars, the War of the Roses, which began in 1455 between the forces allied to the House of Lancaster and the House of York. This time of trouble and constant unrest was brought to an end

by the defeat of Richard III at the Battle of Bosworth Field in 1485 when Henry Tudor, Henry VII (1457–1509), proclaimed himself king of England.

Although a Lancastrian, Henry VII wisely married Princess Margaret of York, thus uniting the two warring dynasties and launching Tudor rule that was to last for over 100 years of relative peace and prosperity. Henry VII's son, the infamous Henry VIII (1491–1547), divorced his wife Catherine of Aragon (1485–1536) in 1533. The English Reformation followed during the reign of his son, Edward VI (1537–53), followed by a ruthless counter-Reformation under his half-sister Mary Tudor (1516–58), who, although a Roman Catholic, began the English conquest and settlement of Ireland. Eventually relative calm returned to England during the reign of Elizabeth I (1533–1603). Under Elizabeth the British settlement of North America was begun. Trade with India, which eventually led to the growth of the Indian Empire, also started. Elizabeth gave peace to her grateful subjects. Meanwhile, English pirates, led by such national heroes as Sir Francis Drake (1540–96), John Hawkins (1532–95), and Sir Walter Raleigh (1554–1618), plundered and raped their way around the Caribbean, Spanish, and Portuguese settlements of Central and South America.

English sea power reached its climax with the defeat of the Spanish Armada in 1588. The Armada was an invasion force intent on conquering England to bring an end to English piracy. Through a combination of skill and luck, the Armada was crushingly defeated. Once the Spanish fleet was destroyed and the danger of invasion over, Elizabeth refused to allow her victorious sailors to come ashore, keeping them at sea for months until most had died of starvation or scurvy. This harsh measure was taken to prevent any possible resistance to her rule by a group known to favor Puritanism that had close ties to Dutch rebels, who were republican. To make matters worse, Elizabeth refused to pay widows' pensions to the families of those who died fighting the Armada. These harsh facts were, however, quickly overlooked in the national myth of a victorious Protestant queen, which Elizabeth promoted at home.

From the time of Edward I of England, in the 13th century, the Scots faced constant harassment and regular invasion by English kings. The dynasty founded by Bruce lasted until 1371 when it was succeeded by the Stewarts (which became the Stuarts). Because of the early deaths of a number of kings, necessitating rule by regents during the minority of the successor, the power of the Scottish monarchy was seriously weakened. James IV stabilized the situation but was killed during the massacre known as the Battle of Flodden Field, when an English army annihilated the Scots. A few decades later, the week-old

Mary Stewart (1542–87) was proclaimed queen, and in 1554 her French mother, Mary of Guise, became regent. Always alert to an opportunity, Henry VIII attempted to arrange the betrothal of his son Edward VI to Mary. But, as a good Roman Catholic, the Scottish regent rejected this idea, leading to a series of English raids that devastated southern Scotland. The net result was that the Scots sought an alliance with France, and Mary was duly betrothed to the dauphin in return for military support. Thus in 1548 Mary sailed for France, where she received her education and appeared to have been very happy. At age 16, she married Francis II, the 14-year-old king of France, and all seemed to be going very well.

In 1560 Francis died and Mary, a very young widow of 17, was returned to Scotland, where the Reformation was in full swing and anti-French feeling was running strong. Backed by English arms, a rebellious group of nobles, calling themselves the Lords of the Congregation, had deposed the regent and established their own rule under the guise of acting on Mary's behalf. Consequently, when Mary returned she found a very changed country where the power of the monarchy was at a low ebb. Mary sought a compromise with her Protestant subjects but made a disastrous marriage to the politically inept dandy Lord Darnley. Soon disillusioned, she appears to have taken an Italian lover, David Rizzio, who became her chief advisor.

Darnley arranged for Rizzio to be dragged from Mary's chambers, where they were eating supper, and murdered in a vicious attack where he was stabbed 56 times. Shortly afterwards, in 1567, Darnley was murdered. Without remorse, Mary immediately married the earl of Bothwell, who was believed to have killed Darnley.

This caused an uproar and Mary, who was only 25 years old, was forced to flee from a popular revolt against what had become her corrupt and inept rule. Foolishly, she went to England hoping for support from her cousin Elizabeth I. The queen recognized Mary's potential for rallying discontented Catholic lords and promptly placed her under house arrest. Mary remained a prisoner for the next 20 years. Finally, Elizabeth decided to execute her on trumped-up charges of plotting a rebellion after her own position was secured by the defeat of the Spanish Armada.

Back in Scotland, the regency was assumed by Mary's illegitimate half-brother, the earl of Moray, with her infant son, James VI (1567–1625), as the nominal king. James was given a firm Protestant upbringing by Presbyterian tutors, whom he appears to have loathed. Back in England, Elizabeth continued to rule until her death in 1603 as a highly popular monarch who had given the country the prosperity which comes from stability and peace. According to arrangements made before her death, James VI of Scotland now assumed the throne of England as James I (1567–1625), thus uniting the two countries under a common crown. The attempt by Guy Fawkes (1570–1606) to blow up the Protestant Parliament, thus making way for the return of Roman Catholic rule, prevented James from relaxing laws against Roman Catholics and ensured that he remained firmly Protestant.

During his reign the colony of Virginia was founded in 1608. The Pilgrims emigrated to America in 1620, beginning a process of mass emigration of over 100,000 English people, mainly Puritans, to settle in America. Roman Catholics who also wanted greater religious freedom created the colony of Maryland.

James was succeeded by his son Charles I (1600–1649), who lacked even his father's limited discretion and relied on increasingly unpopular favorites. When Charles imposed the English prayer book on the Scottish Church in 1637, the nobles responded by signing a national covenant and denouncing the imposition of "popery." Charles denounced the Covenanters as rebels but was unable to effectively act against them. The Covenanters responded by raising their own army, and Charles called the English Parliament to finance a war against his Scottish subjects. But the new Parliament was dominated by Puritans, who shared many of the concerns of the Scots. Consequently, they refused to go along with the king's plans and began passing legislation limiting his power.

Charles responded in 1642 by moving to Nottingham, where he raised his banner and declared war on Parliament. The first English civil war had begun. Many nobles who had military training and were able to finance their own troops gave him an initial advantage, leading to a Royalist victory at the Battle of Edgehill. Dismayed, the Parliamentarians regrouped, and under Oliver Cromwell (1599–1658), the New Model Army, known as the Ironsides, was formed. Cromwell defeated Charles at the Battle of Marston Moor and then decisively at the Battle of Naseby. The Royalist army disintegrated, and Charles fled to Scotland, where he was imprisoned before being surrendered to the English. Initially, Cromwell and his supporters were inclined to cooperate with the king. But soon it became clear that he was plotting with Scottish sympathizers to raise a new army and defeat the Parliamentarians. Charles was tried for high treason, found guilty, and executed in January 1649.

The struggle against Parliament now transferred to his son Charles II, who succeeded in raising a Scottish army and invading England. Cromwell drove it back and defeated the Scots near Dunbar, causing Charles to become an exile and leaving Cromwell to create the Commonwealth, which he ruled after taking the title "the Lord Protector."

Although personally tolerant, Cromwell was dogged by the fact that many of his supporters were religious fanatics who sought to reform the Church of England "root and branch" while totally transforming English society in a revolutionary manner. Consequently, he trod a narrow path that required the support of the army for his moderate and essentially progressive rule. A new university at Durham was established, several colleges created, and schools opened to teach all children, boys and girls, to read. Numerous social reforms and humane welfare programs were created while cruel sports like bear bating were outlawed. Yet to no avail. Rebellions in Ireland led to bloody reprisals that blacken Cromwell's name to this day. Worst of all, his able son-in-law, Henry Ireton (1611–51), died of fever in Ireland, leaving no obvious successor to the Lord Protector following his relatively early death.

After deliberations, the army under General Monck (1608–70), backed by Parliament, naively invited Prince Charles to return to England and assume the crown in the apparent belief that things would continue more or less as before under a monarch. As soon as Charles II (1630–85) was enthroned and in power, he moved quickly to undo the legacy of the Commonwealth. Cromwell's body was removed from Westminster Abbey, publicly displayed, and beheaded. His head was placed on a spike overlooking the Palace of Westminster, where it remained for the next

20 years. Durham University was closed, as were other Puritan-founded schools and colleges, social reforms were abandoned, and rich landowners once more asserted their power over the common folk. Most of the men who had signed Charles I's death warrant were arrested, summarily tried, and horribly executed. Puritan books were banned and preachers expelled from their churches. Many Puritans fled to America; others went into hiding, only to be hunted down. A few, like John Owen (1616–83), the chancellor of Oxford, and the poet John Milton (1609–74), managed to vanish undisturbed, possibly because Charles is rumored to have personally liked both men and their writings, even though he strongly disagreed with their views.

The next 20 years saw a return to all the excesses that led to the Civil War. A corrupt court, flagrant abuse of the law by the nobility and wealthy landowners, and a gradual move within the Church of England toward Roman Catholicism enraged many people. Plague struck in 1665, devastating much of Europe and decimating England's population. A year later the Great Fire of London destroyed over 80 percent of the medieval city. James II, James VII of Scotland (1633–1701), succeeded his brother in 1685, and the simmering discontent erupted with the rebellion of the duke of Monmouth, one of Charles II's illegitimate sons. His ragtag army was decimated by forces loyal to the king at the Battle of Sedgemoor in July 1685. This led to the bloody reprisals meted out by Judge Jeffreys and his so-called "Bloody Assizes," which executed and deported hundreds of people whether or not they really were rebels.

In 1687 James enacted the Declaration of Indulgences, removing all restrictions on Roman Catholics. This led to a protest by seven Church of England bishops, who were immediately arrested on a charge of "seditious libel." Popular support forced James to release them after their acquittal. At this crucial time James's wife had a son, thus ensuring the succession of a Roman Catholic king. This was too much for most Englishmen, and a delegation from Parliament was sent in 1688 to William of Orange (1650–1702), inviting him and his Protestant wife, Mary (1662–94), the daughter of James II, to assume the throne. After some units of the English army began to desert and join the Dutch forces of William, who landed at Torbay in Devon, James panicked and fled to France. Thus England was spared a third civil war, and Parliament could confidently proclaim that the king had abandoned his subjects, thereby signifying his abdication.

The arrival of William and Mary, who were jointly crowned, was hailed as the "Glorious Revolution" of 1688 and seen as an event that restored liberty and good government to England. Before William and Mary were crowned, however, legislation was passed to limit the powers of the monarch as well as prevent a Roman Catholic, or anyone married to a Roman Catholic, from ever becoming king or queen of England. The reign of William and Mary, who were not personally liked, saw the beginning of England's constitutional monarchy and the growth of Parliamentary government. William and Mary were succeeded by Queen Anne (d. 1714) in 1702.

Five years later the Scottish Parliament, by a majority of 41 votes, passed the Act of Union with England, uniting not only the crown but also both parliaments. Anne was childless, so after her death in 1714, the succession passed to George I (1660–1727), duke of Hanover. This provoked the first Jacobite uprising in Scotland that aimed to enthrone James Stuart, who is known as "the Old Pretender." After capturing Perth, the rebels were quickly defeated and James retreated to France.

A period of relative calm and prosperity followed, largely as a result of the decision of George I to remain out of politics and leave the day-to-day affairs of state to his able minister Robert Walpole (1676–1745), who is often called the first British prime minister. In 1745 the peace was brought to an abrupt end during the reign of George II when Charles Stuart (1720–88), "the Young Pretender" who is also known as "Bonny Prince Charles," landed in Scotland to lead the second Jacobite rebellion. This time the rebels had more success and

managed to march as far south as Derby, where they were confronted by a superior Loyalist army. The rebels fled back to Scotland pursued by the duke of Cumberland (1721–65), who engaged them in a battle that turned into a bloody slaughter at Culloden in April 1746. Following his victory, Cumberland ruthlessly subdued Scotland, building new roads and fortifications to prevent further rebellions. The political power of the clan system was destroyed, and both the playing of bagpipes and wearing tartans were banned.

George III (1738–1820), who became king in 1760, was soon confronted by the American Revolution, which began in 1776. The Industrial Revolution, which was launched by the building of the Bridgewater Canal in 1765 and the invention of the spinning jenny in 1787, followed. At the beginning of the 19th century, England emerged victorious from the Napoleonic Wars, and a new order was imposed on Europe. At home, the release of a large number of soldiers and sailors from the army and navy led to mass unemployment and social unrest, with the monarchy reaching an all-time low in popularity.

The young Queen Victoria (1819–1901) assumed the throne in 1837 with her able and intelligent German husband, Prince Albert (1819–61), as consort. Her long reign saw the formal establishment of the British Empire, which had been growing steadily for two hundred years, and the rapid growth of Britain as the world's leading industrial power. A series of able prime ministers, including William Gladstone and Benjamin Disraeli, added to the successes of Victorian Britain. They passed a series of Reform Bills beginning in 1867 that eventually created a parliamentary democracy.

The 20th century began well but soon disintegrated into the chaos of World War I following the assassination of Archduke Ferdinand, the heir to the Austrian throne, in Sarvajevo by Serb fanatics. The subsequent slaughter in the trenches wiped out a generation of leaders and left England decisively weakened at the end of the war in 1918. After the formal armistice, harsh terms were imposed on Germany that led some British leaders, like Lord Keynes and General Smuts, to argue that a French desire for revenge and American naivete had laid the foundations for a future war. Their dire warnings came only too true in 1933 with the seizure of power by Hitler and the Nazis.

The war came in 1939 with the German invasion of Poland and left England exhausted financially, hastening the end of the British Empire. During the war, Germany had recruited over 40,000 Indian servicemen from among Indian prisoners of war to serve in the German Army as a "liberation force" against British imperialism. At the end of the war, the British government decided to court-martial and execute as traitors all Indian officers and a large number of Indian troops who had served under German command. Some Indian historians claim that over 10,000 men were shot after summary court-martials. More than anything else this act, which was justifiable in terms of British law, provoked a bitter reaction in India, turning many moderate nationalists into committed opponents of British rule. The result was Indian independence in 1948.

After World War II, a succession of socialist Labor and paternalistic Conservative governments oversaw the dismantling of the Empire, with the last major African countries gaining their independence in the mid-1960s. At home Parliament created the welfare state and enacted far-reaching educational reforms that included the creation of a series of "new universities" in the 1960s. Increasing trade union militancy led to some crippling strikes in the 1970s and the gradual economic decline of Britain. Great Britain joined the European Common Market relatively late, in 1973, after a long debate.

This trend toward socialism was drastically stopped and then reversed by the election victory of Margaret Thatcher (b. 1925) in 1979. Her 13 years in power transformed English society, creating a new British version of capitalism. She was followed by another conservative, John Major, who was eventually defeated in 1997 by a newly reformed Labor Party under Tony Blair, who modeled his success on Bill Clinton. Since then Britain has been ruled by an economically conservative but socially left-wing government that has overseen the devolution of political power to Ireland, Scotland, and Wales, including the reestablishment of a Scottish Parliament, which many see as the beginning of the breakup of the United Kingdom.

CHRISTIANITY IN BRITAIN

Christianity arrived in Roman Britain with soldiers, traders, and missionaries early in the 1st century. It quickly spread throughout the entire country, with the first Christian martyr, St. Alban, being executed in 209. By the time the Roman legions withdrew from Britain in 410, the country seems to have been fairly well evangelized, with three British bishops attending the Council of Arles in 314.

Pagan Saxon invaders caused extensive destruction throughout Britain, and for many years it was believed that they wiped out native British Christianity. Recent excavations, however, suggest that after the initial wave of destruction, many Christian communities survived and were gradually incorporated into Saxon society. Nevertheless, the conversion of the Saxons dates from the baptism of the king of Wessex by the German missionary Brinus (d. 650). Around the same time, in 597, St. Augustine of Canterbury arrived with a mission to the court of King Ethelbert (560–616) of Kent, who was married to a Frankish Christian princess. Shortly afterwards, Ethelbert and his nobles were baptized. Further north, in Northumbria, King Edwin (c. 585–633) also married a Christian princess, who insisted that he embrace her religion. On July 21, 625, Edwin was baptized with his leading nobles. Thus, as Richard Fletcher points out in his *Pagan Conversions* (1999), within a few years the leading figures in the main kingdoms of England all embraced Christianity.

It is easy to scorn these dynastic conversions as acts of political expediency. But, as Fletcher reminds us, many of these new converts were soon asked to die for their faith, and their children and grandchildren went on to display unusual devotion and dedication to the Christian mission. Nevertheless, the Christianity they embraced was very different from that recognized by many people today. Slavery was accepted, and both polygamy and the keeping of concubines were tolerated. Many parish priests were married men whose children inherited both their calling and their church buildings, and most people believed in the healing powers of saints and holy relics. Nevertheless, despite these glaring differences, there were many similarities, as anyone who reads Bede (673–735) knows.

The Venerable Bede entered the small monastery of Jarrow in Northumberland as a child and spent his life at the monasteries of Wearmouth and Jarrow, where he devoted himself to scholarship. He is best remembered for his classic work *The Ecclesiastical History of the English People,* which gained him the title "the Father of English history." He became one of the leading Christian scholars in Europe, writing dozens of works that kept Christian learning alive for centuries.

Anyone who reads Bede's biblical commentaries, many of which have been recently translated into English by the Cistercians, is immediately struck by the contemporary relevance of his writing and his warm evangelical faith. From his style and insightful comments, it is clear that he could easily be the pastor of a large American Baptist church. Yet there are some things in his works that many Baptists would not appreciate, such as his love of stories about the healing power of God and other contemporary miracles that make him sound like a charismatic. His love of the sacraments and high view of the church, although not overly stressed, would also cause some concern. Nevertheless, anyone who is comfortable reading C. S. Lewis finds in Bede a similar understanding of Christianity that is remarkable in the way it spans the centuries.

This period was a golden age of Christian mission in Britain. Numerous British missionaries like Boniface (680–754) evangelized large areas of Europe. Later men like Alcuin of York (735–804) provided the leadership and educational skills needed to revitalize the church in Western Europe.

All of this came to an end with the Viking raid on Lindesfarne in 793, marking one of the darkest eras of Christian history in Britain. For the second time in 1000 years, pagan invaders began to eradicate Christianity. Carefully organized military and diplomatic resistance by able and wise kings like Alfred the Great (849–99) meant that within two centuries many of the invaders had become Christians. As a result, by the year 1000, England was once more an essentially Christian country. Saxon Christianity was shattered by a third wave of invaders, the Normans, in 1066. This time the invaders were Christian. Nevertheless, they often went to great lengths to obliterate Saxon Christianity, destroying many churches and local communities that they then replaced with their own churches, castles, and towns.

Medieval Christianity in Britain was both dynamic and superstitious. Many elements, such as the adoration of saints' relics and masses for the dead, strike Protestants as particularly unbiblical. Therefore, it is important to place the development of the church in England against the background of the times and constantly remember the chaos caused by repeated pagan invasions and centuries of social and economic unrest. It is against this background that the work of Archbishops Anselm of Canterbury (1033–1109), who played an important role in developing Christian philosophy, and William of Wykeham (1324–1404), who helped create solid academic traditions, needs to be seen. Wykeham became chancellor of England in 1367, a post similar to that of the modern prime minister, and used his ecclesiastical and political power to encourage learning by founding schools and colleges. Although his work was not particularly evangelical, it was men like him who laid the necessary foundations for the revival of learning that took place in the 16th century, leading to the Reformation.

The work of John Wycliffe (1330–84) in the 14th century and the spread of his teachings by the Lollards testify to the dynamic character of English Christianity and the growth of grassroots opposition to the established church. Similarly, writers like Aelred of Rievaulx (1109–67) and Julian of Norwich (1342–1416) tell us a lot about popular piety in England prior to the Reformation. Aelred came from a line of ministers who served the church in Hexham at a time when clergy were allowed to marry. Things changed during his lifetime when his father and mother were forced to separate and enter monasteries while he became a Cistercian monk and eventually the abbot of Rievaulx.

Henry VIII strongly rejected Protestant teachings and in 1521 was even declared Defender of the Faith by the pope for his attack on Luther's teachings. However, in 1533, he lost all real religious zeal when he decided to divorce his wife, Catherine of Aragon, thus launching one of the biggest land grabs in history.

A commission was established in 1535 under Thomas Cromwell (1485–1540) that oversaw the dissolution of smaller monastic houses in 1536 on the grounds that they bred ignorance and immorality. Their lands and buildings were seized and the spoils divided between the king, his nobles, and members of the local gentry, many of whom suddenly found themselves far richer than before. These actions led to a revolt, known as the Pilgrimage of Grace, by peasants of northern England, who were genuinely shocked by the king's impious and cruel acts. The revolt was brutally crushed. Henry then moved against the larger monasteries, which were also dissolved after a mock inquiry by Thomas Cromwell and his commission in 1530. Together the closing of monastic houses are known as the Dissolution.

Although praised by many Protestant historians in the past, the Dissolution can only be seen as outright theft by a greedy king supported by most of his nobles and local gentry, who enriched themselves in the process. Unlike the Reformation in Germany, where monks and nuns willingly left their monasteries after responding to the preaching of the gospel and Luther's teachings, the Dissolution was forced on monastic houses in England against the will of most of their occupants. They were often thrown out of their homes as old people, turning hundreds of monks and nuns into destitute beggars. Leaders who resisted, or who like Sir Thomas More (1478–1535) simply refused to approve of Henry's actions, were given mock trials and executed, creating a number of Roman Catholic martyrs in the process.

At the same time the schools, hospitals, and other charitable institutions run by the monasteries were often closed, thus depriving the common people of much-needed educational, medical, and welfare systems. The fact that most of the schools, hospitals, and eventually charitable institutions were later reopened under secular patronage does not justify Henry's actions.

The English Reformation proper began in 1547 with the reign of Henry VIII's son, Edward VI (1537–53). He permitted the marriage of priests in 1549 and appears to have been a pious Christian who genuinely believed in Protestant teachings. During his reign the English Church was thoroughly reformed, and the beautiful Anglican prayer book was composed by Archbishop Thomas Cranmer (1489–1556) in 1552. At the same time a movement for even further reforms slowly began to take root. This movement was based on the teachings of the Swiss-based, French Reformer, John Calvin (1509–64), and it eventually became known as Puritanism. Edward's short reign ended with his death from TB in 1553, which brought his half-sister Mary Tudor (1516–58) to the throne.

Abandoned by her father when he divorced her mother and forced by him to publicly acknowledge that she was a bastard as a condition for receiving even a minimum of support, Mary was a hardened and bitter woman devoted to Catholicism. Although she married, she was childless, and appears to have died of stomach cancer. During her short reign she did all in her power to return England to the Roman Catholic fold. Protestant leaders and laity alike were arrested, tortured, tried, and burnt at the stake in London and Oxford. London's Smithfield Market alone saw over 300 Protestants die at the stake rather than renounce their faith.

The fury of Mary's vicious attack on Protestants, the courage of those who died, and the spread of biblical teachings led to a widespread revulsion against the queen's fanaticism. Her subjects nicknamed her "Bloody Mary" for the number of people whose blood she spilt in the name of her religion. The net result was that Mary's efforts to reestablish Roman Catholicism ensured that the people of England would remain staunchly Protestant for centuries. A refugee from Mary's brutality, John Foxe (1516–87) began to collect and record the stories of those who died.

After her death he returned to England, collected more testimonies, and published his *Acts and Monuments of Matters Happening in the Church,* commonly known as his *Book of Martyrs* (1563), which became a standard work in educated English homes.

Mary was succeeded by her half-sister, Elizabeth I (1533–1603). Throughout her long reign Elizabeth attempted to heal the wounds in English society opened by both her father and sister. Her greatest achievement was the so-called "Elizabethan settlement" based on an acceptance of the *Book of Common Prayer* and the 39 Articles of 1563. These measures allowed for a modified form of Protestantism and limited toleration of Roman Catholics and other dissenters, provided they kept their religion strictly private.

Following Elizabeth's death, James VI of Scotland became James I of England to the joy of many Puritans, who expected him to initiate further reforms of the church along the Scottish model. But James had other ideas and quickly began to suppress Puritanism. However, he did commission the translation of the Bible, thus creating what in England is known as the Authorized Version and in North America as the King James Version of the Bible, which was published in 1611. Eventually, under his successor, Charles I, the English Civil War was fought and the king defeated, bringing about a short period of Puritan rule under Oliver Cromwell, who refused the crown, preferring instead to be called "the Lord Protector."

After the death of Oliver Cromwell, a vicious reaction set in. Over 2000 Puritan preachers were ejected from their parishes as a result of the Act of Uniformity (1662), which imposed the Anglican *Book of Common Prayer* and various other restrictions upon them. The Five Mile Act of the same year and other pieces of legislation, strict censorship, and partisan attacks on the Puritans and their teaching ushered in a 20-year period of persecution during which many Puritans emigrated to America. The attempt of James II to reintroduce Roman Catholicism failed and led to the Glorious Restoration, when the Calvinist William of Orange was invited to become king of England.

Following the Restoration, the lot of evangelical Christians greatly improved, although the 18th century proved to be an irreligious and impious age. At this time Deism thrived as a rational alternative to Christianity. Later, after the electors of Hanover became kings of England, Deism began to take root in Germany through the University of Göttingen, which was under Hanoverian control.

Religious revivals in Germany, associated with Pietism, spread to England, where they took root following the conversion of John Wesley (1703–91) by Moravian Pietists in London in 1738. The conversion of his brother Charles (1707–88) and several other gifted individuals, like George Whitefield (1714–70), led to vigorous evangelistic campaigns and the conversion of large numbers of people from all walks of life. Although many of these converts joined Wesley's Methodist movement, and later various branches of the Wesleyan or Methodist Church, many others did not; rather they remained in the Church of England. The winds of revival spread through Scotland and Wales and continued well into the 19th century, totally transforming English life and society.

The first British missionary society was the Society for the Promotion of Christian Knowledge founded by Bishop George Berkeley (1685–1753) in 1698 to evangelize North American natives. It was followed by the Society for the Propagation of the Gospel in 1701. These efforts quickly lost momentum, and it wasn't until the publication of *An Enquiry into the Obligations of Christians to Use Means for Conversion of the Heathen* (1792) by a shoemaker, William Carey (1761–1834), and the creation of the Baptist Missionary Society, which he helped found in the same year, that the idea of foreign missions began to take root amongst English Protestants. The Anglicans responded by founding the London Missionary Society in 1792, and the Methodists founded the Wesleyan Missionary Society in 1814. These English efforts, which usually involved sending Scottish or Dutch missionaries to dangerous places, spurred on conti-

nental Christians and led to the founding of the Basel Mission in 1815, followed by numerous other missions throughout Europe.

Prompted by the same zeal for the gospel, other groups in England, often involving the same people as those who set up the missionary societies, engaged in a wide range of reform programs. Thus, John Wesley, followed by Thomas Foxwell Buxton (1786–1845), William Wilberforce (1759–1833), and a small but dedicated group of friends known as the Clapham Sect, agitated for numerous social reforms, including the abolition of slavery, which took place in all British-controlled territories in 1833.

From the start, evangelical reformers and missionaries met dogged resistance from entrenched interests. Initially their opponents, particularly proponents of slavery, argued that Africans had no soul. The publication of Charles Darwin's (1809–82) *Origins of the Species* in 1857 gave them new arguments, as can be seen from debates found in the journals of the London and later Royal Anthropological Institutes. Here one finds travelers and scientists arguing that missionary endeavors impede trade and are doomed to failure because Africans in particular are a subspecies of men while other races are simply inferior to more highly evolved Europeans. Thus, Darwin's work fed a new antimissionary mood by providing critics of Christianity with a strong weapon with which to attack both missionaries and the Bible. The success of these attacks and their influence on public policy can be seen in the fact that shortly after 1857, British Colonial Office documents downgrade African rulers, who are no longer referred to as kings who rule kingdoms, but as chiefs whose followers live in tribes.

The Indian mutiny, or as some Indian writers prefer to call it, the First War of Independence, coincided with the publication of Darwin's work and had a similar effect on the government's thinking about missionary work. The mutiny itself was provoked when evangelical reformers in the Indian administration sought to enact land reforms intended to free peasants from grinding poverty and the burden of generational debt, thus reducing the power of rich landowners. After some initial successes by the rebels, loyal troops, the majority of whom were Indian, succeeded in defeating the rebels. A vicious campaign of reprisals and oppression followed, alienating many Indians from British rule.

The biggest winners in the aftermath of the mutiny were businessmen and the opponents of reform, because the mutiny led to a complete revision of British foreign policy and the renunciation of attempts to change or reform societies under British control. While missionaries were still tolerated, and indeed their numbers increased, a strict separation was introduced between religious and secular affairs. The British

attempted to rule India on the basis of local laws, not morality. They returned to the policy of the old East India Company, which sought to disturb Indian society as little as possible provided it could exploit its wealth.

By the end of the 19th century, the British missionary movement was large, but it had lost much of its reforming zeal and in many places adapted itself to the realities of colonial rule. Worse still, racist ideas emanating from the theory of evolution and writers like the French Count Joseph Arthur Gobineau (1816–82) had taken root in British society, subtly influencing the thinking of many Christians, who now saw Christianity in terms of European cultural superiority. Nevertheless, the missionary movement continued to be popular in mainline churches, reaching its peak with the great Edinburgh Missionary conference of 1910.

Another important development in the 19th century was the rise of trade unions. In Britain the unions were closely associated with Methodism. Thus British socialism, unlike most continental forms of socialism, was often closely associated with Christianity. Kier Hardie (1856–1915), one of the founders of the Labor Party, was a lay preacher, as was British Labor Prime Minister Harold Wilson (1916–95), who chose the title baron of Rievaulx upon his elevation to the peerage, thus linking himself with the Christian tradition. More recently British foreign secretary and diplomat David Owen (b. 1938) was proud to proclaim that his Methodist roots and Christian faith were the source of his socialism. By contrast, the Christianity of most British Conservatives has often seemed an empty affair more linked to the pomp and ceremonies of the Church of England and high office than any deep convictions, which explains why many British evangelicals are distinctly left of center in ways that shock visiting Americans.

The 19th century saw the consolidation of Methodism and apparent success for many British churches. Evangelicals flourished, and new movements like the Salvation Army, founded in 1861 by William Booth (1829–1912), were created. In London Charles Haddon Spurgeon (1834–92) attracted large crowds and built what today we would call a mega-church, seating over 5000. Other large churches, often seating over 2,500, were built by the Methodists. Social reforms proceeded, and the missionary movement seemed to thrive.

Within the Church of England evangelicals met fierce resistance from the so-called Oxford movement, also known as the Tractarians, who sought to return the Church of England to a form of medieval Catholicism which would be Roman Catholic in everything except its allegiance to the pope. Highly successful, the Tractarians placed evangelicals on the defensive and gradually gained control of many bishoprics. At the end of the century, the chief voice against this movement was J. C. Ryle (1816–1900), the outspoken bishop of Liverpool, whose books like *Practical Religion* (1878) and *Holiness* (1890) became spiritual classics. Christian Socialism was an important but small movement. It was led by Fredrick Denison Maurice (1805–72), whose *The Kingdom of Christ* (1838) strongly influenced the great Dutch neo-Calvinist leader Abraham Kuyper (1837–1920).

The publication of Tom Paine's (1737–1809) *Age of Reason* (1794–96) led many people, particularly Methodist lay leaders, to lose their faith. It was followed by George Eliot's translations of David Friedrich Strauss's (1808–74) *The Life of Jesus* (1835) and Ludwig Feuerbach's (1804–72) *The Essence of Christianity* (1840). The works of John Henry Colenso (1814–83), who criticized the Mosaic authorship of the Pentateuch, prepared the way for the reception of German Higher Criticism in the 1880s. Meanwhile books like Charles Gore's (1853–1932) *Lux Muni* (1889) questioned traditional Christian teaching and eroded the faith of educated people.

World War I had a devastating effect on English Christianity. Not only did many men lose faith in the trenches, but a whole generation of evangelical leaders were sacrificed in battle. One of the greatest failures of British Christianity during World War I was the abandonment of German missionaries working in British territories. Because the British government had refused to sign those sections of the Geneva Convention dealing with missionaries, the property of German missions was seized without compensation, and at the outbreak of World War I German missionaries and their families were imprisoned in concentration camps under what were often appalling conditions. Yet so strong was anti-German feeling that few British Christians either assisted German missionaries or protested their government's actions; most simply looked the other way.

A more positive outcome of the missionary movement during the late 19th century was the foundation of the Student Christian Movement, which held great promise for revivals in universities in Britain and overseas. But it succumbed to liberal theology and the latest theological fads from Germany, leading to the founding of the Inter-Varsity Fellowship (IVF) in the 1920s. Strongly evangelical, the IVF was farsighted enough to establish various study centers and projects, such as Tyndale House, Cambridge, which played a key role in reviving the academic aspects of evangelical Christianity in Britain after World War II. Inter-Varsity continues to play a far greater role in British religious life than does its namesake and counterpart in the United States.

Today, however, the state of Christianity in Britain is far from healthy. A steep decline in church attendance began in the late 1950s, eased off in the 1970s and 1980s, and resumed in the 1990s. According to the most recent statistics, most people still consider themselves Christian. But less than two percent attend church on a weekly basis, and at most only ten percent attend fairly regularly. At the same time, Britain has admitted large numbers of immigrants, including over 2.5 million Muslims. Consequently, there is good reason to believe that today more Muslims attend weekly prayers in Britain than Christians attend church.

PART 2

ENGLISH LITERATURE, MUSIC, ART, AND ARCHITECTURE

ENGLISH LITERATURE

The earliest known poem in an early form of English was written by Caedmon (658–80), a lay brother at Whitby Abbey, who according to tradition was in charge of St. Hilda's pigs. Nine lines of what was described as his great poem, the *Song of Creation,* have survived. A few other lines from a poem called *The Dream of the Cross* are found as runic inscriptions on the 8th-century *Ruthwell Cross* and are also thought to have been written by him. All other traces of his work are lost. The other writer from this period, many of whose works have survived, is the historian, biblical commentator, and writer, the Venerable Bede (672–735), a monk in Jarrow. Although Bede wrote in Latin, the range of his works, many of which are now available in English due to a major Cistercian translation project,

is astonishing, making him the first major writer known to have lived in Britain.

In the 8th century four long poems exist written by the poet Cynewulf. One is about the martyr Juliana; another is about St. Helena (250–329), the mother of Constantine the Great (280–337); and two poems deal with the life of Christ. Other poems from this era include the *Dream of the Rood,* which talks about a vision of Christ's cross, and several poems about Christ's life and death. Fragments of heroic poems also exist. The greatest of all of these is without doubt *Beowulf,* which combines heroic deeds with Christian piety.

Other literature of the era includes the writings of King Alfred, who worked hard to revive learning in England and had various Latin works translated into English. Many of his Latin works and other writings survive, some

33

of which are now available in modern English. Usually overlooked as a British writer is St. Boniface, who spent much of his adult life as a missionary bishop evangelizing Germany. Yet, in a sense, his letters and other works are the first British travel literature. Aelfric (d. 1020) and Wulfstan (d. 1023), who was bishop of London, also produced various works, including some of the earliest collections of sermons to have been written in Britain. Several works written in Welsh and Scottish also exist from this time in manuscript form. In this short survey, however, we will only deal with works written in English or readily available in English translation.

With the Norman conquest, the language of the court became Norman French, and native English experienced a period of decline, although Latin remained the common language of educated people. Often overlooked during this period are the Latin sermons, poems, prayers, and philosophical treaties that St. Anselm (1033–1109) wrote as archbishop of Canterbury, such as his *Cur Deus Homo?*, which deals with the Incarnation.

Not until the 12th century did English reappear as a written language that was technically a Creole language, meaning that it was a blend of older English forms with Norman French that together were simplified grammatically. The usual explanation for this process of simplification is that such languages develop in circumstances where a dominant group have children, usually illegitimate, by women belonging to a subservient or conquered group. Hence English is truly a bastard language. The language of this period is known as Middle English.

The greatest of all Middle English writers, who to a large extent stabilized its form and vocabulary, was Geoffrey Chaucer (1342–1400), the author of *Canterbury Tales*. Other writers of this period are William Langland (1330–1400), who wrote *The Vision of Piers Plowman,* and Sir Thomas Malory (1405–71), whose *Le Morte D'Arthur* retold the story of King Arthur. Similar in its evocative use of the past was the work of Geoffrey of Monmouth (1100–1154), who popularized Arthurian plots. He also traced the origins of the English people to fugitives from Troy at the end of the Trojan Wars, thus rooting the British in classical antiquity. One of the greatest sagas of this period is *Sir Gawain and the Green Knight,* written in the 14th century.

The 15th century saw Chaucer's disciples, like John Lydgate (1370–1449), not only produce their own works but also translate many Latin texts into English. Thomas Malory continued the Arthurian tradition with his *Morte D'Arthur,* which was one of the first books to be actually printed in Britain by William Caxton (1422–91). In Scotland, King James I (1394–1437) adopted Chaucer's style to great effect, as did Robert Henryson (d. 1507).

The 14th and 15th centuries also saw the flowering of the *Mystery Play,* dealing with biblical themes, moral issues, or occasionally the lives of saints and martyrs. The earliest such play, *The Play of Adam*, was written in the 12th century in Norman French. Such plays gradually gained popularity, with the *Everyman* plays becoming very popular indeed. In recent years, there has been a revival of interest in mystery plays, with performances on a regular, though not annual, basis in places like Glastonbury and York.

The Italian Renaissance, meaning "rebirth" of learning and a growing interest in the cultures and languages of ancient Greece and Rome, helped fuel a golden age of British literature during the 16th century. Early works included John Skelton's (1460–1529) *Colin Clout* (1519) and Sir Thomas More's *Utopia* (1516), which was originally written in Latin and only translated into English after his death in 1551. William Tyndale (1494–1536) and Miles Coverdale (1488–1568) produced new translations of the Bible. Meanwhile Thomas Cranmer (1489–1556) wrote his much loved *Book of Common Prayer,* which shaped English usage for several generations. In 1588 the Bible was translated into Welsh, providing the basis for rich Christian literature in the Welsh language. Unfortunately, very few Welsh works have been translated into English, although, like the Scots, many Welsh writers have made a big impact on British literature through their English language works.

John Foxe's *Book of Martyrs* (1563) may not be a literary classic, but its powerful use of testimony linked to the memory of Mary I's barbaric burning of Protestants made it into the most commonly read book after the Bible. By contrast, the restrained style of Richard Hooker's (1554–1600) *Laws of Ecclesiastical Polity* (1593–1662, 7 vols.) set the tone for reasoned debate. Edmund Spenser's *The Faerie Queene* (1590–96) and the works of both William Shakespeare (1564–1616) and Christopher Marlowe set new standards for English prose and poetry. At the same time, the works of Lord Herbert of Cherbury (1583–1648) introduced a new anti-Christian tone into English literature that became known in the 18th century as Deism.

The 17th century began poorly with many minor figures but no outstanding ones except John Donne (1572–1631), whose poetry and *Devotions* (1624) set a new trend. Later writers like Thomas Browne, Jeremy Taylor, Francis Bacon, Robert Burton, Thomas Hobbes, John Owen, Samuel Pepys (1633–1703), John Dryden (1631–1700), and John Milton (1609–74) began reshaping the literary landscape. Pride of place, however, must go to John Bunyan (1628–88) whose *Pilgrim's Progress* quickly established itself as the best-loved English book after the Bible, replacing even Foxe in popularity. An interesting side effect of Bunyan's work was its role in encouraging the use of "you" rather than "thee" when addressing God and one's fellows, thus separating English from languages like German that retain both familiar and formal forms of personal pronouns.

The 18th century saw the rise of a bawdy reaction to the moral seriousness of the previous age that drew its strength from Puritanism. Thus Henry Fielding's *Tom Jones* (1707–54) reflects the mood of the times. Samuel Butler (1612–80) scorned the Puritan in works like *Hudibras* (1663), while Lord Clarendon (1609–74) sought to totally destroy the memory of the Puritan Commonwealth in his writings. It is against this background and the growing frequency of works by Deists, like John Toland (1670–1722), that John Locke's (1632–1704) work must be judged. Although most modern writers see Locke as a Deist, a good case can be made that this is a deliberate misreading of Locke's work, as Gary Amos shows in his *Defending the Declaration* (1989). In fact, Locke considered himself a Christian philosopher and was strongly influenced by Calvinism.

Jonathan Swift, Alexander Pope (1688–1744), John Gay (1685–1732), Dr. Samuel Johnson (1709–84), and Daniel Defoe (1660–1731) created a golden age in English literature. Defoe helped create the novel with his *Robinson Crusoe* (1719) and *Moll Flanders* (1722). Samuel Richardson (1698–

1761) began a tradition of moral novels with his *Pamela, or Virtue Rewarded* (1740). In poetry William Cowper (1731–1800) and Robert Burns (1759–96) represented two very different yet equally earnest approaches to life and religion that in strange ways reinforce each other while affirming a basically biblical perspective.

By contrast Horace Walpole (1717–97) began the Gothic novel, with supernatural elements invading the script, as in *The Castle of Otranto* (1765). The Gothic novel was perfected by Mary Wollstonecraft Shelley in *Frankenstein* (1818). The rise of the occult can also be seen in the works of William Blake (1757–1827), who initiated the English Romantic movement. William Wordsworth (1770–1850) and Samuel Taylor Coleridge (1772–1834) lent weight to the Romantic movement while at the same time undermining biblical authority by their understanding of inspiration as a poetic gift. In Coleridge's *Lyrical Ballads*, for example, he saw himself presenting supernatural events in the context of the everyday while Wordsworth gave a supernatural aura to the whole of life. Percy Bysshe Shelley (1792–1822) continued this tradition of Romantic revolt by strongly rejecting biblical religion in the name of an atheism that embraced supernaturalism and a commitment to political revolution. Against romanticism stands the strange figure of the highly Romantic Lord Byron, who scorned the supernaturalism of the Romantic movement in favor of a return to classical norms based on Greek and Roman taste.

The most influential of all Romantic writers was the Scottish novelist Sir Walter Scott (1771–1832), who combined a Romantic love of the Middle Ages with a form of Christianity that comes through very clearly in novels like his all-time favorite *Ivanhoe* (1819). Jane Austen (1775–1817) is also often seen as a Romantic novelist, yet in reality her romanticism is restricted to issues of courtship and love ending in marriage. Although critical of some aspects of the church, which as the daughter of a clergyman she knew well, she is essentially a Christian writer with a keen eye for detail and an understanding of human weakness.

Equally important during the last years of the 18th century and early 19th century were the works of James Macpherson (1736–96), a Scottish clergyman who is now all but forgotten. In 1760 Macpherson began publishing a series of texts which he claimed were a translation of old Gaelic sagas which he had discovered among Highlanders and in the Western Isles. His first publication was *Fragments of Ancient Poetry Collected in the Highlands of Scotland* (1760); this was followed by *Fingal* (1761) and *The Works of Ossian* in 1765. Immensely popular, Macpherson's poems were believed to be the work of a 3rd-century pagan bard and therefore a living record of one of Europe's pre-Christian traditions. While the author of the poems showed great skill, there is little doubt that the poems were the work of Macpherson's active imagination and not, as he claimed, ancient texts.

This fact was pointed out as early as 1775 when Dr. Samuel Johnson disputed Macpherson's claims in his *Journey to the Western Islands of Scotland* (1775) by pointing out that he could find no trace of such a tradition in Scotland and that no one other than Macpherson claimed to know the original texts. Subsequently, Macpherson was challenged to produce the texts, which he failed to do. Nevertheless, *The Works of Ossian* were immediately taken up by Europe's intellectual elite as proof of a great pre-Christian pagan tradition. Today such ideas circulate in the New Age movement and numerous occult groups.

The Victorian Age brought the moral seriousness of Charles Dickens (1812–70), who continually forces his readers to confront the pressing social problems of his age. At the same time, the attack on Puritanism is renewed by Lord Macaulay in his numerous histories, which became standard texts in British schools. Although Macaulay's motivation is not entirely clear, it seems that he was reacting both to his own evangelical upbringing and the growing success of the latter-day Puritanism found in the Methodist movement. Explicitly evangelical writings are to be found in the novels of Charles Kingsley (1819–75), whose *Water Babies* (1850) touched a nerve and the conscience of the Victorian public. Other popular novelists were Anthony Trollope (1815–82) and William Makepeace Thackeray (1811–63) whose *Vanity Fair* (1847–48) is a brilliant parody of social mores that mocks human folly and the earnestness of Christian moralism. In the Brontë sisters, Charlotte (1816–55), Emily (1818–48), and Anne (1820–49), one finds a quiet Christian reflection on the trials of life. In sharp contrast George Eliot (1819–80) presents a brilliant but cynically anti-Christian commentary on Victorian society, reflecting her own loss of faith. The same despairing post-Christian nihilism is found in the works of Alfred, Lord Tennyson (1809–92), who is inspired by the neoclassical love of Greece and the belief that ultimately we are alone in an empty universe where only stoic values can guide us. His most celebrated work *In Memoriam* (1850) captures this ultimately despairing mood in all its forms. Similarly, Matthew Arnold (1822–88) represents the flowering of Victorian humanism, which can no longer embrace traditional religion, and is valiantly looking for a new basis on which to build morality.

Thomas Carlyle's (1795–1881) spiritual autobiography, *Sartor Resartus* (1830–31), is a moving testimony to the crisis of faith that overwhelmed many Victorians. Similarly, John Stuart Mill's (1806–73) *Autobiography* (1873) is essential reading for anyone grappling with the 19th-century crisis of faith. So too is John Henry Newman's (1801–90) *Apologia pro Vita Sua* (1864) essential reading for anyone wishing to grasp the complexity of Victorian religion. Although his decision to embrace Roman Catholicism will dismay many Protestants, the clarity of Newman's thought and consistency of his argument makes this one of the great literary works of the 19th century. Among 19th-century evangelical writers, William Wilberforce's (1759–1833) *A Practical View of Christianity* should not be overlooked.

Transitional writers who in many ways span the 19th and 20th centuries are Joseph Conrad (1857–1924), Thomas Hardy (1840–1928), W. B. Yeats (1865–1939), and Rudyard Kipling (1865–1936). Although not a Christian writer, Conrad's work is steeped in biblical imagery and references to biblical themes. Kipling represents a dying empire which he hoped could be revived through embracing a high moral vision and civilizing mission. Two Americans who made England their home also deserve attention. These are Henry James (1843–1916) and T. S. Eliot (1888–1965). Of these James writes as a remote social commentator acutely observing a restricted society in the style of Jane Austen, while Eliot is the Christian convert eager to proclaim the emptiness of the world and the grace of God.

Mid-century writers included E. M. Forster (1879–1970), Virginia Woolf

(1882–1941), a clergyman's daughter who lost faith, and D. H. Lawrence (1885–1930), who is best known for his explicit use of sexual scenes, such as those found in *Lady Chatterly's Lover* (1928). Following World War II, the complacency of British society was shattered by a group of "angry young men" led by John Osborne (1929–94) and Colin Wilson (b. 1931). Osborne's play *Look Back in Anger* (1956) set the tone for the group, while Wilson's increasing preoccupation with the occult foreshadowed the future. Other writers like Tom Stoppard (b. 1937) and Harold Pinter (b. 1930) set the tone that was to prevail until the end of the century in literary circles. On the other hand, through the excellent productions of the BBC, Granada, and other television studios, British drama reached new heights in the presentation of enjoyable yet sophisticated plays and detective stories that are a far cry from the philosophical nihilism found in most other forms of contemporary literature.

Many 20th-century British writers continued the flight from Christianity begun in the 19th century. The chillingly pessimistic and anti-Christian tone of Hardy's work is matched by H. G. Wells's (1866–1946) triumphant rationalism, which also turns to pessimism in his later years. George Orwell's (1903–50) masterly critique of Marxism, *1984* (1948), was also intended to be simultaneously a critique

of Christianity. Yeats's interest in the occult feeds Aldous Huxley's (1894–1963) equally strong fascination with a non-Christian mysticism.

When reviewing these developments it is important to ponder the significance of the fact that many of the most bitter critics of Christianity were children of evangelical homes. These include George Eliot, the agnostic turned theosophist, Annie Besant (1847–1933), and that leading exponent of Satanism, Alistair Crowley (1875–1947). Equally depressing is the fact that no evangelical writer gained recognition as a major literary figure during the 19th or 20th centuries.

On the other hand a number of outstanding Roman Catholic writers distinguished themselves during the 20th century. These include G. K. Chesterton (1874–1936), Graham Greene (1904–91), Evelyn Waugh (1903–66), and J. R. R. Tolkien (1892–1973). The Anglicans also produced a number of well-recognized writers, including Dorothy Sayers (1893–1957), C. S. Lewis (1898–1963), and T. S. Eliot, whose *Murder in the Cathedral* (1936) created a vivid picture of the martyrdom of Thomas à Becket.

ENGLISH MUSIC

Prior to the Reformation, Scotland was renowned for its schools of polyphonic music created in monastic institutions. When the monasteries were broken up in the 16th century, this great tradition died out. In England playing the harp appears to have been a well-developed musical tradition that also declined after the Reformation. Surviving examples of British music from before the 14th century are rare and often fragmentary. But the Tudor age saw both the development of secular madrigals and serious church music by such famous composers as William Byrd (1543–1623) and Thomas Tallis (1505–85).

A positive effect of the turmoil caused by the Reformation was the employment of laymen as professional singers in English cathedrals, which in turn encouraged the development of the solo performance. At the same time, music as a secular occupation steadily developed. The Puritan Commonwealth encouraged the teaching of music in schools for secular enjoyment. The violin, flute, and oboe, which previously had been reserved for the court, came into common use, while the guitar gradually replaced the lute in popular use. The secular use of music continued to grow after the Restoration, when the court encouraged numerous productions.

Following the Glorious Revolution, particularly as a result of the arrival of the Hanoverians, British music was given a major boost by the arrival of great continental artists like Handel (1685–1759), who arrived in London in 1710. Handel combined the Italian-style opera with popular British choral music to produce such masterpieces as his *Messiah,* which was written as an act of Christian charity to raise money for the Foundlings Hospital.

Another significant development during the 18th century was a growing awareness of the history of music and a desire to preserve older forms. This led to the founding of the Academy of Ancient Music in 1710 and the publication of various works on the history of music, such as John Hawkin's *A General History of the Science and Practice of Music* (1776). A series of music festivals also developed during these years.

During the 19th century, Italian opera gained a foothold in Britain. William Gilbert (1836–1911) and Arthur Sullivan (1842–1900) began to create their own operatic style in 1875. From this type of light-hearted opera, musical comedy developed as a uniquely British form that grew out of the Victorian concert hall. Regional pride led great Victorian industrial cities like Glasgow, Manchester, and Birmingham to create their own orchestras and musical festivals. Many great works, often with explicitly Christian themes, were performed for the first time in the provinces. Among the composers who made their début in this way were Lewis Spohr (1784–1859), whose work *The Fall of Babylon* was performed in Norwich in 1842, and Dvořák, whose work *St. Ludimilla* was performed in Leeds in 1886. Most important of all, Felix Mendelssohn-Bartholdy's (1809–47) great exposition of biblical truth *Elijah* was first performed in Birmingham in

1846. At the local level, the Welsh male voice choir developed as a unique musical tradition deeply rooted in the mining villages of Wales, Calvinistic Methodism, and the Christian faith generally.

Today, music is alive and well in Britain with numerous famous orchestras and opera societies and festivals such as those held at Glyndebourne. The annual Promenade Concerts, held in the Albert Hall since 1895, are another musical tradition that is deeply rooted in British society. British popular music experienced a golden age in the 1960s with the success of the Beatles, and Christian pop experienced a remarkable revival with the Greenbelt Festivals founded in the early 1970s. At the same time, the late 20th century saw a remarkable resurgence of hymn writing in Britain and the development of mass marches for Jesus.

ENGLISH ART

Given extensive prehistoric finds in places like the Cheddar Gorge and caves of Derbyshire, it is remarkable that no prehistoric cave paintings, similar to those found in France, have been discovered in Britain and that the earliest examples of British art are mosaics found in Roman villas. The only surviving British works of art from the 7th and 8th centuries are illuminated manuscripts such as the wonderful *Book of Kells*, which is believed to have been produced at Iona, and the *Lindesfarne*

Gospels. Early Saxon wall paintings may be seen at Winchester Cathedral and Canterbury Cathedral.

The development of Romanesque styles under Norman rule led to a flowering of British art with the production of various illustrated manuscripts in places like St. Alban's Abbey and further wall paintings in places like Winchester Cathedral. This style, which was heavily influenced by French styles, continued to flourish until the mid-15th century, when it existed alongside the development of Gothic art forms. A characteristic of English painters until well into the 15th century is their rejection of the new realism that was emerging on the continent. By contrast, English painters preferred elongated shapes and the graceful drapes that characterized Gothic art.

Surprisingly, the development of realistic painting in Britain developed out of the practice of producing miniatures, or very small portraits, which themselves developed out of the tradition that created illuminated manuscripts. The tradition of portrait painting became very popular during the reign of Henry VIII and continued well into the 17th century. Henry VIII used English portrait painting as a propaganda technique to instill a sense of royal authority. Thus Hans Holbein the Younger (1497–1543) was employed to paint Henry in a regal stance.

The appearance of illustrated books, particularly Foxe's *Book of Martyrs* (1563), popularized a rich tradition of book illustration that was started by William Caxton (1422–91). This tradition continued into the newspapers of the 17th and 18th centuries and ultimately to the satirical sketches of William Hogarth (1697–1764), who comes as close to being a Christian artist as anyone of his age. More traditional portraits by artists like Paul van Somer (1576–1621) continued to be used to enhance the prestige of royalty and the nobility.

Anthony van Dyck (1599–1641), who settled in Britain in 1632, added a twist to British painting through his mastery of continental techniques learned from his mentor Rubens, who briefly lived in Britain between 1630–34. Sir Joshua Reynolds (1723–92) developed these new techniques in his own characteristically English way to make him the most sought after portrait painter of his generation. His contemporary Joseph Wright of Derby (1734–97) pioneered modern painting through his careful studies of the emerging industrial society.

During the 19th century, Joseph Turner (1775–1851) and John Constable (1776–1837) pioneered new forms of landscape painting and fostered a romantic appreciation of the English countryside. William Blake (1757–1827), on the other hand, combined his literary and artistic skill to produce mystical works with occult overtones.

The self-named Pre-Raphaelite Brotherhood attempted to create a self-consciously Christian form of art. They sought to recapture the vivid simplicity of Italian painting, which they believed had been lost as a result of the immense influence of Raphael (1483–1520). The most important member of this group was William Holman Hunt (1827–1910). Ironically, these Christian romantics were strongly influenced by the artist and art critic John Ruskin (1819–1900), whose philosophy led him far from orthodox Christianity. Closer to the spirit of Ruskin were William Morris (1834–96) and his colleague Edward Burne-Jones (1833–98), who also played an important role in reviving book illustration through such works as Burne-Jones' magnificent illustrations in *The Works of Geoffrey Chaucer* (1892–96).

The 20th century saw a drift away from Christianity into modern nihilism. The most famous painter in this respect is Francis Bacon (1909–92). Finally, the far-reaching influence of the self-consciously decadent Bloomsbury Group, with Wyndham Lewis (1882–1957) as its leading visual artist, cannot be overlooked. During the late 20th century, various lecture tours by Francis Schaeffer (1912–83) and his colleague Hans Rookmaaker (d. 1977) led to a revival of interest in art among evangelical Christians and the founding of several Christian arts groups.

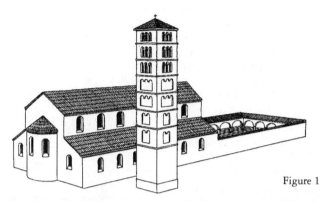

Figure 1

ARCHITECTURE STYLES
THE EARLIEST CHURCHES (TO 800)

Christians originally met in private homes or secret hiding places. Eventually, when Christianity became an accepted religion in the Roman Empire, Christians adapted the Roman basilica, or assembly hall, as their meeting place. From the 2nd century to the 6th century the basilica was the standard form of church building in Western Europe.

Separate from the main building there was usually a tower as shown in Figure 1. Later, during the Middle Ages, the simple style of the basilica formed a basis for the basic form of church buildings, shown in Figure 2.

In 313, with the Edict of Milan, Emperor Constantine granted tolerance and the protection of the state to Christianity. Consequently, many formerly pagan buildings and places of worship were converted into churches. Strange as it may seem, very few early Christian churches have survived in Britain, largely due to the systematic destruction

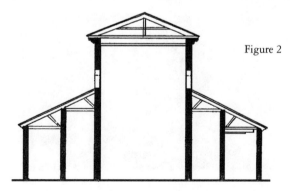

Figure 2

of Saxon churches by Norman conquerors in the 11th century. The earliest British churches are simple preconquest buildings located in remote areas, such as St. Bridge's Church, Beckermet, Cumbria. The crypts of Hexham Priory and Ripon Cathedral also preserve preconquest remains that survived Norman rebuilding programs.

THE ROMANESQUE STYLE (9TH–13TH CENTURIES)

With the arrival of the Normans, the continental architectural style known as Romanesque entered Britain, where it is often call the Norman style. This style was inspired by the abundance of Roman ruins such as the Colosseum in Rome, which inspired awe in all who saw it. Thus ancient Rome provided both the inspiration and sometimes the raw materials for Christian architects and builders for over a millennium. The basic designs were incorporated into church buildings to create what became known as the Romanesque style.

Romanesque churches have very thick walls reinforced by buttresses, which are specially thickened sections of wall which look like a smaller second wall. Buttresses are necessary to help carry the weight of the walls and roof. An excellent example is Durham Cathedral in England, once described by Sir Walter Scott as "half church of God, half fort against the Scots."

Most Romanesque churches were built to a cruciform plan. Normally the altar, or communion table, in such churches faced east while the entrance, known as the West End, is at the other end of the church. Rounded arches and windows are typical of the style. The churches are heavily built, very solid structures; their thick walls often contain vast amounts of rubble. Although the Romans knew how to make concrete, the secret of this valuable aid to building was lost from the 4th century to the early 19th century. Therefore, medieval builders had to rely on porous mortar and carefully placed stone slabs which interlocked with each other.

Durham Cathedral, Durham, England

Romanesque shapes for arches, doors, roofing, and windows were very distinctive. If you learn to recognize these shapes, you will soon know whether a church or part of a church is Romanesque. Below are several examples of typical Romanesque shapes.

Salisbury Cathedral, Salisbury, England

THE GOTHIC STYLE (12TH–16TH CENTURIES)

The Gothic style is regarded as one of the greatest architectural achievements of the Middle Ages and the high point of Christian civilization. The Salisbury Cathedral is a good example of the Gothic style.

The overall impression created by Gothic buildings is one of unbelievable lightness. The whole structure points to heaven and reminds the worshiper of God. The flying buttresses on the outside of the building deflect the weight of the roof from the nave walls to the outer walls, making it possible to build the walls both higher and thinner. Several phases of the Gothic style can be distinguished: the Early, High, and Late, as well as the Gothic revival of the late 18th and early 19th century. In England these styles are often called the Early English, the Middle or Pointed, and the Perpendicular. Gothic cathedrals were built over centuries; consequently, the styles often changed even within one building. When visiting a Gothic cathedral, look for the fan vaulting or roof supports, which have veins like those of a fan. This is often very beautiful and a masterpiece of craftsmanship.

Gothic churches are recognizable by their pointed arches and windows, shown below.

BRITISH BAROQUE (15TH–18TH CENTURIES)

In Britain, Renaissance architecture blended into an early form of neoclassical architecture to produce a uniquely British form of Baroque that lacked many of the more ornate features of continental Baroque. These developments began as early as the 16th century through the work of architects like Inigo Jones (1573–1652) and were continued in the 17th century by Christopher Wren (1632–1723). British Baroque was a distinctive style that was particularly popular for church buildings among nonconformists such as Baptists, Congregationalists, and Presbyterians. Later Methodists embraced the Baroque for their larger churches. The best example of British Baroque is Sir Christopher Wren's masterpiece, St. Paul's Cathedral in London. Work commenced on St. Paul's in 1675 and was completed in 1711.

St. Paul's Cathedral, London, England

NEOCLASSICAL AND NEO-GOTHIC STYLES (18TH–19TH CENTURIES)

In his *A History of Architecture,* Sir Banister Fletcher points out that in Europe the neoclassical style of the 19th century, which was inspired by Greek temples, was closely connected with a growing nationalism and a form of neo-paganism. The new master problem for late 18th-century and early 19th-century architects was the creation of civic pride and national consciousness through museums and cultural monuments. The rediscovery, even reinvention, of ancient Greek culture coincided with a decline in church construction in favor of secular buildings that proclaim the rise of humanity and national pride. Instead of creating great churches to the glory of God, aspiring architects were busy creating temples to man.

Neoclassicism was ideally suited for an imperial age when the grandeur of empire captured the imagination of all European peoples. Somerset House in London was built between 1776 and 1778 to house major government departments. The neoclassical pillars and regular form provide a grandeur suitable for the emerging British Empire, which was just beginning to assert itself as an imperial power.

Although the dominant theme in 19th-century architecture was national glory, not all nations and architects sought to recreate their past in the neoclassical image of ancient Greece and Rome. In England, for example, a spirit of Christian humanism, inspired by novels like Sir Walter Scott's (1771–1832) *Ivanhoe,* revived older architectural styles associated with the Middle Ages and the lost certainty of an age of faith. The deliberate imitation of Gothic styles led to what became known as neo-Gothic. On the next page is a picture of the Houses of Parliament in London which, to the surprise of most people, were actually built between 1840 and 1850 to the design of Sir Charles Barry (1795–1860) and A. W. N. Pugin (1812–52).

Because of its clear imitation of what was seen as a "Christian style," neo-Gothic architecture in Britain tended to soften the impact of neoclassicism and to a certain

Somerset House, London, England

House of Parliament, London, England

extent lessened the tendency toward neo-paganism and the glorification of war, both of which were found in French and German styles of the same period.

HOW TO ENJOY YOUR VISIT TO A BRITISH CHURCH

Visiting British churches can be quite confusing for anyone used to thinking about a church as simply a place to hear a sermon and meet fellow Christians. Even guidebooks are often not very helpful because they are full of unfamiliar terms like *chancel, sanctuary,* and *transept.* Unless you grew up in Europe, you will probably be overwhelmed with this mass of information and seemingly endless detail. So to make things easy, we have provided a brief introduction to the layout of a typical church and cathedral.

The diagram at the top of page 49 shows the layout of a typical parish church. The structure of this church would be familiar to most people. There is a **tower** and **main doorway,** or **narthex,** a baptismal area represented by the **font,** the main body of the church known as the **nave,** and a place for the communion table, or **altar,** known as the **chancel.** Finally there is a **crypt,** or underground chapel used for burying people. Although this structure looks familiar, the way it was understood by medieval people is far from familiar.

The diagram at the bottom of page 49 shows a more advanced and complex church design. To the basic church design, **transepts** have been added and the tower has been moved. The narthex is also called the **porch.** There are also two altars plus an **altar screen,** which separates the nave from the chancel, where the choir would be located. The screen also separated laypeople from the monks and priests who sang in the choir. The **vestry** was a small room used by the

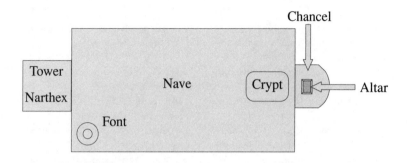

priest to change from his ordinary clothing into the special church clothing, or vestments, used during the service.

Now we must look at the most developed version of a church, which would be found in a cathedral. It is important to remember that in medieval churches the altar, not the pulpit, was the focus of worship. The congregation was separated from the high altar by a screen and could not even see what was happening. Most people stood in the nave or aisles, often conducting daily business or exchanging gossip while the priests performed the Mass. Pews were not added until after the

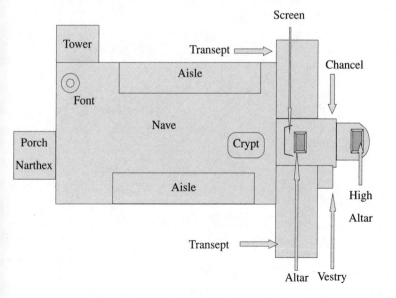

Reformation, when people sat to hear the preaching of the Word.

Below is the layout of a typical cathedral. Let us go through these various areas in turn. First the worshiper entered the church through a doorway with a porch or **narthex**. In Roman basilicas, the narthex was a long porch at the west end of the church. It was the place where women, people awaiting baptism, or those who were under some form of discipline waited before being allowed into the church itself. Symbolically the narthex was associated with the cleansing waters of baptism and the womb where the child waits before its birth.

In some churches there is also a **paradise porch**. It is so named because it was decorated with sculptures and frescoes, or wall paintings, of the Garden of Eden. It often contained a fountain where unbaptized people and sinners could wash themselves before entering the church.

Beyond the narthex one enters the **nave**. This is the main body of the church and is the Latin word for "ship." It represents the ship of salvation, Noah's Ark, and the invisible church of Christ to which all saved souls belong and where humans are protected from the storms of life and material temptations. The nave

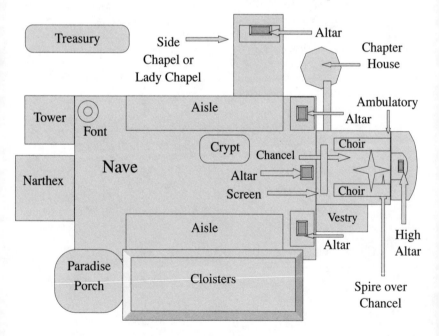

was both a place of worship and general meeting place. Not until after the Reformation were seats added. Before then everyone had to stand, and people often wandered around selling food and other goods in winter.

In large churches there may be more than one nave and most have **aisles**, which are separated from the nave by pillars.

Near the nave is a **baptismal font**. Originally these were wide, low stone basins where new converts stood while water was poured over them. Later, as the general population became Christian, fonts were smaller, raised vessels suitable for baptism.

Near the font and the narthex there is often at least one **tower**. This functioned both as a landmark and a watchtower in isolated villages. Bells were added to call people to worship and warn of danger.

At the end of the nave was an **altar**, where the death of Christ was ritually reenacted with each service.

Until the 10th century, worshipers partook in communion before the **side altars,** where they received both bread and wine. Later they received only bread. Originally this change was made to prevent drunkenness, but later it gained theological importance as only priests were allowed to receive communion in both kinds, bread and wine.

Beyond the altar was a **screen**, which prevented ordinary people from entering the chancel.

The **chancel** was where the choir, which consisted of men only, was located. The **choir stalls** are often richly decorated with wood carvings.

Beyond the chancel was the **high altar,** where the most solemn Masses were performed. In medieval churches the celebration of the Mass was the central event.

Near the high altar is the **crypt**. Originally crypts were underground chambers where Christians met for worship in secret and where they buried their dead. Crypts are often the earliest part of a church building.

The **vestry** is the small room where priests changed from their normal garb into ecclesiastical robes, which were selected on the basis of their color depending on the season in the church year.

Many large churches have a walkway leading behind the choir, chancel, and the high altar. This is known as the **ambulatory** and was used, particularly in pilgrimage churches, to allow worshipers to file past relics.

The **Lady Chapel**, which is often located behind the high altar, was devoted to the Virgin Mary. It was often the most important side altar in a church and usually survived after the Reformation, when many altars were removed from churches.

To one side of large churches, usually the south side, one finds the **cloisters**. This is an enclosed rectangle with a high outside wall and roof, often with very beautiful stonework and ceiling vaulting, surrounding an open garden, usually a grassy lawn, that is enclosed by a low wall and pillars. Here monks and other clergy could walk in bad weather, reciting the Scriptures or praying. In time cloisters became more elaborate and served both as a general meeting place for monks and as a place where copyists transcribed the Scriptures or wrote sacred theological treatises.

Above the chancel it became the practice to build a tall church **spire.**

The spire served as a local landmark and replaced, or at least supplemented, church towers.

Cathedrals also have a **chapter house,** which is the meeting place of clergy during synods and other important functions. Here the business of a diocese was discussed.

Finally, don't miss the **treasury.** Here the treasures of the church are kept, such as ancient crosses, Scriptures, rare books, relics, and vestments.

PART 3

CHRISTIAN HERITAGE SITES IN GREAT BRITAIN

THE TOP 10 CHRISTIAN SITES IN BRITAIN

Because many people only have time for a short visit, the following sites are recommended and clustered together so that they can be visited fairly easily.

1. LONDON: Here you can visit John Wesley's Chapel, the Wesley Museum, and the graves of both John and Charles Wesley, Sir Christopher Wren's masterpiece St. Paul's Cathedral, the Tower of London, Houses of Parliament, and a host of other fascinating places. From London you can also visit nearby Canterbury and St. Albans, two of the oldest Christian sites in Southern England.

2. BRISTOL AND BATH: Anyone who enjoys Jane Austen has to visit Bath to see the Royal Crescent and Roman Baths. Bath Abbey was the last great pre-Reformation church to be built in England. In Bristol you will find John Wesley's chapel, the home of Charles Wesley, a wonderful Late Gothic cathedral, and St. Mary's Redcliffe, once described by Queen Elizabeth I as "the fairest, godliest, and most famous parish church in all my realm."

3. WELLS AND GLASTONBURY: Not far from Bath and Bristol is the magnificent Wells Cathedral with its truly unique internal architecture. Nearby are the ruins of Glastonbury Abbey, which according to legend was the last resting place of King Arthur.

4. GLASGOW AND EDINBURGH: Who can visit Britain without seeing Scotland? In Glasgow there are ancient Christian sites while Edinburgh is the place where John Knox launched the Scottish Reformation.

5. NORTHUMBRIA AND DURHAM: Here you will find an area steeped in history and some of the oldest churches in Britain, like Hexham Abbey. From Northumbria, English scholars like the Venerable Bede preserved Christian scholarship during the Dark Ages, while Northumbrian missionaries evangelized large areas of continental Europe.

6. CAMBRIDGE: Here is the home of English Protestantism and the Puritan movement, with numerous links to North America.

7. OXFORD: This is a far more Catholic city with strong links to medieval Christianity and the oldest university in England.

8. YORK: Once the center of a thriving Christian kingdom, later a Viking stronghold, and for centuries the second most important bishopric in England, this is a city rich in history with well-preserved medieval walls.

9. CUMBRIA: For those who like hiking and prefer a journey through beautiful countryside, this is the place to explore. Here are many ancient and largely neglected stone crosses and other ancient Christian sites in an area of breathtaking beauty.

10. TINTERN ABBEY AND ST. DAVID'S: For centuries Wales was an independent kingdom with its own ancient Christian heritage. More recently Wales was the source for numerous revival movements and remains rich in Christian music.

Many of these and other places are close together. Therefore it is relatively easy to visit Oxford, Bristol, Bath, Wells, and Glastonbury on one trip taking three or four days. Similarly, one can visit York, Durham, and Northumbria together or Chester, Manchester, Lancaster, and Cumbria. From Bristol it is easy to visit places like Tintern Abbey and St. David's as well as other sites in Wales. Finally, Glasgow, Stirling, Edinburgh, St. Andrews, and Aberdeen go well together.

KEY TO THE TEXTS

All entries in the Christian Travelers Guides are written according to the following outline.

The name of each place is given in alphabetical order. Places are listed according to the local spelling.

Background: a short history of the area explains its religious, cultural, and intellectual significance.

Places to visit: individual sites are mentioned with recommendations about things that deserve close attention. Different places are identified in **bold**.

Most dates are A.D. and are given as a plain number, e.g., 800. Only when there might be some doubt about the exact date are B.C. or A.D. used.

MAP OF KEY CHRISTIAN HERITAGE SITES IN GREAT BRITAIN

Orkney Islands

Scotland

Aberdeen

Perth   St. Andrews
Dumfermline

Edinburgh

Iona   Stirling
Bothwell-Blantyre   Glasgow
Alloway

Holy Island/Lindesfarne
Northumbria
Dumfries   Jarrow
Carlisle   Hexham
Cumbria   Durham   Whitby
Fountains Abbey/Ripon

Lancaster   York   England
Manchester

Beverly
Chester   Lincoln
Ironbridge
Derby   Boston

Wales   Lichfield   Leicester   Norwich
Kidderminster   Peterborough

Stratford-upon-Avon   Ely
St. David's   Cardiff   Bedford   Cambridge
Tintern Abbey   St. Albans
Cheltenham   Oxford   London
Gloucester   Cirencester   Rochester
Bristol   Avebury   Canterbury
Bath   Winchester
Glastonbury   Salisbury
Wells   Chichester

ABERDEEN

Until the discovery of North Sea oil in the 1970s, Aberdeen was a quiet northern Scottish town with a long history. Since then it has become the boomtown of Scotland. Prehistoric settlements existed in the area. The Picts, Scots, and Romans all found the area conducive to settlement, but it was not until 1136 that King David I (1080–1153) permitted a tax to be levied on shipping on the Dee. Almost 50 years later, in 1179, the town was granted a charter that confirmed its right to levy taxes. Robert the Bruce (1274–1329) took refuge here on one of his many flights from the English after the defeat of the rebellion of 1306. A year later the town was stormed by troops of Edward III of England (1312–77), who burnt the town and destroyed its castle. The subsequent history of Aberdeen was fairly uneventful until the 17th century, when it changed hands

three times during the Civil Wars (1638–48) that ended with the establishment of the Commonwealth in England (1649–60). Aberdeen remained essentially loyal to the English crown during the Jacobite rebellions.

Andrew Murray (1828–1917), the great 19th-century devotional writer and revivalist preacher, and his brother John Murray (1826–82), one of the founders of Stellenbosch University in South Africa, arrived in Aberdeen in the fall of 1838 after a miserable seven-month journey from South Africa that had left them suffering from scurvy. The day after their arrival, their uncle enrolled them in the local grammar school, where they immediately began to learn Latin. Andrew was only ten years old; his brother was 12. Both of them had no contact at all with their parents for over seven months and were living with an austere uncle in a strange

ANDREW MURRAY JR. (1828–1917) was a South African Dutch Reformed minister and church leader who opposed theological liberalism and led an evangelical revival in the 1860s. An advocate of missions and evangelism, he opposed Afrikaner Nationalism and its political stance that led to apartheid. Mystically inclined, he was greatly influenced by William Law. His books *Abide in Christ* (1882), *With Christ in the School of Prayer* (1885), and *Absolute Surrender* (1895) are classics of devotional piety which continue to have a strong influence in evangelical and charismatic circles even today.

land. Fortunately, one of the teachers was Dr. Melvil, who inspired them to study and serve God. In 1840, William Chalmers Burns (1815–68), a young minister who later became a Presbyterian missionary to China where he inspired Hudson Taylor (1832–1905), had a remarkable evangelistic ministry in Aberdeen, where he strongly influenced the Murray brothers and their lives' work.

PLACES TO VISIT

KING'S COLLEGE CHAPEL, High St., was built between 1500 and 1505 and is the only surviving building from the time of Bishop William Elphinstone (1431–1514). It is a beautiful example of late medieval architecture, with a tower shaped like an imperial crown symbolizing both the universal nature of knowledge and the claim of the Scottish monarchy to be the representatives of the Holy Roman Empire in Scotland. The chapel was badly damaged by a storm in 1633, and it had to be rebuilt.

Originally it was Roman Catholic, later it became Protestant, and today it is an ecumenical chapel that serves the university community.

The pulpit is carved with the heads of all the Scottish kings from James I to James VII. It was originally built for use in St. Machar's Cathedral in 1540 and later moved to the chapel.

Bishop Elphinstone is buried under a slab in the chapel, as is the famous Scottish historian and first rector of the university, Hector Boece (1465–1536).

Today ST. MACHAR'S CATHEDRAL, the Chanonry and King St., is a romantic half-ruined building which evokes a sense of the grandeur of a past age. The cathedral's original nave is still used as a church, and its twin towers are a city landmark. A church was built on this site in the 6th century by followers of St. Columba as part of a missionary outreach to convert the pagan Picts. It became a bishopric during the reign of David I in 1137. The present building dates to the time of Bishop Alexander

> **BISHOP WILLIAM ELPHINSTONE** (1431–1514) founded the University of Aberdeen in 1494. The bishop was a Scottish patriot, statesman, and scholar who worked hard to promote education. He received a papal bull in 1495 from Pope Alexander VI that gave him the authority to create a university. In addition to founding the University of Aberdeen, Bishop Eliphinstone edited the *Aberdeen Breviary,* which contained a fine collection of Scottish church liturgies as well as the lives of various Celtic saints. The *Breviary* was first published in Edinburgh in 1509, when it became the official prayer book of Scotland.

de Kininmond (d. 1362), with additions by Bishop Gavin Dunbar (who added the towers) and Bishop Leighton, both of whose tombs are to be found in the church.

The ceiling, built by Bishop Dunbar from beautiful oak panels, is decorated with 48 heraldic shields, including ones representing St. Margaret of Hungary, the Emperor Charles V, and Pope Leo X. The coats of arms of other European and Scottish kings and nobles are also to be found here. The ceiling vividly reminds the viewer of the universal character of Christendom during the 15th century.

THE ABERDEEN ARTS CENTER is an important Christian site because, until it was converted into a cinema in the 1950s, it was the famous North Church built between 1829 and 1830. Throughout the 19th century it was a center of revival and evangelical activity. For many years its minister was the Rev. John Murray, one of the leaders in the 19th-century Scottish evangelical party. His South African nephews Andrew and John Murray attended this church while students in Aberdeen. The building was recently renovated to restore some of its original features.

MARISCHAL COLLEGE, Broad St., is the oldest college in the university system after King's College. Earl George Keith founded it in 1593 to promote Protestant theology. The two colleges combined in 1860 to create the University of Aberdeen. The college claims to be the largest granite building in northern Europe and the second largest in the world. Only the Escorial palace in Spain is larger. Its neo-Gothic facade has an average height of 80 feet and is over 400 feet long. It was built in 1844 on the site of the original building, which before the Reformation was the Grayfriars monastery. Both Andrew and John Murray graduated from here in 1845 with master's degrees. Here they took courses in biblical languages, theology, and Christian evidences. After graduation they spent another three years studying at Utrecht in the Netherlands, before returning to South Africa.

THE MARISCHAL MUSEUM, which is in the College, houses a fascinating collection of anthropological and missionary items. It explores the role of graduates of Aberdeen University who went abroad as doctors, soldiers, merchants, and missionaries through the items they donated to the University.

ST. NICHOLAS CHURCH, Upperkirkgate, claims to be the largest parish church in Scotland. It was built in the 12th century. During the Reformation it was divided into two separate congregations, with a common meeting area known as the transept.

ST. ANDREWS CATHEDRAL, King St. Although the present building was redesigned by Archibald Simpson in 1817, it was here in 1784 that Samuel Seabury was consecrated as the first Episcopal bishop to be sent to the United States. Thus St. Andrews claims to be the "Mother Church" of the North American Episcopalian Communion.

PROVOST SKENE'S HOUSE, Guestrow, is now a fascinating museum depicting life in Scotland in earlier centuries. It was built in 1545 shortly after the Scottish Reformation and has an excellent collection of period furniture from the 16th century to the early 19th century.

THE ART GALLERY contains a rich collection of modern art, plus some fascinating 19th-century paintings by local artists in the Romantic or Pre-Raphaelite tradition. There is also the famous Macdonald Collection of portraits of famous British artists.

MARITIME MUSEUM. Anyone who loves the sea or whose ancestors emigrated from Europe to North America by ship ought to visit this excellent collection, which is housed in **PROVOST ROSS'S HOUSE** in Shiprow. The house itself was built in 1593.

ALLOWAY

Three miles south of the much larger town of Ayr, which until the 18th century rivaled Glasgow as a major seaport, lies the small village of Alloway, made famous because it is the birthplace of the most famous of all Scottish writers, Robert Burns (1759–96).

PLACES TO VISIT

BURNS COTTAGE AND MUSEUM. The birthplace of Robert Burns reminds visitors of the harsh conditions ordinary people lived under until quite recently. It is a long, two-roomed, thatched cottage where the Burns family and their domestic animals, including cows, sheep, and goats, huddled together for protection against the elements. Nearby another display is to be seen in the Land of Burns exhibit which is also well worth visiting. Although remembered as something of a skeptic, Burns's religious views were complex. He was a harsh critic of the Church of Scotland and its clergy, most of whom he believed to be hypocrites. But he also seems to have maintained a real faith, in contrast to his more critical contemporaries, whose rationalism he rejected.

ROBERT BURNS (1759–96) was the National Poet of Scotland and one of the greatest literary figures ever. He preserved Scottish dialect when it was in danger of being replaced by English. A fundamentally honest man, Burns scorned hypocrisy and cherished fundamental Christian values. Although he lived through what has been called "the Scottish Enlightenment," which saw the popularity of such skeptics as David Hume (1711–76), he appears to have retained a basic Christian faith. Often, however, he was at odds with clergymen and the established church, as his ballad "The Kirk of Scotland's Alarm" (1789) shows with its biting verse "That what is no sense must be nonsense." Burns's objections to the church are not surprising when it is realized that he lived at a time when the average clergyman of the Church of Scotland was more concerned with hunting and fishing than the care of his congregation. He welcomed the American Revolution and lamented English dominance in Scotland. He criticized what he saw as the treachery of the Scottish ruling class in poems like "Such a Parcel of Rogues in a Nation" (1791) with the line "We're bought and sold for English gold." Nevertheless, he also made fun of Tom Paine (1737–1809) and other radicals in his "The Rights of Women" (1792), which he rightly maintained "merit some attention." His republican sympathies and idealism can be seen in his beloved "A Man's a Man for A' That" (1795), which scorns the corruption of wealth declaring, "The coward slave we pass him by. We dare be poor for a' that! . . . The honest man, tho' e'er sae poor, Is king of men for a' that." In like manner he criticized the corruption of universities in a remarkably modern poem "The Dean of Faculty" with its telling line "The more incapacity they bring, The more they're to your liking." Burns' best-known poem is "Auld Lang Syne" (1787), which has become the New Year's anthem.

AVEBURY

During the Bronze Age and earlier, Salisbury plain was densely populated by a people who left behind numerous earthworks and stone monuments, the purpose of which remains a mystery despite extensive speculation.

PLACES TO VISIT

SILBURY HILL AND THE WEST KENNET LONG BARROW, five miles west of Marlborough on the A4. This low 130-foot hill on the Salisbury plain is easily missed. Yet it is the largest prehistoric burial mound in Europe erected around 2500 B.C. and the center of a number of interesting prehistoric remains. You cannot walk on the hill itself, which is a protected site. The "hill" is actually an artificial mound built from large limestone blocks for some unknown purpose by a prehistoric people who left no written records to indicate the purpose of their monument. Although it has yet to be fully excavated, extensive work has already been undertaken without it yielding solid results. In all likelihood, this was an ancient burial chamber. But this is not certain. From the car park you get a good view of this strangely impressive monument. From there you can walk half a mile along a footpath to the West Kennet Long Barrow, which is one of 50 chamber tombs in the area dating from around 3500 B.C.

AVEBURY STONE CIRCLE is located to the west of Silbury Hill. Although less famous, it is actually much bigger and far more complex than the better-known Stonehenge. Here you can actually walk within the circle, while Stonehenge is now fenced off to prevent vandalism and overuse. A huge twenty-foot high earthwork protects the circle, which is 1,400 feet in diameter. The main circle is entered along one of four causeways, two of which become long avenues that run for over two miles away from the circle itself. Archaeologists believe that the circle was built around 2500 B.C. by the same peoples who built the earthworks at Silbury

Hill. The circle consists of 100 pairs of 30–40 stones of differing sizes and shapes that some scholars think represent pairs of men and women. Two and a half miles to the southeast, along one of the avenues, is a burial site known as "the Sanctuary." The circle survived almost intact until the 18th century, when local people began breaking up the stones for building material. Fortunately, the 18th-century antiquarian William Stukeley (1687–1765) managed to prevent the circle's total destruction and drew plans of its earlier design. The ALEXANDER KEILLER MUSEUM on the west side of the circle has a good display explaining what we know about the circle and showing how it probably looked when it was first built.

Although we actually know nothing substantial about the beliefs of the people who created these imposing monuments, it is clear that they had a strong belief in the afterlife. Today, of course, they are part and parcel of the growing mythology of the British neo-pagan movement even though, in reality, they have nothing to do with modern paganism.

ST. JAMES CHURCH, in the village of Avebury, is a pleasant parish church that is worth a visit for its combination of Anglo-Saxon and later Gothic style.

DEVIZES MUSEUM, seven miles from Avebury on the A361. This market town with some pleasant 18th-century buildings houses a good museum that contains many finds from Avebury and other prehistoric sites in the area. Its greatest treasure is the Marlborough Bucket, a highly decorated, unique, Bronze Age find dated to the 1st century B.C.

BATH

Originally a Celtic settlement, Bath was occupied by the Romans around A.D. 44 when they built a fort. In A.D. 60, a Roman city was established, complete with baths and temples that they called Aquae Sullis, after the local Celtic god Sulis Minerva. The city later became a center of Roman Christianity, but was stormed by pagan Saxons in 577, who renamed it Hat Bathum. In 1090 the see, or bishop's seat, which was located in Wells, was moved here to create the new see of Bath and Wells. The town prospered during the Middle Ages due to its importance in the clothing trade, which was the object of Chaucer's wit in his *The Wife of Bath*. Although its famed hot springs brought relief to Roman legionaries and were popular during the medieval period, they fell into disuse during the 15th and 16th centuries when many bath houses were closed throughout Europe due to the spread of plague and other contagious diseases. Their popularity was revived in the late 17th and 18th centuries, when water cures became the rage in medical circles. Taking the cure in Bath quickly led to the development of a sophisticated and often highly immoral social life led by

the famous Beau Nash (1674–1761), who became Master of Ceremonies in 1704. The rich and famous flocked to Bath, leading to a building boom and the creation of such Regency masterpieces as the Royal Terrace. Much of the city was rebuilt under the direction of the able architects John Wood the Elder (1704–54) and his son John Wood the Younger (1728–82).

Among the many famous people to have lived in Bath are the Christian philosopher Joseph Butler (1692–1752), who became the bishop of Bristol; General Wolf (1727–59), who conquered Quebec; and the historian Lord Thomas Babington Macaulay (1800–1859). Macaulay's writing did much to condemn the Puritans in English popular culture through remarks like "The Puritans banned bear baiting not because it harmed the bear, but because it gave pleasure to people." Jane Austen (1775–1817) set her novels *Northanger Abbey* and *Persuasion* in the city. Richard Sheridan (1751–1816) also set his novel *The Rivals* in Bath.

PLACES TO VISIT

BATH ABBEY was the last great pre-Reformation church to be constructed in

B

England. It is an impressive structure with distinctive flying buttresses and some excellent stained-glass windows. The church was built on the site of earlier churches. A nunnery was founded at this site in 675, and it became a Benedictine monastery in the reign of King Edgar (944–75), the first king of a united England, who was crowned in Bath in 973. Work on the present church began in 1499 and wasn't completed until 1616. Outside the abbey is a pleasing piazza known as the churchyard. The abbey's west facade is elaborately sculptured to depict Jacob's ladder with angels descending and ascending to heaven, as seen in a vision by Bishop Oliver King (15th century), who began the construction of this magnificent church.

ROMAN BATHS AND MUSEUM. Excavation of this important Roman site, the best-preserved in Britain, began in 1878 and continues today. The complex is really an extensive Roman temple dedicated to the local god Sul and the Roman god Minerva. Among the many archaeological finds is a bronze head of Sulis Minerva discovered in 1727. There is also a relief of the god Medusa. Other carvings show the god Hercules, while smaller items include pewter trinkets inscribed with prayers, curses, and magical formula, giving insight into religion both in Roman and in medieval times. The King's Bath is the original Roman reservoir built on the site of a local hot spring that maintains a constant temperature of 46.5 degrees centigrade. The Great Bath was the main bathing area; it is flanked by statues of great Romans erected in the 19th century. Other baths of a more specialized nature made up the entire complex.

During the 18th century, the splendid Pump Room was constructed, along with a bathing complex that was in use until the early 1900s. It is now a comfortable restaurant where the waters from the spring, which were long believed to have healing properties, may be tasted. Plans are now afoot to reopen a spa in the area that will use the spring water.

THE ASSEMBLY ROOM was the site of many scenes in the novels of Jane Austen and other authors. The original building was destroyed in an air raid in 1942, but it was carefully reconstructed after the war and now houses a fascinating Museum of Costume with designs from 1580 to the present.

THE ROYAL CRESCENT is a masterpiece of Georgian architecture built between 1767 and 1774 by the Woods. Number 1 is now preserved by the Bath Trust as a museum. Other houses are still in use as private residences or hotels. The ordered design of the terrace conveys the values of the Age of Reason, when order and balance were valued over enthusiasm and irrationality. It is also a reminder of the ethos of the ruling classes during the age of John Wesley (1703–91) and the Methodist revival.

THE VICTORIA ART GALLERY, the Guildhall, Northumberland Place, contains a good collection of English and European paintings, including works by Thomas Gainsborough (1727–88).

THE HOLBURNE MUSEUM, Sydney Gardens, also has a fine art collection, including works by Gainsborough as well as some excellent silver, glass, and porcelain. Jane Austen lived a few doors away in 4 Sydney Place.

THE BUILDING OF BATH MUSEUM, the Paragon, is worth a visit because its exhibits show the 18th-century transformation of Bath from a medieval industrial town whose economy was based on the wool trade into an elegant 18th-century spa. The museum is housed in an early Methodist chapel.

BEDFORD

You won't find Bedford mentioned in many tour guides because it is a rather ordinary English town that holds little of interest to the secular tourist. But for Christians it is a major religious site because of its association with John Bunyan (1628–88), who was born in nearby Elstow. It was in the local jail on High Street that Bunyan wrote such classics as *The Pilgrim's Progress* and *Grace Abounding*.

There was a settlement in the area in Roman times, and according to legend the Saxon won a victory over the local people in 571. The town prospered during the Middle Ages but was plundered by Danes in 1010. Slowly it was rebuilt and has remained a fairly quiet English provincial town.

PLACES TO VISIT

THE JOHN BUNYAN MUSEUM, Mill St. Recently opened, this is the main Bunyan site in Bedford. It is a small but

spiritually important collection lovingly created by believing Christians who raised over one million pounds to create the museum through donations to the Bunyan Trust. Government aid was refused because government funds for museums and art galleries rely on lotteries, which John Bunyan would have considered immoral. The museum contains numerous items of interest, including early editions of such famous works as *The Pilgrim's Progress*.

ST. JOHN'S RECTORY, St. John's St., is now the headquarters of the local St. John's Ambulance, where in the early 1650s John Bunyan was converted. He was plying his trade as a tinker repairing pots and pans when he met the Rev. John Gifford, the newly appointed rector, or pastor, of St. John's Church, an Independent Congregation in Bedford. Gifford was a reformed alcoholic who had been recently converted himself. He pleaded with Bunyan, leading Bunyan to

B

a conviction of sin and his conversion. Today only one small room is open to the public as a Bunyan museum. A plaque on 17 St. Cuthberbert's Street marks the site where Bunyan and his family moved in 1655. The original cottage was demolished in the early 19th century.

MOOT HALL, seven miles from Bedford in nearby Elstow, is the other main Bunyan site in the area. It is an interesting timber-framed hall built in the early 16th century that is now a museum devoted to the life and times of John Bunyan. He was actually born in a small cottage near the Moot Hall that no longer exists, although a small monument erected in 1951 marks the spot. It seems certain that the Bunyan family had lived in this neighborhood for well over 400 years.

THE COWPER AND NEWTON MUSEUM, Orchard Side, Market Place, Olney, Buckinghamshire, not far from Bedford, is devoted to the life and work of the great 18th-century hymn writer William Cowper (1731–1800), author of such favorite hymns as "God Moves in a Mysterious Way," and his friend John Newton (1725–1807), the author of the well-loved hymn "Amazing Grace." The museum houses the personal belongings and books of both men and has an attractive garden.

Although they are all relatively small and seemingly unimportant, a number of other Bunyan sites exist in the area of Bedford which anyone seriously interested in Bunyan may want to visit. On the A428 from Bedford to Northampton, one mile right past Bromham, is the STEVINGTON CROSS. This is a 14th-century stone cross that stands in the center of the village of Stevington and is believed to have inspired the scene in *The Pilgrim's Progress* where Pilgrim was freed from the burden he was carrying. On the B530, just north of Ampthill, is the steep AMPTHILL HILL, which stands on a route regularly taken by Bunyan when he worked as a tinker. This is said to be the source for the Hill Difficulty. Finally, if you turn left off the B530 from Ampthill along the narrow road at Ampthill Hill, you come to HOUGHTON HOUSE, which is open to the public and is believed to be the source of Bunyan's the House Beautiful, because Bunyan is known to have visited Houghton House on many occasions.

BEVERLY

riginally called Inderawood, an abbey was built here around 690 by John Beverly, bishop of Hexham, who was buried in the church he founded after his death in 721. As a result of his reputation as a great scholar, conscientious pastor, and saintly person, people began to visit his grave, where they claimed they had received miraculous cures. The abbey became a major site of pilgrimage throughout the Middle Ages, and a thriving market town soon grew up around it. Danish Vikings destroyed the original church in 866, but it quickly revived to become a flourishing center of Christian activity. A fire in 1188 did considerable damage to the building, and in 1213 the central tower, weakened by the fire, collapsed. Afterwards the church was rebuilt over two centuries, incorporating variations of the Gothic style to create one of the best Gothic churches in England.

A theological school was established here for secular canons in the 10th century, reinforcing Beverly's importance as a center of Christian learning and evangelism. By 1370 the town had over 5000 inhabitants, making it one of the most important centers in the north of England. Because of its important role in educating the laity, the abbey was one of the last to be dissolved during the Reformation. After its dissolution in 1547, it became a parish church. It was restored in 1713 to prevent it falling into ruins.

During the 18th and 19th centuries Beverly slowly lost commercial importance and saw its population decline relative to other northern cities. Consequently, it escaped the ravages of the Industrial Revolution, which destroyed many ancient buildings. Today over 300 buildings in the town are listed as important historic sites and architectural gems. Nevertheless, the town is still off the main tourist routes, thus avoiding the commercialism that often scars better-known historical sites, and is well worth visiting.

PLACES TO VISIT

BEVERLY MINSTER, which stands on the site of the original church, is an architectural treasure that rivals many English cathedrals. Because it was built over a long period during which the architectural styles gradually changed, it is possible to see all the different developments of the English Gothic style under one roof. The east end of the church, which is the oldest, is built in the Early Gothic style. The nave itself, built about a century later, is decorated Gothic, while its upper story, known as the clerestory, is a combination of the decorated and perpendicular Gothic styles. Finally the west front, which was completed in 1421, is pure perpendicular.

John of Beverly is buried under a plaque at the east end of the nave. There is also the elaborate tomb, decorated with angels and mythic animals, known as the Percy (1340–49), which is probably the tomb of Lady Idonea Percy (d. 1365).

The church is rich in stone and woodcarvings. Note the 68 misericords, or folding seats for the choir, which were designed to support someone while standing through long services. They are the work of the 16th-century Ripon

B

school of craftsmen. There are also 16th-century carvings of the evangelists on the west doors. In the north aisle are some fine stone carvings of musicians.

The north choir aisle has an unusual double staircase that once led to the chapter house. There is also a late Norman marble font in the south aisle with a highly decorated cover.

The Fridsol, or peace chair, in the sanctuary on the north side of the altar, is said to date from King Athelstan's (895–939) reign; he was the grandson of Alfred the Great (849–99). The chair is dated around 925. Anyone who sat in it was automatically granted 30 days' sanctuary. Before the modern period, when jails were built, justice was administered on the basis of the biblical principle of restitution, a practice that also involved cities of refuge and the granting of sanctuary in churches.

Finally, an original medieval crane in the central tower was once used to raise the stones used to rebuild the church.

St. Mary's Church, Hengate and

North Bar, stands beside the one remaining medieval gate that once was one of five gates in the town's fortified walls. Today it is the only surviving medieval church in the town and is noted for its particularly rich collection of medieval carvings and musical instruments, said to be the best in England. Note the carving of the "pilgrim rabbit" on the pillar of St. Michael's Chapel. This fascinating figure is believed to have inspired both Charles Dodgson (1832–1898), better known as Lewis Carroll, to create the White Rabbit in his classic story *Alice in Wonderland*, and the artist Sir John Tenniel (1820–1914), who drew the original illustrations for Carroll's book. The painted ceiling of the church contains portraits of English kings, from legendary figures of pre-history to Henry VI (1421–71). When the ceiling was restored in 1939, the face of George VI (1895–1952) was added among the legendary kings. The misericords are also exquisitely carved.

BOSTON

Various suggestions have been made about the origins of the name of Boston. Some suggest that it is a corruption of "Botolph's stone"; others say it refers to "Botolph's town." In either case it seems that an Anglo-Saxon monk, Botolph, built a monastery here in the mid-7th century.

The town grew up around the monastic settlement, which was strategically located on an important river crossing. As a result of its location, it became the center for the export of wool to Flanders and by the 13th century was the second largest port in England. Following the discovery of the American continent,

B

the focus of English trade switched to the west coast. Boston declined in importance until the draining of the Lincolnshire fens, or marshes, in the 18th century, when Boston became a thriving agricultural center. Today the port once again plays an important role in the local economy as a result of trade within the European community. Boston is the birthplace of John Foxe (1516–87), whose *Acts and Monuments of Matters Happening in the Church*, commonly known as his *Book of Martyrs* (1563), ably documented the suffering of Protestants during the Reformation and became one of the most popular English books of the 16th and 17th centuries. The composer John Taverner (1495–1545) also lived and worked here from 1537 until his death.

PLACES TO VISIT

ST. BOTOLPH'S CHURCH, South St. Built in the 14th century by local merchants in gratitude to God for their prosperity, St. Botolph's is a splendid building that was once the largest parish church in England. The church tower is known as "the stump" because its spire was never completed. In the 16th century, the tower was given a lantern that could be seen from many miles away and acted as a lighthouse for sailors and people crossing the treacherous fens. The church has some exquisitely carved misericords (choir stalls), decorated with a variety of religious and secular scenes, including a medieval schoolmaster caning a boy while others await a similar fate. The COTTON CHAPEL is dedicated to John Cotton (1585–1652) who was the local vicar. He emigrated to Boston, Massachusetts, in 1633, where he became the leading Puritan theologian of the American colonies. There is also a plaque commemorating George Bass (d. 1812), a surgeon, who played an important role in the exploration of Australia and gave his name to the strait between the Australian mainland and Tasmania.

GUILDHALL, South St., is where the Pilgrim fathers were jailed for 30 days. Several of their cells are now part of a small museum that is important to anyone interested in Puritan or American history.

JOHN TAVERNER (1495–1545) composed Christian music before and during the English Reformation. He was imprisoned by Cardinal Wolsey (1475–1530) in 1530 because he was suspected of being a Protestant and therefore a heretic. But he was quickly released because Wolsey considered him "a mere musician." Following Wolsey's death, he worked for Thomas Cromwell (1485–1540) promoting the Protestant cause. He is generally considered the greatest musician of the Tudor period in England.

BOTHWELL-BLANTYRE

This uninteresting suburb of Hamilton, 12 miles southeast of Glasgow, was a small village in the early 19th century and is the birthplace of David Livingstone (1813–73).

PLACES TO VISIT

THE NATIONAL DAVID LIVINGSTONE MEMORIAL, Shuttle Row, is housed in the 24-room tenement block where Livingstone lived as a child. It has various exhibits about his life as well as the 19th-century missionary movement. The room where the entire Livingstone family lived comes as a shock to modern visitors. From these squalid conditions Livingstone escaped by dint of hard work and natural intelligence, studying in his spare time after long days at work to help support the family. Apart from the missionary interest, the museum helps visitors understand the utter poverty in which many people lived early in the 19th century and the impact the gospel was able to have even under such difficult social conditions.

BOTHWELL BRIDGE, which spans the Clyde, is a few miles to the north. Here in 1679 the army of Monmouth and Claverhouse routed the Covenanters, who rebelled against the imposition of Episcopacy and what they saw as unbiblical church practices by the government of Charles II (1630–85). Over 500 men were killed and another 1000 taken prisoner. This defeat led to their brutal suppression, known as "the killing time." Their religious rights were not restored until the English revolution of 1688 that forced James VII of Scotland, II of England, to flee and brought William of Orange, the III (1650–1702), to the throne.

BRISTOL

According to legend St. Augustine of Canterbury (d. 605) met with representatives of the ancient Celtic Church in Bristol in 603, six years after the arrival of his evangelistic mission to England, to discuss mutual concerns and differences in religious practice, such as the date of Easter. The negotiations were a failure. But they helped establish Bristol as an important town at a very early period in English history. Almost 500 years later, in 1140, a monastery was established on the site of the supposed meeting. Following the Reformation, this abbey church became Bristol Cathedral.

The town itself grew up in the 700s during Saxon times, when it was the center of a flourishing slave trade. In the 18th century, the city again grew rich through trade in slaves. This time Africans were brutally shipped to North America on Bristol ships, whose owners built magnificent houses in Bristol and the surrounding countryside. A reminder of the slave trade is to be found in street names like Whiteladies Road and Blackboys Hill.

At the time of the Norman Conquest, in 1066, Bristol was the fourth largest city in England. To secure the area, the Normans built a castle, which was rebuilt in 1126 by Robert, earl of Gloucester (d. 1147). King Stephen (1097–1154) was held prisoner here for a short while in 1141 during the civil war that pitted him against the Empress Maud (1102–67).

John Cabot sailed from Bristol on June 24, 1407, to discover Newfoundland, and later his son explored the coast of North America after sailing from Bristol. During the English Civil War (1642–46), the citizens of Bristol sided with Parliament. But the city was stormed by Prince Rupert (1619–82), who made it a Royalist stronghold until it was recaptured by General Fairfax

(1612–71) in 1645. After retaking the city, the Parliamentarian army systematically dismantled the castle. Today the place where the castle once stood is part of the University of Bristol.

Serious rioting broke out in 1831 as a result of the opposition of Anglican bishops in the House of Lords to the Reform Bills that granted voting rights to dissenters and Roman Catholics. As a result, the Bishop's Palace and jail were torched. The 19th century also saw Bristol boom as an industrial center. This development was symbolized by the launching of the world's first steamship, Isambard Kingdom Brunel's (1806–59) *The Great Western*, followed by his construction of the Clifton Suspension Bridge. During World War II, Bristol's importance as a shipping and industrial center led to heavy air raids that destroyed the center of the old city.

During the 18th and 19th centuries, Bristol was a center of evangelical Christianity. Baptists, Methodists, and the Plymouth Brethren all took root here. Thus, John Wesley (1703–91) and his Methodist movement made Bristol a center of opposition to the slave trade, while George Müller's (1805–98) orphanages pioneered child welfare by taking care of and educating abandoned children.

PLACES TO VISIT

BRISTOL CATHEDRAL, College Green, is a Late Gothic building that originated as an abbey. It was elevated to

B

the rank of a cathedral by Henry VIII in 1542 following the Reformation and the Dissolution of the Monasteries. The nave and west tower were constructed in the 19th century in neo-Gothic style. A church stood on this site from at least the 10th century, although legend dates its origins to the evangelistic work of St. Augustine of Canterbury in the year 603. The original church, excluding the east end, is a hall church that has chancels and aisles of equal height. Although this style is common on the continent, it is very rare in England.

There are some excellent 15th-century misericords and a unique 14th-century vaulted ceiling in the choir that is the earliest of its kind. The 12th-century Elder Lady Chapel, which runs off the north transept, has some fine carvings, including one of a monkey playing the bagpipes. The east Lady Chapel has some highly colored carvings dating from its construction in the 13th century. It also contains some of the best English medieval stained-glass windows. The cloister, where medieval monks walked, studied, and prayed, and chapter house, where clergy met with

the bishop to discuss theological and practical issues, are fine examples of medieval architecture. In the south transept is an unusual Saxon coffin dating from around the year 1000, with carvings depicting the harrowing of hell.

Note the monument to the philosopher and Christian apologist Bishop Joseph Butler in the north transept. The Newton Chapel contains the tombs of the Newton family.

LORD MAYOR'S CHAPEL/ST. MARK'S CHAPEL, College Green, almost diagonally opposite the cathedral, was founded as a hospital and welfare center in 1260. The entire complex, of which only the church remains, was capable of housing over 100 people. Much of the present building dates from the 15th century. It has some of the best French and Flemish 16th-century stained-glass windows in England. The chapel itself reminds the visitor that throughout history, Christians have played a prominent role in caring for the poor and providing medical aid to those in need.

ST. MARY'S REDCLIFFE, Redcliffe Way. Queen Elizabeth I called this

BISHOP BUTLER (1692–1752) was a famous Christian apologist and author of the *Analogy of Religion* (1736). He became bishop of Bristol in 1738, and in 1750 the bishop of Durham. Although his writings helped destroy British Deism as an intellectual movement, he came into sharp conflict with John Wesley (1703–91) and George Whitefield (1714–70), whose style of preaching he considered too emotional.

beautiful Gothic church "the fairest, godliest, and most famous parish church in all my realm." It was built between 1325 and 1375 through donations from William Canynge the Elder (d. 1396) and his grandson William Canynge the Younger (1399–1474), who held office as the Lord Mayor of Bristol. In the St. John the Baptist's Chapel, which is commonly known as the American Chapel, whalebone was presented to the church by John Cabot (1425–1500) after his successful voyage of discovery from Bristol to North America. It also contains a wooden statue of Elizabeth I.

The transepts are unusual in that they have aisles, something occasionally found in cathedrals but very rarely in parish churches. In the south transept is the tomb of William Canynge and his wife. There is also the tomb of Sir William Penn (d. 1670), whose son William Penn (1644–1718) was converted by the Quakers while at Oxford University and eventually founded Pennsylvania. There is also a monument to the admiral, where he is seen in full armor at the west end of the nave. Above the north porch is the room where Thomas Chatterton (1752–70) claimed to have discovered the 15th-century manuscripts that made him famous.

JOHN WESLEY'S CHAPEL, Broadmead, is the oldest Methodist meeting house in Britain. From here John Wesley railed against the evils of the slave trade. Consequently local gentry, who thrived on the trade, regularly sent gangs of local thugs to break up the services. This is why the back of the church, where Wesley had his rooms, is built like a small fortress, and the pulpit itself is a door in the wall high above

---

THOMAS CHATTERTON (1752–70). Known as "the wonderful boy," Chatterton was born in what is now Redcliffe Way. As a teenager he claimed to have discovered a collection of ancient poems written by a 15th-century monk whom he called Thomas Rowley. Literary opinion was divided about the authenticity of the poems, some of which were written on old parchment. Eventually the majority of critics decided that they were forgeries written on parchment Chatterton had taken from a collection he found in the muniment room above the north porch of St. Mary's Redcliffe, where Chatterton's uncle was the sextant. After losing his job as an apprentice lawyer, Chatterton went to London, where, in dire poverty, he eventually committed suicide. Seven years later, Dr. Johnson went to Bristol to investigate the case and concluded that the poems were indeed forgeries. Nevertheless, the poems took on a life of their own and helped stimulate the growth of the Romantic movement.

B

the congregation, thus protecting Wesley from rioters who might well have lynched him. The chapel is now a fascinating museum that testifies to the social impact of Christianity and the courage of Wesley and his fellow preachers in a hostile society.

CHARLES WESLEY'S HOUSE, 4 Charles St., is now a center for prayer, discussion, and other activities. The house may be viewed by appointment.

QUAKER FRIARS, off Broadmead, is a square with the remains of a 13th-century Dominican priory and the Old Friends' Meeting House built in 1747. An earlier Quaker chapel was opened here in 1670, and William Penn was married here in 1670.

HANNAH MORE'S HOUSE, 43 Park St., was the home and boarding school of the great Christian social reformer Hannah More (1745–1833), who is credited with founding popular education in Britain. All one sees today is a plaque on the wall, which is a shame, because this house ought to be a museum to social reform and the achievements of a great Christian woman.

HANNAH MORE (1745–1833) was one of the great evangelical social reformers of the late 18th and early 19th centuries. Born in Stapleton, Gloustershire, she was educated by her father at his school in Bristol. Later, while visiting London, she became a friend of the great conservative politician Edmund Burke (1729–97), who was Bristol's member of Parliament, and Samuel Johnson (1709–84), who encouraged her to publish her poems and plays, which were then staged by the famous actor David Garrick (1717–79). After Garrick's death, she concentrated on writing Christian literature while living off the proceeds from her earlier writings and new publications. Her *Sacred Dramas* (1782) and *Thoughts on the Importance of the Manners of the Great to General Society* (1788) were best-sellers. In 1787 she became a close friend of William Wilberforce (1759–1833) and through him John Newton (1725–1807), who became her main sources of spiritual inspiration. During a visit to the Mendip Hills with Wilberforce and a group of friends, she became aware of the widespread ignorance and general illiteracy of ordinary people. Subsequently, supported by Wilberforce, Newton, and other evangelical leaders, she set about establishing a network of parish schools to educate the children of the poor. In her schools literacy, religious education, and practical trades were taught as a way of improving daily life. Following the outbreak of the French Revolution, she wrote numerous tracts designed to counter what she saw as the deadly effects of Deism and the revolutionary spirit that attacked Christianity.

B

GEORGE MÜLLER (1805–98) was a German-born pastor, philanthropist, and leader in the Plymouth Brethren in Britain. After a dissolute life, he was converted during a prayer meeting by German Pietists in 1825. In 1832 in Bristol, England, he began a church-planting ministry and in 1835 opened his orphanage, for which he is chiefly remembered. The orphanage grew from a rented house to a great complex of buildings. Müller renounced a regular salary and refused throughout the rest of his life to make any requests for financial support. His ideas and example provide the basis for modern "faith" missions, greatly influencing people like Hudson Taylor (1832–1905), who founded the China Inland Mission, and Francis Schaeffer (1912–83) and the L'Abri movement. Müller's *A Narrative of the Lord's Dealing with George Müller* (1905) is a spiritual classic.

The City of Bristol College, Ashley Down, Ashley Down Rd., occupies the final complex of the **GEORGE MÜLLER HOMES**. The Müller Orphanage buildings have "listed status," which means that their outward appearance cannot be changed, and the grounds have a "preservation order" on them, which protects their integrity. But beyond this minimal recognition, Müller's heritage is neglected and his study is now a storeroom. Nevertheless, a move is afoot to change things by creating a George Müller museum on the site.

Bristol is also the home of three British theological colleges. The most recently founded, but paradoxically the best known today, is **TRINITY COLLEGE**, Stoke Hill. It was founded in the 1970s through an amalgamation of two older colleges and is known because the popular writer and theologian Jim (J. I.) Packer was on its faculty and for a while

its principal before he moved to Regent College in Vancouver, Canada. This is one of the leading evangelical Anglican colleges in Britain. The oldest of the Bristol colleges is the **BRISTOL BAPTIST COLLEGE**, which possesses an original copy of William Tyndale's New Testament and a fine bust of Oliver Cromwell. Finally, there is **WESLEY COLLEGE**, College Park Drive. Built in 1790, this richly furnished house shows how wealthy merchants lived in the 18th century and is a great introduction to the social and intellectual climate that flourished during the Enlightenment. It was here that the poets William Wordsworth and Samuel Coleridge first met. This meeting helped launch the Romantic movement in England.

BRISTOL INDUSTRIAL MUSEUM, Prince's Warf, is a fascinating collection housed in an old warehouse. It contains

B

a large number of manufactured goods made in Bristol, including several cars and a bus.

SS *GREAT BRITAIN*. The pride of 19th-century Bristol industry is Isambard Kingdom Brunel's *Great Britain*, the world's first ironclad steamship, launched in 1843. Before it was wrecked in the Falklands in 1886, it circumnavigated the world 32 times. It was "rescued" from oblivion in 1970 and returned to Bristol, where it was

restored to become a major tourist attraction and monument to the 19th-century Industrial Revolution.

CITY MUSEUM AND ART GALLERY, Queen's Rd., contains many good paintings, including a fine portrait of Martin Luther (1483–1546) by his friend Lucas Cranach the Elder (1472–1553). The museum contains excellent Egyptian and Roman collections as well as local history and an interesting display of Bristol glass.

CAMBRIDGE

Recent excavations reveal a pre-Roman settlement in the area and a Roman town from around A.D. 60. Following the Norman conquest, a castle was built to control the river crossing. Under its protection a thriving market town developed. The university was founded in the 13th century by scholars who are said to have fled Oxford after riots between the townspeople and the university. It received a royal charter from Henry III (1207–72) in 1231, but it was not until 1284 that Peterhouse, the first college, was founded. By 1352 seven more colleges were in existence, and the university began to dominate the town. This led to riots in 1381 between the townsfolk and university community and the plundering of several colleges. Eventually the university community gained

the upper hand, and the town developed as a small market town dominated by the university. The fame of Cambridge as a center of European learning was established when Erasmus of Rotterdam (1466–1536) chose to live in the city rather than in Oxford. During the Tudor era, Cambridge was a center of Protestant scholarship, graduating Archbishop Thomas Cranmer (1489–1556) and Bishops Hugh Latimer (1485–1555) and Nicholas Ridley (1500–1555), all of whom were burnt at the stake in Oxford by Queen Mary (1516–58). Later, Cambridge became a center of Puritanism and counted Oliver Cromwell (1599–1658), the Lord Protector, among its graduates. During the English Civil Wars (1642–46 and 1648), the university sided with the crown, while the town and surrounding countryside were Parliamentarian. Following the restoration of the monarchy in 1660, the university was rewarded for its loyalty to the king by the granting of numerous privileges, but decay soon set in, and the academic reputation of the university steadily declined until the late 19th century. Today Cambridge is a center of scientific research and hi-tech industries and boasts that 90 of its graduates are Nobel laureates. Although anyone can view the outside of the colleges, admittance to many areas is restricted during term; therefore visitors need to check with the local tourist office about when and where they are allowed to visit before venturing to Cambridge.

PLACES TO VISIT

KING'S COLLEGE CHAPEL, King's Parade, has become Cambridge's most famous landmark due to the careful marketing of its justly famous boys choir, which broadcasts and records its carol service every Christmas to the delight of music lovers throughout the world. Built between 1446 and 1515, the chapel is a wonderful example of Late Gothic architecture that was financed by kings Henry VI (1421–71), Henry VII (1457–1509), and Henry VIII (1491–1547). The beautiful exterior was the subject of a painting by the artist Joseph Turner (1775–1851) and praised in the poems of William Wordsworth (1770–1850), thus stimulating the so-called 19th-century Gothic revival. The chapel has some particularly splendid fan vaulting. In 1962 an anonymous benefactor donated Paul Rubens's (1577–1640) *Adoration of the Magi*, which now hangs behind the high altar.

TRINITY COLLEGE, King's Parade-St. John's St., is the third largest landowner in England and boasts among its graduates the poets John Dryden, Lord Byron, and Alfred Lord Tennyson; the novelist William Thackeray; scientists Isaac Newton and Lord Rutherford; composer Vaughan Williams; Prime Ministers Pandit Nehru, Balfour, and Baldwin; Kings Edward VII and George VI; and Prince Charles, as well as philosophers Bertrand Russell and Ludwig Wittgenstein. It was founded in 1546 by Henry VIII, whose statue can be seen over the college's gate. Today the college is probably best known as the

THOMAS CRANMER (1489–1556) was the archbishop of Canterbury and the prominent Protestant Reformer whose prose in the *Book of Common Prayer* (1552) helped shape the English language. He was burnt at the stake for heresy during the reign of Mary Tudor, queen of England and Ireland.

scene of the first race in the film *Chariots of Fire*. According to legend, Lord Byron used the fountain in the center of the college square to wash the pet bear he acquired when the college forbade students from keeping dogs. To add spice to the tale, it's said that he always bathed with his bear in the nude. More seriously, it was in the cloisters of the college where Isaac Newton calculated the speed of sound. At the end of the courtyard is the famous **WREN LIBRARY,** which appears small from the outside, but in fact is remarkably large.

ST. JOHN'S COLLEGE, St. John's St., was founded in 1511 by Lady Margaret Beaufort (1443–1509) on the site of a 13th-century hospital. It possesses one of the best examples of Tudor oak paneling in England in its 16th-century combination room. In the richly paneled hall there is a portrait of William Wordsworth, who studied here and lived above the college kitchens. John

Ruskin (1819–1900) described the college's second court as the most beautiful in Cambridge. The college library contains an original copy of the Bible, published for reading in churches by Archbishop Cranmer in 1539. The malevolent Titus Oates (1649–1705) studied here, as did the Parliamentarian General Lord Fairfax (1612–71), the apologist Samuel Butler, and Erasmus Darwin (1731–1802), the grandfather of Charles Darwin (1809–82) and an early advocate of a form of evolution.

QUEENS COLLEGE, Silver St., Queen's Lane, founded in 1446, takes its name from two queens, Margaret of Anjou (1429–82), the wife of Henry VI, and Elizabeth Woodville (1437–92), Edward IV's (1442–83) wife, both of whom patronized the college. It is known for its wonderfully romantic Elizabethan courtyard and superb half-timbered buildings. Here you can also see the **MATHEMATICAL BRIDGE**, built

TITUS OATES (1649–1705) was born into an Anabaptist family. He studied at Cambridge University and became a minister in the Church of England before claiming to convert to Roman Catholicism. He then moved to France, where for a while he studied at a Jesuit College, from which he was expelled for unacceptable behavior. He returned to England in June 1678, where he claimed to have uncovered a "Popish Plot" to assassinate the king and massacre Protestants. As a result of his testimony, over 35 prominent Catholics were tried and executed before the whole thing was proved to be a hoax. Oates was imprisoned for perjury and sentenced to life imprisonment in 1685. After the Glorious Revolution of 1688, he was freed and granted a pension.

over the river Cam in the 18th century on strict mathematical principles which are said to ensure that even if all the nails from this wooden construction were removed, it would remain fully functional. This monument vividly illustrates the grip mathematical thinking exercised over Europe during the Enlightenment.

MAGDALENE COLLEGE (pronounced "maudlin") Magdalene St., was first established as a monastic institution in 1428. It was reestablished in 1542 and only began admitting female students in 1988, testifying to the conservatism of this venerable community. Built in the 16th century, the college houses the library of Samuel Pepys (1633–1703), which is on display to the public in the **PEPYS BUILDING**.

EMANUEL COLLEGE, St. Andrew's St., was founded in 1584 on the site of a former Dominican monastery by Sir Walter Midmay (c. 1520–89), the chancellor of the exchequer, or chief financial officer, of Queen Elizabeth I, to train clergy for the newly reformed Church of England. It became a center of Puritan scholarship and later of the so-called "Cambridge Platonists." One of its most famous graduates was John Harvard (1607–38), after whom Harvard College, now Harvard University, was named, as a result of the role he played in its creation by donating £779 and over 300 books to create the core of its library. Emanuel claims that its graduates represented 67 of the original 100 Puritan clergy who emigrated to America to escape religious persecution. The chapel has a fine altarpiece by the Italian artist Jacopo Amigoni (1682–1752), painted in 1734, as well as a memorial window dedicated to him. Another influential graduate was William Law (1686–1761), whose devotional writings such as *Christian Perfection* (1726) and *A Serious Call to a Devout and Holy Life* (1728) influenced John Wesley, George Whitefield, and Andrew Murray. Swift used the college as the setting for the education of Gulliver in his classic *Travels*.

SIDNEY SUSSEX COLLEGE, Sidney St., is one of the more unimposing colleges that was badly "restored" in the

CAMBRIDGE PLATONISTS flourished at the University of Cambridge in the 17th century in reaction to Puritanism and the dominance of Aristotelian philosophy in Christian thought. Although they remained Protestant, the Platonists sought to root their faith in a tradition other than that of the dominant Calvinism of the Reformers. They rejected the Calvinism prevalent in the Church of England in favor of a form of faith that emphasized God's love and a theology close to Dutch Arminianism.

C

19th century. It was founded by Francis Sydney (1531–89), count of Sussex, in 1589 on the site of a Franciscan monastery where the medieval philosopher Johannes Duns Scotus (1265–1308) once taught theology. The 18th-century hall has a portrait of its most famous graduate, the Parliamentarian general and statesman, Oliver Cromwell (1599–1658). In 1960 Cromwell's head was buried at a secret location in the college chapel. More recently Lord David Owen (b. 1938), who was known for his outspoken Christian views as the British foreign secretary from 1977–79, was a student here.

PEMBROKE COLLEGE, Trumpington St., was founded in 1347 by the countess of Pembroke, Mary de St. Pol (14th century). Its chapel was the first significant building designed by Sir Christopher Wren (1632–1723) in the neoclassical style. Pembroke prides itself on producing bishops for the Church of England, including Edmund Grindal (1519–83) and John Whitgift (1530–1604). Students here included the Christian poet Edmund Spenser (1552–99); the modern skeptical poet Ted Hughes (1930–98); and the politician William Pitt the Younger (1759–1806), who became prime minister at the age of 25. Pitt's statue can be seen outside the college's library. The Puritan Roger Williams (1604–83), who as a strong advocate of religious liberty founded the city of Providence, Rhode Island, in 1636, and the first Baptist church in America in 1639, graduated from Pembroke College in 1627. Lancelot Andrewes (1555–1626), one of the translators of the King James, or Authorized, Bible, became master of the college in 1589.

OLIVER CROMWELL (1599–1658) was the English Puritan general and democrat who championed the rights of commoners against King Charles I and aristocracy. He founded the New Model Army that he led to victory in the English Civil War. After Charles I (1600–1649) threatened a second civil war, Cromwell supported his execution. He ruthlessly subdued the Royalist rebellion in Ireland (1649–50), believing that his actions would prevent further bloodshed. He was made Lord Protector in 1653 and ruled by ordinances confirmed by Parliament. He reorganized the Church of England, protected Quakers and Jews, and favored religious toleration. His actions ensured that Parliament and not kings with absolute power eventually ruled England.

FAMOUS BISHOPS OF THE CHURCH OF ENGLAND

C

EDMUND GRINDAL (1519–83) studied at Cambridge University, where he was converted to the Protestant cause before becoming a fellow (professor) at Pembroke College. During the reign of Mary Tudor (Bloody Mary), he fled to the Continent, finding refuge in Frankfurt-am-Main, where he became a staunch Calvinist. Upon the accession of Elizabeth I, he returned to England, where he became bishop of London in 1559 and played an important role in revising Cranmer's *Book of Common Prayer* for use in churches. He became the archbishop of York in 1570, and finally archbishop of Canterbury in 1575. His Puritan sympathies and strong biblical preaching made him very unpopular at court, as did his refusal to persecute independent Bible study, or "prophesying," groups among the clergy. Consequently, he was suspended from his administrative, but not spiritual tasks, from 1577 to 1582.

JOHN WHITGIFT (1530–1604) was educated at both Queens and Pembroke College, Cambridge, before becoming a fellow of Peterhouse and in 1563 the Lady Margaret Chair of Divinity at Cambridge University. In 1570 he became the master of Trinity College, where he came into sharp conflict with Thomas Cartwright (1535–1603), one of the leading Cambridge Puritans. His opposition to Puritanism brought him to the attention of Queen Elizabeth, who appointed him archbishop of Canterbury in 1583 after the death of Edmund Grindal (1519–83), whose Puritanism she loathed. As archbishop he strove to uphold Episcopacy and the rule of bishops, and suppress Puritanism, which leaned toward Presbyterian forms of church government. Although Whitgift used church courts to interrogate clergy suspected of Puritan leanings, he was, paradoxically, a Calvinist in most essential doctrines.

THE ROUND CHURCH, Bridge St., was built in 1130 as a replica for the Church of the Holy Sepulchre in Jerusalem. It is one of four churches of its type in England. Unfortunately, it was badly restored in the 19th century, losing much of its historical value.

FITZWILLIAM MUSEUM, Trumpington St., is one of the oldest and richest public museums and art collections in England. This splendid neoclassical building erected between 1837 and 1847 houses the original collection, donated to the university by Viscount Richard Fitzwilliam (1745–1816).

On the ground floor, the lower galleries include a fine ancient Egyptian and Mediterranean collection as well as some remarkable exhibits of pottery and European porcelain. There is also a Chinese and Korean gallery. The upper galleries house some outstanding English and European paintings, including works by Pieter Brueghel the Younger, Peter Paul Rubens, Franz Hals, Rembrandt van Rijn, Pierre August Renoir, and Claude Monet. Among the English works are paintings by Thomas Gainsborough, Sir Joshua Reynolds, William Hogarth, and John Constable. Modern works include those by Pablo Picasso, Benjamin Nicholson, and Graham Sutherland.

UNIVERSITY LIBRARY, Memorial Court, contains among its many treasures a copy of the Gutenberg Bible and the first book to be printed in England, William Caxton's (1422–91) *The Historyes of Troye* (1475). It also contains the 5th-century *Codex Bezae,* one of the earliest copies of the Gospels, and the private libraries of many famous people, including Charles Darwin (1809–82) and Isaac Newton (1642–1727). More

recently, the libraries of the British Bible Society and the Royal Commonwealth Society have been added to the collection. Because this is a working research library, people cannot wander around at will. But there are exhibitions on display to the public and a daily guided tour that begins at 3 P.M.

Today Cambridge is the home of the TYNDALE FELLOWSHIP and TYNDALE HOUSE, Selwyn Gardens. This is the world's leading evangelical research center for the study of the Bible and the publisher of the prestigious *Tyndale Bulletin* and numerous scholarly books on theological and biblical issues. Tyndale House is a ten-minute walk from the city center and only a five-minute walk from the University Library. Founded in 1944 as a private library dedicated to "foster research in a spirit of loyalty to the historic Christian faith," today it is a recognized center of biblical research worldwide. The library contains over 30,000 volumes and subscribes to over 200 academic journals. It also has a very up-to-date collection of biblical manuscripts and related materials on CD Rom.

CANTERBURY

Situated on a key crossing on the river Stour between London and Dover, a settlement existed here in pre-Roman times. The Romans conquered the area and built a fortified town on what was a strategic military road during the reign of the Emperor Claudius in A.D. 43, calling it Durovernum. After the withdrawal of the Roman legions in 450, Canterbury became the capital of the Saxon kingdom of Kent. Ethelbert (560–616) married Bertha, the daughter of the Frankish King Charibert (6th century), who insisted that she be allowed to practice her Christianity. Ethelbert agreed and allowed his wife to build a church in his capital and bring along her priests. He welcomed the arrival of Augustine of Canterbury's (d. 604) evangelistic mission in 597 and was soon converted along with many of his followers, although he made no attempt to force Christianity upon his people. Thus Ethelbert became the first Christian king in England and was later canonized. His feast day is celebrated on the 25th of February.

Augustine built several churches, including a Benedictine abbey in 598 that became the burial place of Saxon kings. Later he established another church that grew into the present cathedral. Augustine's church was destroyed by a fire in 1067 and replaced by a larger stone building. In 1070 this older Saxon church was leveled by the Norman Archbishop Lanfrac (1005–1089) to construct an even larger structure. Of the original only the crypt remains. Further extensions were carried out by the philosopher primate Anselm of Canterbury (1033–1109). After the brutal murder of Archbishop Thomas à Becket (1118–70), his shrine became the most important pilgrimage site in northern Europe until it was destroyed during the English Reformation on the orders of Henry VIII (1491–1547). The importance of Canterbury as a pilgrimage des-

tination and the joy, spirituality, and downright abuse of the practice is vividly illustrated in Geoffrey Chaucer's (1345–1400) unforgettable *Canterbury Tales* (1386–90). The monks of Canterbury, who lived in a monastic community, do not seem to have accepted the Rule of St. Benedict until 998; after that they continued to live as Benedictines until the Dissolution of their monastery in 1540. During the reign of Queen Mary (1516–58), the 83rd archbishop of Canterbury, Thomas Cranmer (1489–1556), was burnt at the stake for heresy because of his work in promoting the Protestant Reformation. The 103rd archbishop now presiding is George Carey (b. 1935), an evangelical with charismatic sympathies.

PLACES TO VISIT

CANTERBURY CATHEDRAL. The southwest porch is the cathedral's main entrance. It was built to commemorate the English victory at Agincourt in 1415 and offers the best view of the interior upon entry. Here one sees the magnificence of the Gothic architecture with its soaring columns and vaults. The northwest window contains 12th-century glass depicting Adam at work. The Trinity Chapel on the east side of the choir, which is one of the longest in England, was built to house the shrine of Thomas à Becket. Until the Reformation, this area was the destination of numerous pilgrims. Its stained-glass windows depict miracles attributed to

Becket, who was declared a saint after his murder.

Immediately behind the high altar is a chair said to have been used by St. Augustine of Canterbury that is used during the enthronement of archbishops. The tomb of Henry IV (1367–1413) is located between the north piers. On the south side is the tomb of the Black Prince, Edward (1330–76), son of Edward III (1312–77), and a famous gilded statue of the prince in full armor. The rather dark crypt is the only surviving part of the earliest church and is particularly large. At the end of the cathedral is a chapel, called a "temple," that was created as a place of worship for French Protestant refugees in 1568. The Chapel of St. Anselm is dedicated to the great 13th-century Christian philosopher and devotional writer who is best known for his ontological argument for the existence of God. It is built in the Norman, or Romanesque, style and has a rare 12th-century wall painting.

On the north side of the cathedral there is a well-preserved complex of monastic buildings. The great cloister, built between 1397 and 1414, can be entered from the northwest transept. The chapter house leads off the cloister and is a fine example of Gothic architecture. In 1935, T. S. Eliot's play *Murder in the Cathedral* was first performed here as part of a special commission; in 1964 it was made into a film, *Becket*, starring Richard Burton as Thomas à Becket.

ST. AUGUSTINE'S ABBEY, Monastery St., was founded by Augustine of Canterbury in 597 and is now a well-preserved ruin. Originally it stood outside the city walls and was the burial place of early archbishops of Canterbury and the kings of Kent.

ST. MARTIN'S CHURCH, North Holmes Rd. and Pretoria Rd., is an ancient English church built on the site of a Roman villa. It was here that King Ethelbert was baptized, supporting the view that this is really the oldest Christian site in Canterbury.

THE ROMAN MUSEUM, Longmarket, is built around the remains of a Roman house with a valuable floor mosaic discovered during recent building developments. It contains a good collection of material relating to the Roman period.

CANTERBURY HERITAGE MUSEUM, Stour St., housed in the 14th-century Poor Priests Hospital, provides an excellent overview of the history of Canterbury and its Christian traditions from pre-Roman times to the present.

THE CANTERBURY TALES EXHIBITION, St. Margaret's St., is located inside the former St. Margaret's Church. Opinions of the multimedia display vary from denouncements that proclaim it to be kitsch to appreciative comments that praise its creativity and ability to bring Chaucer alive in the modern world.

FAMOUS ARCHBISHOPS OF CANTERBURY

AUGUSTINE OF CANTERBURY (d. 604), a missionary to the English, was made archbishop of Canterbury in 596 by Pope Gregory the Great. He tried, but failed, to reconcile the old English Celtic Church with the practices of Roman Catholicism, including the Roman Catholic dating of Easter.

ANSELM OF CANTERBURY (1033–1109) was archbishop of Canterbury and an important figure in medieval Church-State disputes. He is best remembered for his philosophical works, including his work on the atonement, *Cur Deus Homo?* He argued that Christ died as a satisfaction due to the outraged majesty of God, who could not abide human sin.

THOMAS À BECKET (1118–70) was an English nobleman and friend of King Henry II. Appointed archbishop of Canterbury in 1162 to help control the Church of England, Becket took his responsibilities seriously and upheld the rights of the Church, much to the surprise of his contemporaries. Disputes with the secular authorities led to his murder on December 29, 1170. Soon after his death, miracles were reported from his tomb, and he was eventually elevated to sainthood.

CARDIFF

The capital of Wales since 1955, Cardiff is rich in history and tradition. Founded in pre-Roman times, it became a strategic settlement after the defeat of the local Silures people around A.D. 60. Very little is known about the area from the withdrawal of the legions in 450 to the arrival of the Normans in the 11th century, although there is some evidence of Christian missionary activity in the surrounding district, and legends associate it with stories about Lancelot and King Arthur. The Norman conqueror Robert FitzHamon (11th century) built a castle on the site of an earlier Roman fortification to control the crossing of the river Taff. The castle and surrounding town continued to grow. By the 13th century Cardiff had a population of over 2000, making it a major medieval city. A royal charter was granted in 1340 that was periodically renewed until the Municipal Corporations Act of 1835, which

C

ended the close association between the town and the lord of Cardiff Castle. In 1158 Welsh troops stormed the castle under the leadership of Ifor Bach, who conquered the surrounding area. It was captured again by Owen Glendower (c. 1359–1416) in 1404 and seized by Jasper Tudor for Henry VII in 1488. During the Civil War, the town supported the Royalist cause and changed hands several times. During the 19th century, Cardiff saw a period of rapid industrialization, with the population growing from under 1000 in 1801 to over 30,000 50 years later, and 180,000 in 1900. During World War II large parts of the city were damaged in heavy bombing raids aimed at destroying its industrial base.

PLACES TO VISIT

LLANDAFF CATHEDRAL, Cathedral Rd. The full name of this fascinating cathedral is the Church of Saints Peter and Paul, Dyfrig, Teilo, and Euddogwy. Everyone who has read the Bible knows the first two, but the last three are something of a mystery. In fact, they were three early Welsh missionaries, all of whom lived in the 5th and 6th centuries. But beyond their names, we know very little about them. Archaeology shows that the site of the cathedral once housed a pagan shrine, and tradition relates that St. Teilo (6th century) built a church here after converting the local people. Because he was associated with Dyfrig (d. 546) and Euddogwy

(6th century), the cathedral's coat of arms bears three crowns, representing these three men.

The present church was built by Bishop Urban (12th century), a Norman appointee. The arch behind the high altar and the doorway to St. David's Chapel, which is also the Welsh Regimental Chapel, survive from the original building. Around 1220 the cathedral was renovated and the striking west front was added. The Lady Chapel dates from later in the 13th century. All of the earlier Romanesque windows were replaced with Gothic ones in the 14th and 15th centuries, and Jasper Tudor donated a new bell tower. Before this, a separate bell tower on the nearby hill served both the church and as an alarm in case raiders were spotted in the Bristol Channel.

Until the Reformation, the tomb of St. Teilo, which still stands in the sanctuary, was an important pilgrimage center. The abolition of organized pilgrimages and the resultant loss of income created a sharp drop in church revenues, and the building slowly decayed over the next two centuries. To make matters worse, the nave was turned into a tavern by Parliamentarian troops during the Civil War, and the stones were used for military purposes. An attempt at restoration began in 1734 by the Bath architect John Wood (18th century) but soon floundered. In 1835, however, serious restoration work began under the guidance of the Precentor

Douglas (19th century), who donated two years of his own salary to the task and raised further funds from local gentry and manufacturers. Most of the 19th-century restoration was carried out by John Prichard whose father had been a minister in the cathedral. He employed a group of artists associated with the Pre-Raphaelite movement to produce a truly remarkable work of art, which was almost completely destroyed by German bombs in 1941. Following the war, the piece was restored to its original 19th-century grandeur by John Chace.

An unusual feature of the cathedral is its lack of transepts, making it unique in Britain. During the restoration Chace added an impressive concrete arch, and in 1952, a new baptismal font was created by Alan Durst; its decoration fittingly depicts the fall of man, the saga of redemption, and scenes from the lives of Welsh saints. The windows in the south aisle are Pre-Raphaelite, as are the designs on the organ. There is a Madonna and child over the south door by Bartolome Esteban Murillo (1627–82).

The Lady Chapel is probably the most intact 13th-century section of the cathedral complex and has some fine Gothic vaulting. In the northwest corner is the tomb of its original builder, Bishop William de Braose (13th century). On the west side is the Urban Arch, the lone surviving feature of the original church. The modern stained glass above the arch is by John Piper and Patrick Reyntiens (both 20th century).

The Dyfrig Chapel at the end of the north aisle is said to contain the relics of St. Dyfrig, who was buried there by Bishop Urban in an attempt to attract pilgrims to finance his building projects. Outside the church on the south green is a restored 13th-century cross and the remains of a bell tower from the same period.

CARDIFF CASTLE lies at the center of the city. The main keep is 12th century, but most of the outer walls are a 19th-century reconstruction on the site of ancient Roman walls. The castle apartments can only be visited on a conducted tour that takes 45 minutes. Here one sees the lifestyle of the rich and powerful from the 15th to the 19th centuries. Inside the castle, the Welsh Regiment and the Queen's Dragoons also have interesting museums.

WELSH NATIONAL MUSEUM, Cathays Park, opened in 1922. It is one of the best in Britain, with a wealth of historical material and an exceptionally valuable art collection. The main hall contains a permanent collection of modern sculpture, including works by Henry Moore that speak of the lostness and alienation of modern people. There are a series of fine science galleries and an excellent exhibition of Welsh archaeology.

The history of Wales and the Cardiff region is outlined, showing rare Stone Age finds said to be 200,000 years old, Bronze Age metalwork dated around 1400 B.C., and items from the Middle Ages. An interesting aspect of

C

the early material is the evidence it provides about extensive trade links to distant parts of Europe. Bronze Age beads are of Mediterranean origin, while later Celtic finds from 300 B.C. originated in Switzerland. The artistry of many of these pieces is breathtaking. The Roman period is particularly well represented. There are not many items in the early Christian period, but those that have survived, mainly stone and stone carvings, are absolutely fascinating.

The art collection is outstanding especially in terms of 15th- and 16th-century Italian Christian art and modern art. The Italian gallery contains Giovanni Cima's (1459–1517) *Madonna and Child* (1505), Alessandro Allori's (1535–1607) *Virgin and Child with St. Francis* (1585), and works from the studio of Botticelli (1444–1510). The Dutch collection has works by Hals (1591–1656), de Bray (1597–1664), and Rembrandt (1606–69). The 18th-century gallery concentrates on Welsh landscapes, while Turner's (1775–1851) *Tobias and the Angel* (1832) is to be found in the 19th-century gallery. The modern art section is widely recognized as one of the best in the world, with works by van Gogh (1853–90), Monet (1840–1926), Degas (1834–1917), and many others.

WELSH FOLK MUSEUM, located on an 80-acre site four miles west of the center of Cardiff, at St. Fagans, is a rare treat. A branch of the Welsh National Museum, it is divided into three distinct areas. First, there are a series of exhibitions and galleries. Second, there is an extensive outdoor exhibition, with buildings ranging from a Celtic village to a Welsh chapel. Finally, there is the Elizabethan mansion, built between 1560 and 1590, which is furnished with period furniture from the 16th to 18th centuries.

The **RHONDA VALLEY HERITAGE PARK** is located in the Rhonda Valley some 12 miles northwest of Cardiff. During the 19th and early 20th centuries, "the valleys," as they were known, were the heart of industrial Wales and Welsh nonconformist religious ferment, which were lovingly portrayed in Richard Llewellyn's *How Green Was My Valley* (1939). Here the famous male voice choirs grew out of the great 17th-century revivals and 18th-century Methodism, singing such moving hymns as "Abide with Me" and "Land of My Fathers." Here too Baptist, Methodist, and other nonconformist preachers brought the gospel to miners living in near poverty yet proud of their traditions, strong faith, and strong sense of community.

The **HERITAGE CENTER** is another open-air museum centered on the disused Lewis Merthyr mine. Valley buildings, such as a school, chapel, and miner's cottages, are being reassembled to recreate a sense of the past. Although many of the exhibits are not explicitly Christian, anyone who knows anything about the valleys recognizes the deep Christian roots of a way of life which has now passed away forever.

CARLISLE

A Celtic settlement existed here long before the arrival of the Romans, who conquered the area. They built a military town, Luguvalium, that they used as a base while building Hadrian's Wall, which ran along the north bank of the river Eden. The town continued to thrive after the withdrawal of Roman legions and was evangelized by St. Kentigern (518–603), a semi-legendary figure who spread Celtic Christianity in northern England and southern Scotland and eventually became the bishop of Glasgow. The Christian settlement thrived until 875, when the Danes sacked it. But it seems to have quickly recovered its former prosperity due to its location in a rich farming area. The Normans under William Rufus (1060–1100) constructed a strong castle on the site of the older Celtic hill fort, using stones from the Roman town in 1092. Throughout the Middle Ages, the town was constantly under threat from the Scots. William Wallace (1274–1305) besieged the castle in 1297, and Robert the Bruce (1274–1329) attacked it in 1315. Queen Elizabeth I used the castle as one of the jails for her cousin, Mary Queen of Scots, after Mary fled to England to escape her own rebellious subjects in 1568. During the English Civil War, a Scottish army captured it after a nine-month siege in 1644–45. Bonnie Prince Charlie captured the city and its castle in the 1745 rebellion and proclaimed his father the true king of England. The town was easily recaptured by the duke of Cumberland a few weeks later. Both the prince and his adversary the duke of Cumberland stayed in Highmoor House while in Carlisle.

PLACES TO VISIT

CARLISLE CATHEDRAL, Castle St., is a beautiful red sandstone building. It is one of the smallest cathedrals in England due to the fact that a large section of its nave was demolished and the stones used for military purposes; it was later rebuilt to its present proportions. The original church was part of an Augustinian monastery founded around 1100 and elevated to the rank of cathedral in 1133, making it the only Augustinian foundation to achieve cathedral status in England. The choir was built in 1225 and is unusual in that it is 12 feet wider than the nave. The east window, first installed 1340–45, contains some excellent stained glass depicting the Last Judgment. The glass in the main window, however, is of 19th-century origin and was designed by John Hardman in 1861. Below this window is a monument dedicated to the great Christian apologist and philosopher

William Paley (1743–1805), who was archdeacon of Carlisle and is buried in the north choir aisle.

The outstanding feature of the cathedral is its exquisite painted barrel-vaulted ceiling, first decorated in 1360 and lovingly restored in 1970. Its blue background with golden suns and stars is truly magnificent. High-quality paintings from 1420 are also to be found on the misericords; they depict the apostles and the lives of the saints Anthony, Augustine, and Cuthbert. In the south transept, which is of Norman origin, one can see runic inscriptions on the wall. In 1990 the cathedral opened its fine treasury, which is housed beneath the north aisle and contains an excellent exhibition depicting the history of Christianity in Cumbria.

ST. CUTHBERT'S CHURCH, St. Cuthbert's Lane, was originally founded in 685 and dedicated to St. Cuthbert, who is said to have preached here. It was rebuilt in 870 and expanded in 1095. The present church dates from 1778 and is a good example of the Georgian style. Only a 14th-century stained-glass window has survived from earlier times. An interesting feature of the church is its recently restored church hall, which is in the old Tythe Barn built between 1485 and 1507.

TULLY HOUSE MUSEUM, Castle Way, is a 17th-century house that was donated to the city earlier this century for the purpose of creating a local history museum. It contains an excellent collection and exhibition which are particularly rich in material relating to the Roman occupation of the area, the turbulent Middle Ages, and the Civil War period.

CARLISLE CASTLE, Castle Way, is one of the great castles of England that was built in 1192 to prevent raids by marauding bands of Scots. It has been used as a military base for over 1000 years. The original Norman keep was redesigned in Tudor times to allow for the placement of artillery when a half-moon battery was also added to the outer defenses of the complex. The medieval hall now houses the King's Own Royal Border Regiment Museum, which vividly recalls the life, triumphs, and even defeats of this proud regiment. The dungeons, where Scottish prisoners were often held for years at a time, are very sobering.

ST. MICHAEL'S CHURCH, BURGH-BY-THE-SANDS, six miles east of Carlisle, is a 12th-century structure built with stones from Hadrian's Wall on the site of the Roman granary. The church is of particular interest because it is one of only three surviving examples of a fortified church. The west tower was clearly designed to serve both as a church tower and as a stronghold where people could take refuge in times of danger. The massive, thick walls of the tower and its narrow doorway, which is protected by a sturdy iron gate, are indications of its defensive nature. The church is of historical interest because after his death in

1307, on campaign against Robert the Bruce, the English King Edward I (1239–1307) lay in state here before his body was taken back to London. The church has some interesting stained-glass windows depicting the lives of saints Cuthbert, Kentigern (518–603), and Ninian (6th century), as well as King Edward I (963–78).

ST. MARTIN'S CHURCH, BRAMPTON, 11 miles northeast of Carlisle on the A69, is the only Pre-Raphaelite church designed by the Victorian architect Philip Webb (1831–1915). It is notable for its magnificent stained-glass windows designed by Sir Edward Burne-Jones (1833–98) and created in the workshop of William Morris (1834–96). The church was consecrated on November 11, 1878, and is built on an ancient Christian site that was part of a Roman fort.

LANERCOST PRIORY, three miles northeast of Brampton, on the B6264. This border priory and mission was built between 1200 and 1220 with stone from Hadrian's Wall. At the Dissolution, part of the priory became a parish church, while the rest was allowed to fall into disrepair until it was restored in recent times because of its historical value as a good example of early English architecture.

ST. CUTHBERT'S CHURCH, BEWCASTLE, is located in a remote and difficult-to-find area several miles north of Lanercost Priory. This inaccessible church is well worth a visit because the 7th-century yellow sandstone Bewcastle Cross stands in its graveyard. The origin of this remarkably well-preserved stone cross, which is 14 feet high and missing its upper sections, is unknown. The artwork is exquisite and clearly influenced by the Coptic art of Egypt, a fact that raises all sorts of very intriguing questions. The cross is inscribed with runes praising King Alcfrith (7th century), a son of Oswi (612–70). John the Evangelist is depicted on the west side of the cross. Above John is the inscription and above that a carving of Christ holding a scroll in one hand while the other hand gives a blessing. Christ is stepping on the head of an adder and a lion. Above him is another smaller inscription and a carving of John the Baptist. The south side has a panel containing a finely carved symmetrical knot and vine panels. The east side is carved with a vine scroll decorated with the heads of animals and birds. Finally, on the north side there are panels with more knot and vine work.

The church itself is built within what was once a Roman outpost founded by the Emperor Hadrian in A.D. 122. During the 2nd and 3rd centuries, this frontier post had a garrison of 1000 troops. The church was built in the 12th century and renovated in the 18th, when it was dedicated to St. Cuthbert, whose life is told on a tapestry inside the church. The surrounding graveyard has a number of interesting old tombstones.

CHELTENHAM

The discovery of a hot spring in 1716 led to the development of Cheltenham as the most popular spa in the early 18th century. Today's town is built in the 18th-century Regency style, reflecting affluence and the taste of a rich leisure class. The town hosts a music festival in July and literature festival in October. Gustav Holst (1874–1934) was born here, as was Edward Jenner (1748–1823), who pioneered the vaccination for smallpox.

PLACES TO VISIT

ST. MARY'S CHURCH, off High St., built in the 14th century, has an excellent rose window installed in 1320.

CHELTENHAM MUSEUM, 4 Clarence Rd., contains some good 17th-century Dutch paintings considered by the Christian art historian Hans Rookmaker to be among the best examples of Protestant art.

GUSTAV HOLST MUSEUM, High St., is located in the Regency house where Holst was born.

CHELTENHAM UNIVERSITY, founded as a women's college to train teachers in 1853, is the home of one of the leading evangelical theological faculties in Britain.

SUDELEY CASTLE, seven miles northeast, is a country house that originated as a medieval castle and home of Catherine Parr (1512–48). Parr was a highly intelligent and deeply committed Protestant who became the 6th wife of Henry VIII; she persuaded Henry to recognize his daughters as legitimate heirs. She survived his death in 1547 and married her original sweetheart, Lord Seymour (1508–49) of Sudeley Castle, only to die in childbirth a year later. After her death, Lord Seymour sought to marry the princess Elizabeth (1533–1603), who eventually became Queen Elizabeth I, but was arrested and executed for treason. The castle contains an excellent art collection, including works by Rembrandt van Rijn, Paul Rubens, John Constable, and Joseph Turner.

HAILES ABBEY, nine miles northeast near Winchcomb, is the ruin of one of the largest Cistercian monasteries in England. It was made rich by its claim to possess a phial of Christ's blood. It attracted numerous pilgrims and is mentioned in Chaucer's *Pardoner's Tale*. At the Dissolution of the Monasteries, the blood in the phial was shown to be fake. Although the site of the monastery is impressive, the ruins are not. There is, however, a really excellent local museum and an interesting 13th-century church with some fascinating wall paintings warning against breaking the Sabbath.

CHESTER

B uilt at a strategic crossing on the river Dee as a port with easy access to the sea, Chester was the largest Roman fortress in Britain and the headquarters of the 20th Legion. The original name of this Imperial city was Deva, meaning "camp on the Dee." Later it became Castra Legionum, which in time was changed to Caeleon and later Legaceaster, which then became Ceaster and ultimately Chester. The Roman city was laid out on a grid pattern that in essence has survived until the present, giving the town a plan that is quite unusual for an English city.

Following the Roman withdrawal from Britain, Chester fell to various marauding raiders until it was once again fortified in 907 by Aethefleda (10th century), queen of Mercia and daughter of Alfred the Great (849–99). A period of peace followed until the Norman conquest, when Chester resisted the invaders longer than any other English town and as a result was sacked by William the Conqueror's (1027–87) troops. In 1070 William awarded his nephew Hugh Lupus (11th century) the earldom of Chester and all the lands to the west that Lupus could conquer. Chester reverted to the crown in 1237 when Lupus's line died out without male heirs. During the Civil War,

Chester was fiercely Royalist and withstood a two-year siege by Parliamentarian armies.

From Roman times until the 17th century, Chester was a seagoing port with important trade links to Ireland. When the river Dee silted up, it became necessary to develop what was then the village of Liverpool as the city's port. Consequently, the town decayed economically until the mid-19th century, when it became an important rail link. The medieval historian Ralph Higden (d. 1364) was a native of Chester. Higden's *Polychronicon* (1482), which is a history of the world from the Creation, was one of the first books to be published in English. The 19th-century artist Randolf Caldecott (1846–86) and the modern conductor Sir Adrian Boult (1889–1983) were also natives of Chester. Chester is also the birthplace of the famous Chester cycle of medieval mystery plays depicting the story of salvation.

PLACES TO VISIT

ST. WERBURGH'S CATHEDRAL, Northgate St., is named after a Saxon saint who died around 700. The present cathedral was built, in beautiful red sandstone, between 1091 and 1184 by Norman architects when Hugh Lupus, aided by St. Anselm, founded a Benedictine abbey on the site of an earlier

C

Saxon church. The nave and porches are classic Romanesque, but the choir, tower, side chapels, and Lady Chapel are Gothic. It did not become a cathedral until the Reformation, when Henry VIII created the new diocese of Chester. After falling into a dangerous state of decay in the 17th and 18th centuries, the cathedral was restored by Sir Gilbert Scott (1811–78) between 1868 and 1876. Consequently, many of the interior decorations are actually Victorian. These include J. R. Clayton's mosaic on the west wall and the Byzantine font in the baptistery that was manufactured in Italy in 1885.

The choir, which dates from 1390, has some of the best stalls in England. The famous 17th-century Christian theologian and apologist Bishop John Pearson (1613–86), whose *Exposition of the Creed* (1659) was a standard text at British and American universities until the late 19th century, is also buried in the cathedral. He is commemorated by a monument by Arthur Blomfield (1829–99) that was erected in 1864. Ralph Higden (d. 1364) is buried in the south choir aisle. The lovingly restored early English Gothic Lady Chapel, built 1275–80, has a rare painted ceiling and also contains the reconstructed shrine of St. Werburgh.

ST. JOHN THE BAPTIST'S CHURCH, Grosvenor Park, claims to have been founded in the 7th century, but the present building dates from 1075, when for ten years it was the cathedral church of the kingdom of Mercia. The bishopric was relocated to Litchfield in 1085. The tower collapsed in 1523, destroying the west end. The bell tower collapsed in 1881, destroying the north porch. What remains is a beautiful but greatly reduced church attached to some romantic ruins that are rich in history. According to local tradition, King Harold fled here after the Battle of Hastings. He became an anchorite, or hermit, in a small cell that can be seen on the south wall of the churchyard.

THE ROWS are a unique feature of Chester that give the town its medieval feel and charm. They are a half-timbered, Tudor-style, shopping arcade with an upper gallery built above a row of ground-level shops. Today they are a major tourist attraction.

CITY WALLS. Chester has the most complete set of city walls in England that go back to Roman times, although they were rebuilt by both the Saxons and Normans.

GROSVENOR MUSEUM, Grosvenor St., is an award-winning exhibit that includes many fascinating items from the Roman period, including a graveyard.

DEWA ROMAN EXPERIENCE, Bridge St., is a multimedia exhibit of life in Roman times. Some love it; others regard it as kitsch.

CHESTER HERITAGE CENTER, Bridge St., Grosvenor St., is housed in the former Church of St. Mary, a 12th-century building with a fine timber roof. It has displays showing the growth of Chester through history. Opposite is the **FALCON INN**, where Handel stayed on his visit to Chester in 1741. The inn was built in 1626.

CHESTER CASTLE, Castle St., was built in neoclassical style in the 18th century. It houses the local courthouse and town hall, as well as the Cheshire Military Museum. A small section of Hugh Lupus's original castle wall and a 13th-century tower survive from the Middle Ages, as well as the Chapel of St. Mary de Castro, which has some interesting wall paintings. The history of the castle is displayed in a couple of old guard rooms that now serve as a museum.

CHICHESTER

Founded by the Romans in the 1st century as Noviomagnus, a sea port, it was called Cisseceaster by the Saxons and, like Chester, is built on a grid pattern. Since Roman times, the sea has receded, and the town is now seven miles inland. It was here that King Canute (995–1035) is said to have attempted to command the sea to obey him. The Episcopal see of Selsey was founded here in 1175 following the conquest. During the 18th century it became a popular health spa, and the town was rebuilt in the pleasing Georgian style that is seen today. The famous Chichester festival of the arts is hosted every July.

PLACES TO VISIT

CHICHESTER CATHEDRAL was founded by Bishop de Luffa in 1075 when the foundations of the cathedral were laid. A fire in 1184 destroyed the bishop's Romanesque building. It was rebuilt in Gothic style by Bishop Seffrid II between 1180–1204, although some Romanesque sections, such as the porches, remain. The Late Gothic Lady Chapel contains an excellent series of 12th-century carved stone panels depicting the raising of Lazarus. The outer aisles are also Late Gothic. The south transept has an excellent 14th-century set of stained-glass windows, plus some unusual ancient paintings that were restored in 1519. The grave of the composer Gustav Holst (1874–1934), best known for *The Planets Suite*, is found in the north transept. There is also a memorial to the little-known composer Thomas Weelkes, who was the organist here from 1602–23. In the choir is a modern tapestry by John Piper that was completed in 1966. There is also a modern stained-glass window by the Jewish artist Marc Chagall (1887–1985). The cathedral also has some well-preserved cloisters that originally surrounded its cemetery.

ST. MARY'S HOSPITAL, St. Martin's Square, was built in 1158 to care for the poor, reminding us of the long history of Christian healing and welfare. It is still in use today as a retirement home. Its small chapel, which is open by appointment only, is a good example of medieval style.

FISHBORNE ROMAN VILLA, one mile west of the town center on the A259, is the main reason for visiting Chichester. This is by far the best-preserved Roman villa in England, if not northern Europe. A workman laying pipes in 1960 discovered it. It was excavated between 1961 and 1969. The adjoining museum contains many items from the excavations. Archaeologists believe that this was a supply base for the Roman army, which once had its own harbor. A large house was built here around A.D. 50, but the villa itself was not built until A.D. 79. A fire destroyed the main building in 285. A number of excellent Roman mosaics are on display.

CIRENCESTER

During Roman times Corinim was a provincial capital second only to London in importance. Situated at the intersection of three major roads—Ermine Street, Akeman Street, and Fosse Way—Corinim had one of the largest forums north of the Alps. The town was destroyed by Saxon invaders in the 6th century, but regained importance as a center of the wool trade during the Middle Ages. Today Cirencester, as it is now called has a wealthy, quaint, market town atmosphere.

PLACES TO VISIT

ST. JOHN THE BAPTIST'S CHURCH, Market Place, is a 15th-century Cotswold Wool Church that was built by wealthy traders at great expense. It is a magnificent Gothic structure. The tower is supported by some ingenious flying buttresses that were added after construction was complete because it had begun to subside and was in danger of collapsing. The large three-tiered porch was designed to serve as a public meeting place as well as the entrance to the church. The pulpit is a rare example of a pre-Reformation pulpit made entirely out of stone and is known as a wineglass pulpit because of its shape. The Chapel of St. Catherine has some traces of early wall paintings. Throughout there are many excellent carvings and examples of fan vaulting.

MALMESBURY ABBEY, 12 miles southwest on the A429, was founded by the Saxon St. Aldhelm (639–709). It was destroyed by fire in 1050 and extensively rebuilt between 1115 and 1140 in the Romanesque style as one of the most important Benedictine abbeys in England. Today the nave of the original abbey, which survives as the local parish church, is considered one of the best examples of Romanesque buildings in Britain. The rest of the abbey fell into ruins after the Dissolution of the Monasteries. The porch is said to contain the tomb of King Athelstan (895–939), the grandson of Alfred the Great (849–99), who came close to unifying England into one kingdom and married his daughter to the Holy Roman Emperor, Otto the Great (912–73). The south porch contains some outstanding Romanesque carvings. The church owns four rare medieval Bibles.

The historian William of Malmesbury (1090–1143) was a monk here, as was Elmer, or Oliver, who is said to have made himself wings and attempted to fly by jumping off the church tower. He survived the fall but was lame thereafter. Malmesbury was also the birthplace of the philosopher Thomas Hobbes (1588–1679).

WESTONBIRT ARBORETUM holds one of Europe's finest collections of trees and shrubs. Founded in 1829 by Robert Holfield, it claims over 18,000 trees on a 600-acre site. In 1956 this collection was given to the Forestry Commission by the Holfield family. Its most famous sites are the rows of rhododendrons and azaleas which flower in the springtime.

CUMBRIA

Cumbria is one of the richest areas for the history of early Christianity in Britain with an extraordinary number of ancient stone crosses. Unfortunately, most of the crosses and other ancient Christian sites are in remote areas. Therefore, all we can do here is to direct visitors to a few of the more readily accessible sites. Even then the use of a car and a willingness to ask directions from local people are practical necessities. Apart from the popular Lake District, most of Cumbria is relatively difficult to reach, and some of the places mentioned here are not even marked on most road maps. Nevertheless, the rarity

and historical importance of these sites, most of which are fairly neglected, make a journey through Cumbria a rich spiritual experience. The fact that Cumbria is one of the most scenically beautiful areas in Britain compensates for the difficulty and time taken in finding these remote outposts of ancient Christian civilization.

The origins of Cumbrian Christianity are undocumented. All we know is that Christianity took root among Roman legionnaires and traders in the area during the 2nd and 3rd centuries, as can be seen from the early gravestones bearing Christian inscriptions on display at the Tully House Museum in Carlisle

C

and other similar objects scattered around the area. What is unclear is whether Roman Christianity survived the withdrawal of the legions in A.D. 410, and if so, for how long was it able to flourish? The evidence is inconclusive, although some historians think that Carlisle and Cumbria may have preserved a more or less unbroken tradition of Christian worship and a reasonably high level of civilization throughout post-Roman times.

Evidence for this view can be found in the fact that when St. Cuthbert (635–87) visited Carlisle in 685, he found a prosperous community with a functioning administration. Recent excavations have confirmed that the Roman pattern of settlement in this area continued long after it had broken down in the rest of Britain. Further, very few clearly pagan burial sites have been found in the area, suggesting continuing Christian influence, and many of the place names are of Christian origin. It is also probable that by the time the Anglo-Saxons reached Cumbria after battling their way across England, most of them had accepted Christianity.

Consequently, it seems that the Viking raids and eventual invasion of the 9th century were the first real challenge to Christianity in Cumbria in 600 years. Thus when the Vikings destroyed the Christian center of Lindesfarne, Christians from the devastated kingdom of Northumbria took refuge in Cumbria. Even the Viking raids do not seem to have disrupted Cumbrian Christian-

ity too much, because as early as 883, a Danish king, Guthfrith, was enthroned in Carlisle by the local abbot. This act suggests that by that time the raiders recognized the importance of Christianity and had begun to cooperate with church leaders. The transition from paganism to Christianity is vividly illustrated by the carvings on the Gosforth Cross.

A century after the Norman invasion of 1066, we find a Cumbrian, Athelwold, was appointed bishop of Carlisle by the Norman Archbishop of York, suggesting the tenacity of the Cumbrian church. During the same period, a monk at Furness Abbey wrote a life of St. Kentigern (518–603) that extolled the ancient origins of the Church in this remote area.

Cumbrian Christians seem to have accepted the Reformation but strongly resented the Dissolution of their ancient monasteries. As a result, many laymen and clergy alike supported the abortive rebellion known as the Pilgrimage of Grace (1536–37), which was brutally crushed by the armies of Henry VIII (1491–1547). As a result of the vicious persecution of Roman Catholics which followed, Cumbria retained far fewer Catholic families than most areas of England. In fact, until the Irish immigration of the 19th century, Catholics made up less than one percent of the entire population of the area.

George Fox (1624–91) made frequent journeys to Cumbria in the

1850s. His teachings quickly took root among Bible reading groups known as the "Westmoreland Seekers." From Cumbria he sent out his first 35 teams of missionaries to evangelize Europe. Despite or perhaps because of their popularity, the Quakers experienced strong opposition from clergy of the Church of England, who were unable to stamp out the movement. Later in the 18th century, the Quakers welcomed and gave considerable support to John Wesley and other Methodist preachers who roamed around the area. Wesley himself made no less than 30 separate preaching tours of Cumbria, converting the unchurched and establishing small groups of believers that eventually formed the nucleus of the Methodist Church in the area. Other nonconformist churches including the Congregationalists, Presbyterians, and Plymouth Brethren flourished in Cumbria during the 19th and early 20th centuries, although the Baptists never really took root in the region. From the mid-1950s, however, Christianity in Cumbria went into severe decline, and according to the 1990 church census, remains relatively weak. In fact, regular church attendance was almost half the national average at a mere seven percent of the population.

A striking feature of Cumbria is its stone buildings with slate roofs built in a style known as Cumbrian vernacular. Even the earliest surviving church building, built between the 10th and 12th centuries, is in a distinct Cumbrian style that is a form of Romanesque, with a minimum of rounded arches that tend to be low and squat. The most striking feature of these churches is their clear age and lack of extensive renovations, making them archaeological treasures.

PLACES TO VISIT

Kendal is a good place to begin your tour of Cumbrian Christian sites, because it is the gateway to both the Cumbrian Coast and the Lake District. The tour described here will take at least two to three days.

To begin a circular tour that leads along the Cumbrian coast, take the A590 southwest to Lindale and then the side road B277 to Grange-over-Sands and on two miles west to the small town of Cartmel. Rejoin the A590 beyond Cartmel and follow it for 14 miles to Dalton-in-Furness, and another four miles to Barrow-in-Furness. From Barrow follow the A595 15 miles to Kirby-in-Furness, then on six miles to Broughton-in-Furness. From there Ravenglass and Eskdale are another 19 miles through spectacular rugged coastal country. From here Gosforth is another seven miles and beyond it Calder Bridge. Six more miles on the B5345 leads to St. Bees and then another six miles to Whitehaven. Finally, a short drive of around 25 miles then takes you to either Carlisle or Keswick. Those who choose to visit

C

Keswick can either return to Carlisle or go back to Kendal by way of Ambleside.

KENDAL is famous as the home of the Kendal Mint Cake, a block of mint-flavored sugar that was taken with Sir Edmund Hillary (b. 1919) on his ascent of Everest in 1953. It is also the birthplace of Catherine Parr (1512–48), Henry VIII's (1491–1547) sixth and last wife. She narrowly escaped the block by his death. A pious Christian, she was the person who persuaded Henry to recognize his daughters as legitimate heirs to the throne, thus ensuring the succession of first Mary Tudor (1516–58) and then her sister Elizabeth I (1533–1603). There is an excellent **MUSEUM OF LAKELAND LIFE.** The **KENDAL MUSEUM** has an interesting display relating to the life of the author and outdoorsman Alfred Wainwright (1907–91), who through his books and articles almost single-handedly revived interest in the preservation of Cumbria and the Lake District.

THE PARISH CHURCH is a five-aisled Gothic building. In its Bellingham Chapel is an ornate 13th-century tomb. The church also contains a plaque to the painter George Romney (1734–1802), who is famous for his portrait of Lady Hamilton (1765–1815), the mistress of Lord Nelson (1758–1805). Romney was born in nearby Dalton-in-Furness and moved to Kendal, where he was an apprentice before becoming a portrait painter. At the urging of Sir Joshua Reynolds, in 1762, he deserted his wife and two small children because Reynolds had convinced him that art and family life were incompatible. In many ways this action marks the beginning of the Romantic movement in England. He returned to Kendal 35 years later to be reconciled with his wife and die.

QUAKER TAPESTRY EXHIBITION, The Friends Meeting House, Stramongate, contains a series of 77 separate tapestries each 25 inches by 21 inches. The tapestries tell the story of the Quaker movement. It took 15 years to complete and involved the combined effort of over 4000 people in 15 countries. Among the many tapestries is one devoted to the Quaker scientist John Dalton (1766–1844), a native of Cockermouth, who is the father of atomic theory. The astronomer Sir Stanley Eddington (1882–1944) and physicist Kathleen Lonsdale (1903–71) are also depicted.

John Wesley preached in Kendal on at least 30 occasions. On April 13, 1768, he recorded in his journal that he found a group of "Seceders and mongrel Methodists" that were disrupting the congregation. He gave his sermon and moved on with the comment, "I once more 'cast' my 'bread upon the waters,' and left the event to God." From Kendal he rode on to Ambleside in pouring rain.

CARTMEL. Here the 12th-century Church of St. Mary and St. Michael, the old Cartmel Priory, is a real gem. It was saved from destruction during the Dissolution of the Monasteries when the townspeople petitioned for it to become their parish church. The wisdom of their action is apparent to anyone who enters this wonderful example of English Gothic. The 45-foot-high east window is particularly striking, as are the exquisite misericords. The church contains a number of very interesting tombs. Beyond the church, the market square still has Elizabethan cobbles that today are very rare in England.

SWARTHMOOR HALL, Ulverston, is a 16th-century country house that belonged to Thomas Fell (d. 1658), vice-chancellor of the duchy of Lancaster, who with his wife, Margaret (1614–1702), were members of a Bible study and prayer movement known as the Westmoreland Seekers. In 1652 George Fox had a vision while walking on Pendle Hill in Lancashire. This vision led him into what was then Westmoreland, today part of Cumbria, where he met the Seekers and stayed with various families in the area before finally reaching Swarthmoor Hall, where the Fells befriended him. Although Judge Fell never became a Quaker, Swarthmoor Hall became the headquarters of the movement. In 1669, 11 years after Thomas Fell's death, Fox married Margaret and established Swarthmoor Meeting House, which is still in use as a place of worship. Today Swarthmoor Hall is owned by the Society of Friends and is open to the public.

GREAT URSWICK lies a few miles southwest of Ulverston. Here you will find the oldest church in the Furness region, the 10th-century CHURCH OF ST. MARY AND ST. MICHAEL. The remains of two 9th-century Viking crosses discovered in the graveyard in 1909 and 1911 are on view in the church. There is an ancient font, the medieval cover of which is decorated with carvings of dolphins swimming around the heads of children. This oak-beamed rough stone church contains various other carvings and an interesting altar painting by a local artist.

BARROW-IN-FURNESS grew up around its Cistercian monastery, founded in 1123 by a group of Savigny monks. The monastery was taken over by the Cistercians in 1150 after a fairly bitter ecclesiastical feud. The abbey quickly became one of the richest in Britain and was responsible for the founding of numerous other smaller monastic institutions as far away as Ireland, the Isle of Man, and Yorkshire. Recurrent raids by Scottish armies left the abbey unscathed, probably because of its links to Scottish houses, until 1316, when the Scots sacked the abbey. In 1322 the abbot paid Robert the Bruce a large ransom to spare the abbey. Bruce took the money and sacked the abbey anyway. Bruce's raid led to the building of nearby Dalton Castle to protect the area against Scottish incursions. Serious Scottish raids continued until 1346, when order was eventually restored to the area by the English army. In 1537 Furness Abbey was the first of

C

the great houses to be dissolved by Thomas Cromwell (1485–1540) on the orders of Henry VIII (1491–1547). At that time the lead was stripped from the roof and the buildings used as a stone quarry to build local stately homes. In 1923 the English Heritage Society acquired the abbey and now runs a small museum in it.

During the 19th century, Barrow became a center of British shipbuilding due to readily available sources of coal and iron ore after the construction of the Furness Railway in 1846. Within 40 years Barrow grew from a small village to the world's largest iron and steel center and a major shipbuilding port. During World War II, Barrow was heavily bombed. Following the war, the shipbuilding industry fell into rapid decline. Today British Nuclear Fuels runs nearby Sellafield, the world's first nuclear reactor. British Gas, whose Morcambe Bay pipeline comes ashore here, operates the docks. The port has turned to tourism by becoming a major center for the cruise industry.

In the bay lies PIERS ISLAND, where Lambert Simnel (d. 1475) landed in 1487 in an abortive attempt to overthrow Henry VII. Today the island, where the ruins of Piers Castle inspired the poet William Wordsworth, can be reached by a ferry. To the north of Barrow is DALTON-IN-FURNESS, a small market town which developed after the construction of the 14th-century Dalton Castle. The painter George Romney

(1734–1802), who was famous for his portraits of beautiful women, is buried in the churchyard. Although off the usual tourist track, a visit to the Furness area is well worthwhile because it is rich in Christian history.

FURNESS ABBEY is located on the A590 between Dalton and Barrow, one-and-a-half miles from Barrow. Nothing remains of this once imposing Cistercian abbey but the romantic red limestone ruins. The abbey was founded in 1123 by Stephen of Blois (1097–1154). In 1135, he became King Stephen, who is known to anyone who reads the *Cadfael* detective stories or watches the BBC series on PBS. At the bookshop you can rent an excellent audio guide. The museum includes some rare medieval stone carvings of knights in full armor with their visors closed, ready for battle; they are believed to be the oldest of their kind in England. The abbey ruins are themselves late Norman, while the ruined chapter house is early English.

BARROW DOCK MUSEUM, North Rd., housed in a renovated Victorian dock, provides an excellent overview of the development of shipbuilding in Barrow.

SWINSIDE STONE CIRCLE, near Broughton-in-Furness on the way to Millom, was built around 3000 B.C. It contains 55 stones and is 90 feet in diameter.

ST. JOHN'S CHURCH WABERTH-WAITE, Millom. In this delightful village 23 miles from Barrow is an ancient Cumbrian church built sometime before the 12th century. In the churchyard stands the shaft of an ancient stone cross similar in design to the better-preserved cross found in Irton. The church contains rare early-19th-century pew boxes. The rest of the church has remained intact through the centuries. The font is Norman and is believed to have been made out of a Roman pillar.

RAVENGLASS is the site of the Ravenglass miniature railway, known locally as the "larl rati" or "Little Ratty," which offers a very pleasant excursion through some beautiful countryside. Originally this was a working railway, opened in 1875, to bring ore along a 15-inch narrow gauge line seven miles from Dalegarth in the Eskdale valley to the sea. Today it is a tourist attraction that provides a 40-minute ride through beautiful country, much of which is a nature reserve.

Ravenglass was developed as an important Roman port and military base known as "Glannaventa" in the 2nd century with a garrison of over 1000 troops. All that remains of the Roman occupation are the ruins of a large bathing complex, known as Walls Castle, which is one of the largest remaining unexcavated Roman ruins in Britain. In the Middle Ages, Ravenglass was the site of a Benedictine hospital. During the 19th century, it was a center for "Bible Christians" among the Cornish miners who flocked to the area to work in the mines.

ST. PAUL'S CHURCH IRTON/RAVEN-GLASS. You really have to look for this one because you are unlikely to find it on any map, although the locals will point the way from Ravenglass. In fact, you can go by car or take the Little Ratty. Irton is a village, if you can call it that, of houses scattered between two and four miles from Ravenglass. Its treasure is St. Paul's Church, which is a classic Victorian structure, built in 1865 when a much older building, parts of which went back to the earliest Christian settlement in the area, was demolished. Two things make a visit to this church a must.

First, in the churchyard stands the famous Irton Cross, which is ten feet high and was erected sometime in the 9th century, just before the Norse invasions. The cross is very important in the history of Christian art because it bears no figures or mythological scenes. Instead, it is decorated with vine scrolls and elaborate patterns, suggesting the Irish origin of its creator.

Second, the church itself contains two remarkable Victorian stained-glass windows designed by Sir Edward Burne-Jones (1833–98) and created in the workshop of his friend William Morris (1834–96). Burne-Jones belonged to the circle of artists around Morris and, like his mentor, was influenced by Italian styles and a European Romanticism that looked back to the Middle Ages as a golden period in European life. The windows were donated to the church by the shipping magnate Sir Thomas Brocklebank (19th century), the father-in-law of George Westinghouse III (b. 1882). The church has some other fine windows by lesser-known artists. Brocklebank also donated a peel of eight bells to the church.

MUNCASTER/RAVENGLASS is another couple of miles away and once again is unlikely to be on your map. It too can be reached by car or the Ratty. Here you will find both MUNCASTER CASTLE, the foundations of which go back to Roman times, and St. Michael's Church, within the castle grounds. The castle itself, which has belonged to the Pennington family since 1208, is well worth a visit. An audio guide is available to help you as you go around its stately rooms. One of the glories of the castle is its wonderful 77 acres of wooded gardens containing magnificent displays of rhododendrons, camellias, and azaleas. The castle is also the center of the World Owl Trust, which strives to preserve the owl population worldwide. There is an owl-breeding program and study center, as well as a resident population of over 48 species of owl protected in the conservation area.

ST. MICHAEL'S CHURCH is a squat 12th-century English construction that was renovated in the 19th century. It is remarkable for its rare "Doom" windows, which portray Christ in majesty looking down on the Archangel Michael carrying a banner of victory and wielding a sword of judgment as he divides the saved and the lost at the final resurrection. The church also houses the shaft of a 10th-century stone cross, which is decorated in the style of the Gosforth Cross. Unfortunately the cross itself was broken at some time in its long history. The head, which is now beside the shank, was found a few miles away in Irton.

While in the area you can also visit the MUNCASTER MILL, a restored flour mill that grinds flour in the traditional way.

ESKDALE, a few miles further inland, is the site of the 12th-century ST. CATHERINE'S CHURCH located at the foot of the ruggedly beautiful Scafell, a popular hiking destination. Originally a chapel belonging to St. Bees Monastery, the church has some fine stained-glass windows and an unusual octagonal font. The font is decorated with marigold designs usually found on pagan Roman altars, suggesting that it was once part of a Roman temple in the area before its stone was made into a font.

Further up the valley, along a steep road, one comes to Hardknot Pass, from which the road, originally built by the Romans, leads on to Ambleside. At the beginning of the pass, just outside the village of Eskdale, are the ruins of HARDKNOT FORT, known to the Romans as "Medibogdum." This isolated outpost was built between A.D. 120 and 138 to protect the supply route from Ravenglass to the fortresses of Ambleside and Penrith. The low ruined wall encloses a series of buildings that were once granaries and barracks. Outside the defensive perimeter are the remains of a three-roomed bathhouse and parade ground.

GOSFORTH is a quaint English village well off the tourist beat because of its remote location. In the churchyard is a very rare Anglo-Danish stone cross 14 feet high that is richly carved with Norse and Christian symbols. This is the tallest Viking cross in England and is a visible reminder of the complex transition of the Viking invaders (who occupied the area from the 8th century onwards) from pagans to Christians.

On the east face of the cross is a carving of Christ crucified. Two Roman soldiers and a woman, assumed to be Mary Magdalene, look on. The rest of the lower carvings tell the story of Ragnarok and the destruction of the Norse gods. Above Christ is a puzzling carving, which some believe is the Norse god Vidaar taking revenge against the wolf that in Norse legend slew his father. The carefully selected themes depicted in the carving are not accidental but clearly are intended to portray the triumph of Christ over the old gods and his coming judgment at the end of the world.

The graveyard contains two 10th-century tombstones covering the graves of Norse chiefs. The church also contains a Viking "fishing stone."

CALDER BRIDGE is the site of a ruined Cistercian monastery that stands on private land and is therefore not open to the public, although the ruins can be viewed from a distance.

ST. BRIDGET'S CHURCH, Beckermet, is an ancient vernacular Cumbrian church that was built on the site of an even older monastery probably founded in the 6th century. Today, St. Bridget's is only used three times a year. In the village of Beckermet the more modern St. John's Church serves everyday needs. Two Norse cross shafts are to be seen on the south side of the church; one of them has a round base and is similar in design to the Gosforth Cross. The other cross has runic inscriptions and scroll designs. The interior of the church is simple, with an ancient sandstone altar and plain glass windows.

ST. BEES is situated in a stunningly beautiful bay. This is the site of one of the oldest Christian settlements in Britain. It gets its name from a corruption of St. Bega (7th century). The origins of the monastery go back to around the 3rd century. Danish raiders destroyed the first church, dedicated to saints Mary and Bega, in 651. According to legend, St. Bega was an Irish princess who in mid-August asked the local lord to give her enough land to build a monastery. The lord recklessly said that he would give her all the land she could find covered with snow. During the night there was a freak snowfall, and Bega was able to claim a three-mile stretch of land along the coast.

The present church was built in 1120 and restored between 1855 and 1858 by the architect William Butterfield (1814–1900), who was a devout

Anglican and a leading figure in the 19th-century Gothic revival. It is an early English cruciform structure with an intricately carved west entrance and dominating central tower. Inside the church is a lintel that has a preconquest carving of St. George slaying the dragon. This is known as the Beowulf Stone.

In 1587 the Reforming archbishop Edmund Grindal (1519–83), who was born in St. Bees, founded the grammar school that continues today as St. Bees School.

WHITEHAVEN, once a thriving sea port and mining town, experienced severe economic decline as a result of the closure of its deep undersea mines that began in the 1950s. The last mine closed in 1986, and the town took on a seedy appearance. But in the early 1990s a major effort was made to restore the Georgian heart of the town to its former glory as a way of encouraging tourism. More recently, Whitehaven was awarded a large grant to renovate its harbor area. Today Whitehaven is one of the best examples of Georgian town planning in England.

The Benedictine monks of St. Bees originally owned the area around Whitehaven, while the town itself consisted of six fishermen's cottages. At the Dissolution of the Monasteries, the land was bought by Sir Thomas Chaloner. It was acquired by Sir George Lowther in 1600. In 1635, Sir John Lowther was granted the right to develop local salt-pans and coal deposits. Subsequent generations of the Lowther family developed the area into a booming industrial and commercial port to exploit local coal reserves, most of which were exported to Ireland.

The present town was laid out in a grid pattern by Sir John Lowther, who was inspired by the designs of Sir Christopher Wren, making Whitehaven the first modern planned community in Britain. Today, the town boasts no less than 250 listed buildings that are considered historical treasures and has been declared one of Britain's 51 Gem Towns by the Council for British Architecture.

Whitehaven is of particular interest for American visitors because of the town's close links to America and American leaders in the 18th century. Mildred Warner Gale, George Washington's grandmother, was a native of Whitehaven, and was buried in St. Nicholas churchyard on January 30, 1700. Unfortunately, the site of her grave is unknown. There is, however, a small display devoted to the Gale family housed in the clock tower of the now ruined church. Augustine Washington, the future president's father, slept at No. 1 Scotch Street, a fine Georgian house, the night before he returned to America in 1704. Benjamin Franklin visited Whitehaven in 1772 to see William Brownrigg (d. 1800), a pioneer of modern mining, who invented the safety lamp that Sir Humphry Davey (1778–1829) eventually improved upon to make his famous safety lamp. Brownrigg also experimented with the manufacture of carbonated water, better known as "soda pop."

Later in the century, Whitehaven was the only town in England to be attacked by Americans during the War of Independence. On April 23, 1778, John Paul Jones, a former resident of Whitehaven, entered the harbor at night, destroyed the shore batteries, and attempted to set fire to several ships. In the early 1970s, a severe storm washed up several cannons that Jones had dumped in the sea. These are now displayed on the town's main pier. Before the American Revolution, Whitehaven was one of the major seaports in England that traded with America.

The last notable American connection lies in the fact that the red sandstone flags used to pave the piazza of George Washington's home in Mount Vernon were exported from Whitehaven. The stones themselves were quarried at nearby St. Bees.

During the 17th and 18th centuries, Whitehaven was a center of British nonconformity. Its independent colleges educated the sons of nonconformist families, who were denied access to the universities of Oxford and Cambridge.

ST. JAMES CHURCH, High St., has been described as having the finest Georgian church interior in Britain. It was consecrated on July 25, 1753. Over the altar hangs Guilio Proccacini's (1548–1626) *Transformation.* According to local gossip, the painting was plundered from the El Escorial Palace outside Madrid by the French army during the Napoleonic Wars. Lord Lowther, third earl of Lonsdale, bought it and presented it to the church in 1869, making it the only painting by this famous Italian artist to hang in an English parish church. The organ, installed in 1909, is one of the best in the north of England.

ST. NICHOLAS CHURCH, Lowther St., was originally built on the site of an earlier chapel in 1693. This unimpressive building was torn down in 1883 and rebuilt as a neo-Gothic church in beautiful red sandstone at the personal expense of a wealthy donor, Miss Margaret Gibson. Until it was destroyed by fire in 1971, the church was one of the most beautiful in England. All that remains today is the clock tower and a few other ruins. The tower now serves as a resource center with a small museum and chapel. It stands in the church graveyard that has been transformed into a pleasant garden. Inside the tower is a plaque to George Washington's grandmother, Mildred Gale.

WESLEYAN CHURCH, Scotch St. This grand Victorian neo-Gothic structure testifies to the strength of Cumbrian Methodism in the 19th and early 20th centuries. Today there is a preservation order on the building, which is considered a classic of its kind.

THE BEACON MUSEUM, West Pier, is housed in an old industrial area that was recently renovated. It contains fascinating displays relating to Whitehaven's role in the development of mining and even the involvement of local merchants in the North Atlantic slave trade.

HAIG COLLIERY MINING MUSEUM is a fascinating museum that is currently under construction by the Haig Pit Restoration Group. Volunteers are restoring the mine and its equipment, including railway engines, the winding house, and various mine workshops. The museum has some excellent photographs that retell the often-tragic story of mining over the centuries.

The monks of St. Bees Monastery in the 13th century developed the first mines in the Whitehaven area. After the Reformation, the Lowther family exploited both local coal and iron deposits, often at great cost of life. Deaths were so common in the mines that the local newspapers scarcely mentioned the deaths of fewer than ten men. Estimates suggest that between at least 1,200 men, women, and children died in Whitehaven's deadly mines, which were among the deepest and most dangerous in Britain. By the time the mines were finally closed, their seams stretched over seven miles under the Irish Sea. The Haig Pit was the last of the deep mines in the area and was closed in 1986.

COCKERMOUTH lies 13 miles inland from Whitehaven at the junction of the rivers Cocker and Derwent. The Romans built a fort, Deventio, at Papcastle approximately a mile northwest of the present town. A Norman castle was built here in the 13th century only to be stormed by Robert the Bruce during his invasion of the north of England in 1313. The town received a royal charter permitting it to hold a market in 1221. Its real claim to fame is as the birthplace of the poet William Wordsworth (1770–1850) and his sister, Dorothy (1771–1855), who spent their childhoods in the town. The Quaker scientist John Dalton was also born here, as was Fletcher Christian (1764–94) who led the mutiny on the *Bounty*. All three men attended the same small school at about the same time.

WORDSWORTH HOUSE, High St., is easy to find and full of fascinating exhibits and period furniture. The house was built for the High Sheriff of Cumberland, Joshua Lucock (18th century), in 1745, when it was one of the grandest in the area. William Wordsworth's father, John, was installed in the house as the local agent of Sir John Lowther, who bought the property in 1761. The Wordsworths had four sons and a daughter. William and his sister lived here until his mother died when he was eight, at which time they were sent to live with relatives in Penrith. Five years later, his father died. When the local bus company attempted to buy the house in 1938 with the intention of demolishing it to build a bus station, their plans caused a national uproar. A fund was established to buy the house for the National Trust. They took possession in 1938 and opened it as a memorial to the poet on July 3, 1939.

Wordsworth is important to the history of British Christianity because he was the foremost spokesman of English Romanticism and an advocate of the cult of nature. Although Wordsworth never formally rejected Christianity, he influenced many people towards a pantheistic worldview. At the same time, Wordsworth's interest in antiquity and ancient monuments inspired others to develop an interest in and preserve many of Cumbria's historic Christian sites.

ST. OSWALD'S CHURCH, Dean/ Cockermouth. This 12th-century church with a 15th-century chancel and 17th-century sanctuary was renovated between 1967 and 1973, making it one of the better-preserved interiors in the region. It contains a Norman font and 15th-century chancel window and is one of only three Cumbrian churches with gargoyles. The graveyard, which was used as a center for preaching before the construction of the church itself, contains many ancient tombstones and a 12th-century cross.

ST. MUNGO'S CHURCH, Dearham/ Cockermouth, is another 12th-century church with a 13th-century chancel built on the site of an earlier Saxon building. When the church was renovated in 1882, a large stone, four feet high, was discovered. Known as the Adam Stone, it is covered with carvings depicting the Fall. Also discovered was an ancient stone cross decorated with the story of the 6th-century hermit and holy man St. Kenneth. Both the stone and the cross are displayed in the church along with a well preserved wheel-head, or Celtic cross, which is decorated with the Norse Tree of the Universe. The ornate Norman font is also carved in the Norse style with mythological beasts and devils.

KESWICK is 13 miles further inland past the beautiful Lake Bassenthwaite. This picturesque town is the heart of the English Lake District and the site of a settlement that goes back to about 2000 B.C. The town itself is located on the shores of Lake Derwentwater, where, according to Bede, St. Cuthbert's friend St. Herbert lived on an island that now bears his name.

The town itself is mainly Georgian or Cumbrian vernacular with many quaint buildings that delight visitors. From a Christian viewpoint, the main attraction of Keswick is its world-famous annual Keswick Convention.

Robert Battersby, the vicar of St. John's Church, and his Quaker friend Robert Wilson founded the Keswick Convention. Battersby came to Keswick in 1849 as curate to its evangelical vicar, Frederick Meyers. Under Meyers's influence, Battersby moved away from his earlier High Church Tractarianism towards a lively evangelical faith. After Meyers's death, Battersby went on to become a leading evangelical in the

19th-century revival that was sweeping Victorian England. Despite considerable opposition from local people and fellow Anglicans, he organized the first Keswick Convention as an interdenominational holiness meeting in July 1875. The convention was an instant success and has been held every year since that time. Thus for two weeks in July, thousands of British Christians converge on Keswick to stay in local hotels, guest houses, and campsites while they attend daily Bible readings, prayer meetings, and a variety of other events intended to deepen their spiritual life and strengthen their faith. So successful was the convention that other "Keswicks" were soon set up as far away as America and Australia.

ST. KENTIGERN CROSTHWAITE, Keswick. This delightful church on the northwest outskirts of Keswick was built in 1181 and extensively renovated in 1553. Later it was tastefully restored in 1844 by Sir Gilbert Scott (1811–78). According to legend, a congregation was founded on this site by St. Kentigern (518–603) in 553. The church has a unique and complete set of 16th-century consecration crosses that stand on places blessed by the bishop, who consecrated the remodeled church. There are 12 crosses outside and nine inside the church. Some of its stained glass dates from the 12th century, but most of it is from the 16th century. The church has a 16th-century sundial and beautiful floor mosaic. The baptistery font dates from 1400 and is highly decorated.

The baptistery was built in 1909 as a memorial to Canon Drummond Hardwicke Rawnsley (1851–1920), who was vicar here from 1883 to 1917. A tireless conservationist, he founded the Lake District Defense Society, the forerunner of today's Friends of the Lake District. To him we owe the preservation of much of the Lake District from exploitation by industrial and commercial concerns. He was the cofounder of Britain's National Trust, which owns and preserves for public enjoyment many historic buildings and stretches of particularly beautiful countryside. With his wife, he created the Keswick School for Industrial Arts and helped found the Keswick High School. It was through Canon Rawnsley's encouragement that Beatrix Potter (1866–1943), whom he first met when she was only 16 years old, published her first book, *The Tale of Peter Rabbit,* in 1902. He is buried with his wife in the graveyard.

The poet laureate Robert Southey (1774–1843) is also buried in the graveyard. Apart from his poetry, Southey wrote *Goldilocks and the Three Bears.* Southey lived for 40 years at Greta Hall in Keswick, which is a private residence and may only be viewed from the outside. Among his many friends were the Wordsworths, Charles Lamb, and Sir Walter Scott, all of whom frequently visited Keswick.

ST. JOHN'S CHURCH, Keswick, is a superb example of neo-Gothic designed by Anthony Salvin (1799–1881) and built in glowing pink sandstone. The church was consecrated on St. John's Day, December 27, 1838, and soon became one of the centers of evangelical preaching in the north of England. Robert Battersby, the founder of the Keswick Convention, was its vicar from 1851 until his death. The novelist Hugh Walpole (1884–1941) is buried in the graveyard.

CASTLERIGG STONE CIRCLE, about a mile outside Keswick off the road to Grasmere, was built around 3000 B.C. and is one of the oldest stone circles in Britain. It was bought by Canon Rawnsley, who gave it to the National Trust in 1913 to prevent its destruction. The circle's 38 stone structures are 100 feet in diameter, with an inner rectangle of ten stones. The tallest stone is seven feet in height. No one knows its true purpose, although the alignment of the stones suggests some sort of astronomical function.

GRASMERE is a small village that lies four miles north of Ambleside. It was here that William Wordsworth lived with his wife, Mary, and sister, Dorothy, from 1799–1808. Their home, DOVE COTTAGE, is now a museum and one of the most popular tourist spots in the Lakeland. The Wordsworths are buried in the nearby St. Oswald's churchyard. Wordsworth played an important role in the creation of British romanticism and the popularization of the Lake District among poets and the educated classes of Victorian England. He was the center of a group of poets and writers, including John Ruskin, Hugh Walpole, Samuel Coleridge, Robert Southey, and Thomas De Quincey. Together these men had a profound effect on Victorian spirituality, influencing many educated people away from evangelical Christianity towards both High Church ritualism and a vague religion of nature that tended towards pantheism.

ST. OSWALD'S CHURCH, Grasmere, is a 13th-century parish church named after a king of Northumberland and Christian convert, St. Oswald, who according to legend led an evangelistic mission to Cumbria and preached here in the 7th century. The church has a beautiful old wooden beamed ceiling and some good stained-glass windows by the 19th-century artist Henry Holiday (1839–1927). There are several interesting monuments, including one to the Wordsworth family.

Four miles south of Grasmere is the picturesque town of AMBLESIDE with many fine stone Victorian houses. The Romans built a wooden fort here, GALVA, in A.D. 79 with a garrison of over 200 troops. Later in the 2nd century it was rebuilt, using local stone, and the garrison increased to over 500. The ruins of this military complex can be seen next to Borrans Park in nearby Waterhead at the north end of Lake Windermere.

ST. MARY'S CHURCH, Vicarage Rd., Ambleside, was one of the first churches built in northern England as part of the

C

JOHN RUSKIN (1819–1900) was arguably the most influential writer on artistic and architectural issues in the 19th century and the advocate of a simple, pre-industrial lifestyle. His views on art influenced William Morris and a whole generation of British and American artists, many of whom worked to produce some very beautiful neo-Gothic churches. His views on modern society had a profound impact on Count Leo Tolstoy (1828–1910), Mahatma Gandhi (1869–1948), and leaders of the British Labor movement. Positively, Ruskin stressed the relationship between art and architecture and the spiritual ethos of an age. In his view, architecture manifests the moral qualities of its designers. Negatively, Ruskin totally rejected modern industry and encouraged a sentimental nostalgia for a mythical past. In his early life Ruskin appears to have embraced Christianity. But around 1850 he lost his faith and embraced a cosmic naturalism that led him to become increasingly reactionary in his social and political views.

growing Oxford, or Tractarian, movement. This movement rejected what its members saw as the "modernism" of evangelical religion by attempting to reintroduce medieval rituals and forms of worship. It was built between 1850 and 1854 in the neo-Gothic style according to designs by Sir Gilbert Scott. Two of the stained-glass windows are by Henry Holiday. On the choir stalls are carvings of 14 saints associated with Cumbria. These are Ethelberga, Benedict Biscop, Cuthebert, Caedmon, Hilda, Bede, Adian, Edwin, Wilfred, Oswald, Paulinus, Finan, Columba, and Kentigern.

THE RUSKIN MUSEUM, Yewdale Rd., Coniston, is located eight miles southwest of Ambleside. This museum, opened in May 1999, replaces an earlier museum opened by Ruskin's devoted follower, Canon Rawnsley, in 1901. It is dedicated to the life and work of John Ruskin (1819–1900). It contains a fine collection of Ruskin's watercolor paintings, sketches, drawings, and manuscripts.

DERBY

Well off the usual tourist route, Derby is rich in Christian history, particularly nonconformist or evangelical history, although this is not as well acknowledged by local museums as one would like. A Roman settlement existed in the area on the north bank of the river

Derwent, but the present town was not founded until the Danish invasions, when in 854 Derby became one of five Daneburghs, along with Leicester, Lincoln, Nottingham, and Stamford. It was stormed by Saxons in 917 and later became an important medieval city. In the *Doomsday Book*, produced after the Norman conquest, Derby had a population of 2000 served by six churches. Most of its history was uneventful until 1746, when it became the most southerly town to be captured by Bonnie Prince Charlie, Charles Stuart, the Young Pretender (1720–88), before he was forced to retreat back to Scotland. In 1717 John Lombe and Thomas Cotchet founded the first factory in England, a silk mill, and the Royal Crown Derby porcelain works were founded in 1752. During the 19th century, Derby became a major rail junction and in the 20th century the home of Rolls-Royce, which was established here in 1908. During the 18th and 19th centuries, Derby was a center of Methodism and English nonconformity. The artist Joseph Wright (1734–97) and skeptical philosopher, freethinker, and father of sociology Herbert Spencer (1820–1903) were both born here in Exeter Row and lived on Wilmot Street. Erasmus Darwin spent 20 years in Derby.

The family of Florence Nightingale (1820–1910) came from nearby Cromford. She was the great Christian reformer and advocate of nursing, known as "the lady with the lamp." The museum has a bust of her.

John Clifford (1836–1923), the first president of the Baptist World Alliance, was born in Sawley in 1839. He became president of the Baptist Union in 1888 and took a leading role in opposing the 1902 Education Act that reduced the role of Christian churches in British education. Other natives of Derby include John Flamsteed, a rival of Newton and founder of the Royal Observatory who established the Greenwich meridian, and Henry Cavendish (1731–1810), the eccentric Christian who founded modern chemistry.

On August 1, 1556, an old woman, Joan Waste, was burnt at the stake on Burton Road, in the Windmill Pit, because she questioned the doctrine of transubstantiation and said that Christ was spiritually, not physically, present in the Communion. She died praying for her persecutors and the bishop of Derby, who condemned her.

PLACES TO VISIT

DERBY CATHEDRAL. Although there has been a church here for over 1000 years, the cathedral was actually built between 1723 and 1733 as the parish church of All Saints. The tower, however, dates from 1510, and at 212 feet is said to be the second highest in England. It also claims to have the oldest peel of ten bells in the world. It became a cathedral in 1927 when the new diocese of Derby was created. The inside has a fine nave designed by James Gibbs (20th century) and some good modern stained glass. The wrought-iron screen was created by Robert Backwell (d. 1752) and is an excellent example of 18th-century decorative ironwork. The cathedral contains the grave of Bess of Hardwick, who for over ten years was the jailer in charge of Mary Queen of Scots (1516–58) after her imprisonment by Elizabeth I (1533–1603). Henry Cavendish is also buried in the cathedral.

ST. WERBURG'S, the Strand, is a 12th-century church, now used as a shopping center, where Samuel Johnson, who was a native of nearby Litchfield, was married on June 9, 1735.

ST. MARY ON THE BRIDGE. This is one of only six surviving medieval bridge chapels in England. The present bridge dates from the 18th century, but a bridge has stood here since Saxon times. In the Middle Ages the chapel charged a toll for people and animals to cross. It also provided a place for prayer before travelers entered the dark and dangerous Sherwood Forest on the road to Nottingham. The original Saxon bridge was made of wood. The Normans built a stone bridge in 1230. On July 26, 1588, three Roman Catholic priests, Nicholas Garlick (1555–88), Robert Ludlam (1553–88), and Richard Simpson (1556–88), known as the Padley Martyrs after the place where they were arrested, were hung, drawn, and quartered in Derby. Their bodies were then displayed outside this chapel. The adjoining rectory, or minister's home, was in active use by the clergy until in 1985, when it became the Padley Day Care Center for homeless people. In 1995 the center was moved, and the

house is now vacant. Today Derby's small Lutheran community uses the chapel.

ST. MARY'S, Bridge St. Built in the 19th century for Irish immigrants, St. Mary's was the first Roman Catholic church designed by the architect Augustus Pugin (1812–52). It is considered by many to be his masterpiece.

DERBY MUSEUM AND ART GALLERY, the Strand, has a superb collection of china and porcelain and a splendid gallery devoted to the work of Joseph Wright, whose paintings of the early industrial age are highly significant social documents as well as stunning works of art.

PICKFORD HOUSE, 41 Friar Gate, is one of the few Georgian houses that has been made into a museum which is not a stately home belonging to the nobility. This house was built by the middle-class architect Joseph Pickford in 1770 as his home. In it there are fine exhibits of life in the late 18th and early 19th centuries that give vivid insights into the lifestyles of the type of people who supported John Wesley (1703–91). The main rooms are furnished as they were during Pickford's lifetime. The kitchens are a reconstruction from the 1830s and show how the servants of well-to-do families actually lived. The upstairs rooms have been restored as they would have looked around 1815 at the end of the Napoleonic wars. There is also a costume and toy collection on display.

INDUSTRIAL MUSEUM, Full Street, is housed in an old warehouse that contains a reconstruction of Lombe's early factory, as well as an excellent display devoted to the history of engineering in Derby, including the Rolls-Royce and the development of the railways. Anyone wanting to understand the 19th century with its rapid industrialization needs to visit this informative museum.

ROYAL CROWN DERBY MUSEUM, Osmaston Rd., contains a fascinating collection that documents the porcelain industry, which once played an important role in the growth of other industries throughout Europe.

DALE ABBEY, six miles east, was originally a thriving abbey. Today only a small church and the ruins of a hermitage remain. A Derby baker who claimed to have received a vision of the Virgin Mary founded the hermitage. It is generally believed that the church was once the abbey's hospital. It contains a 13th-century painting and according to legend is where Robin Hood's men used to marry.

KEDLESTON HALL, four miles northwest, was designed by Robert Adam (1728–92) and built between 1759 and 1765 for the Curzon family. It contains rare Dutch and Italian paintings, plus a large collection of Indian art and artifacts acquired by Lord Curzon of Kedleston (1859–1925) when he was viceroy of India.

Prince Gunthlac, who retired from military duty to become a hermit on St. Bartholomew's Day 669, founded REPTON. The town grew up around his foundation and eventually became the capital of Christian Mercia. The pagan Danish invaders destroyed it in 875. The present church of St. Wystan was built around 950 and has one of the best-preserved Saxon crypts in England. Later it became the site of a great Augustinian priory, founded in 1153. After the Dissolution of the Monasteries in 1557, the local landowner, to prevent the monks returning, tore down the monastery buildings. A few years later Repton School was founded, one of the most famous public schools, i.e., private foundations, in England. The guest hall of the priory survived destruction to become the school library. There is also one of the earliest brick towers in England dating from 1438 and the remains of the priory gateway. The school houses a small but interesting museum.

DUNFERMLINE

This ancient town, whose name means "fort of the crooked Linn," was made capital of Scotland by Malcolm Canmore (d. 1093), Malcolm III, after he married the English princess Margaret (1045–93) in 1067. Together they built a palace and founded a priory that eventually replaced Iona as the burial place of Scottish kings. David I raised the priory to an abbey in the 13th century. In 1303 the city was sacked by Edward I, who destroyed the abbey. Robert the Bruce had the abbey rebuilt. His body was buried here, although his heart was buried in Melrose Abbey. Dunfermline remained the capital of Scotland until the Act of Union in 1603. In 1651 Charles II stayed here before his disastrous march south and his defeat at Worcester. Dunfermline is also the birthplace of Andrew Carnegie (1835–1918).

PLACES TO VISIT

DUNFERMLINE ABBEY, Monastery St., St. Margaret St., was originally built by Margaret and her husband. In 1128 David I extended it. The buildings were destroyed by Edward I in 1303, who stripped the lead of the abbey church roof to use it as ammunition in his catapults. The nave of the original Romanesque church was renovated by the addition of a neo-Gothic choir by William Burn when the building was restored between 1817 and 1822 to create a new parish church. Beneath the pulpit is the grave of Robert the Bruce. Outside the church at the east end are the ruins of the shrine of Margaret, where she was buried with her husband and children. The tomb of the great 18th-century evangelical leader Ralph Erskine (1685–1752), who was the minister here, is to the northeast of the shrine.

ABBOT HOUSE HERITAGE CENTER, St. Margaret St., provides a good overview of the history of the abbey and the Christian heritage of the area.

ST. MARGARET'S CAVE MUSEUM, Glen Bridge Car Park off Bridge St. This unusual museum is entered by descending 84 steps to a cave where St. Margaret regularly retired for prayer and meditation. It is now equipped with displays about her life and times.

DUNFERMLINE COUNTY MUSEUM, Viewfield Terrace, has some interesting exhibits about the area and the history of Scotland.

THE ANDREW CARNEGIE BIRTHPLACE MUSEUM, on the corner of Moodie St. and Priory Lane. This is the simple weaver's cottage where Andrew Carnegie (1835–1918) was born and lived before his family emigrated to America. The museum has a fascinating collection of items relating to the man who richly endowed his hometown with numerous gifts, including the local public baths and library, as well as an annual music festival.

RALPH ERSKINE (1685–1752) was an evangelical leader who objected to patronage in the Established Church of Scotland, which he saw as corrupting the preaching of the gospel. In 1773, with his brother Ebenezer (1660–1754), he helped form the Associate Presbytery, which developed into the Secessionist Church.

D

ST. MARGARET OF SCOTLAND (1045–93) was born in Hungary but raised in England. After the Norman conquest, she helped organize resistance in the north before fleeing to Scotland with her mother and younger brother, who was the heir to the English throne. Shipwrecked on the Firth of Forth, her party was brought to Dunfermline, where she met and married Malcolm III, a widower. Her piety and devotion to the Christian cause did much to revive the church in Scotland while at the same time bringing Celtic elements in line with Roman Catholic practice. She commissioned the building of numerous churches and restored the monastery of Iona that had been destroyed by Vikings. Pope Innocent IV (d. 1254) declared her a saint in 1252.

DUMFRIES

Dumfries is thought to have originated as a Roman settlement and inland seaport. Later a castle was built here, and the town developed around it. In 1301, Edward I of England captured the castle and installed an English garrison. A few years later, in 1306, Robert the Bruce (1274–1329) murdered his rival Lord John Comyn (1277–1306), sparking off a war of independence. The town received a royal charter in the early 12th century, which was renewed in 1395 by Robert III (1340–1406) of Scotland. Dumfries was twice captured by the English and razed to the ground. It was first destroyed in 1448 and then, almost a century later, in 1536. The Young Pretender, Charles Stewart (1720–88), captured the city on his retreat from Derby in 1745, causing considerable damage because of the townspeople's lack of enthusiasm for his cause. During World War II, Dumfries was the headquarters of the Norwegian army in England. Robert Burns (1759–96) worked here as an excise man, or customs officer, until his death. During that time he wrote over 100 poems.

PLACES TO VISIT

ROBERT BURNS CENTER, Mill Rd. This is a superb audio-visual presentation that introduces visitors to the life and work of Burns, whose rich poetry both shapes the Scottish people and reflects the intellectual conflicts of the Age of Reason.

ROBERT BURNS HOUSE, Burns St., is a simple sandstone house where Burns spent the last days of his life. It contains a host of items intimately connected with the great poet.

ST. MICHAEL'S CHURCH, St. Michael's St., is essentially an uninteresting 18th-century building that has gained fame because the BURNS MAUSOLEUM is located in its graveyard. Here in an uncharacteristic neoclassical tomb, Burns, his wife, and seven children are buried. Around the site are the gravestones of many of Burns's friends.

DUMFRIES MUSEUM, Church St., contains a fine exhibit depicting the early history of Christianity in north Britain.

SWEETHEART ABBEY, eight miles southwest along the A710, New Abbey Road. This great romantic ruin was once one of the largest Cistercian houses in Scotland. It was founded in 1273 and became the last Cistercian monastery to be built in Scotland before the Reformation. It gains its name from the practice of its patron, Devorgilla de Balliol (d. 1290), aged 90, who also founded Balliol College at the University of Oxford. She carried the embalmed heart of her husband wherever she went for the last sixteen years of her life; at her death it was buried with her in her grave. However ghoulish this may seem, it certainly explodes the lie promoted by some modern writers that medieval people felt no real affection or love for their spouses. The ruins of the church itself are remarkably intact in beautiful

red sandstone, although there is little trace of the other abbey buildings. The abbey suffered particularly severely because its last abbot, Gilbert Brown of Carsluith (d. 1612), strongly opposed the Reformation.

LINCULDEN ABBEY, six miles northwest on the A76. Here lies the ruin of this 12th-century Benedictine house. Very little remains of the original abbey except a small church that was once part of the abbey's choir and south transept. This 15th-century church, which contains the tomb of Margaret, daughter of Robert III, is superb.

THE RUTHWELL CROSS. Sixteen miles southeast on the A75 and B74 is the village of Ruthwell. One of Europe's most important early Christian works of art, the richly decorated 8th-century Ruthwell Cross, stands in the parish church. In 1642, the cross was actually smashed to pieces and buried in the church floor because it was considered idolatrous. But in 1823 it was dug up and lovingly pieced together. The 18-foot shaft is entirely original, although parts of the cross arms have been restored. The runes on the shaft of the cross are a poem written in the first person, so that they appear to be spoken by the cross itself. They are known as the Dream of the Cross and are in West Saxon language, making them among the earliest inscriptions in English. It is generally believed that the poem is by the Christian poet Caedmon (658–80).

DURHAM

Following the destruction of Lindesfarne monastery by Viking raiders in 793, the monks who escaped carried with them the body of St. Cuthbert (635–87) and various other treasures. They wandered around northern England and southern Scotland for many years seeking a place of refuge. For a while they settled in Carlisle, but wisely moved on before the city was sacked by the Danes in 875. Eventually, they settled on a rocky crag overlooking the river Wear. From this monastic settlement, with an easily defended location, the city of Durham eventually grew. The Normans recognized the value of the site and built a castle in 1073. After demolishing most of the Saxon town, they began work on the cathedral in 1093. Because of the strategic importance of Durham, which blocked the route of Scottish invaders, the bishop was given unique privileges as a prince bishop with important secular powers. The city had a turbulent history and was attacked by the Scots and other groups several times. But it escaped the ravages of the Industrial Revolution and remains today a small picturesque town. A university was founded here by Oliver Cromwell (1599–1658), but closed after the Restoration and not reopened until 1832, when it was the only other English university after Oxford and Cambridge.

PLACES TO VISIT

DURHAM CATHEDRAL was described by Sir Walter Scott (1771–1832) as "half church of God, half fort against the Scots." This is a magnificent example of Romanesque architecture. The cathedral is situated in a splendid location on a rocky crag overlooking the city surrounded by university buildings that occupy former ecclesiastical houses, many of which go back to the Middle Ages. The high central tower is a late 15th-century addition, while the Chapel of the Nine Altars is Gothic. The nave conveys a sense of solidity and power. Although Romanesque, the pointed ribs of the vault are strikingly similar to what became the Gothic style, making Durham unique and highly innovative for the time of its construction. In the south transept is a 16th-century clock that is fun to look at.

The Chapel of the Nine Altars was built in the 13th century in the Early Gothic style by the same craftsmen that built Fountains Abbey. Note the way the floor is sunken to increase the sense of space and soaring heights of the roof that reaches to heaven. The stone carving on the bosses and capitals is superb and gives some idea of what Fountains

Abbey and similar church ruins must once have looked like.

The tomb of the Venerable Bede (672–735) can be seen in the Galilee Chapel in the west of the church. Seeing it reminds the viewer of the reality of church history and makes one ponder the mystery of life and death, as well as the impact one man can have on the world through their writings and dedication to God. The tomb, or rather shrine, of St. Cuthbert, which is equally impressive, is located behind the Neville Screen at the back of the high altar. Visiting Cuthbert's grave is an occasion to reflect on the missionary work of a man who went to the wildest parts of a decaying Europe, where he created a Christian movement that impacted the world.

Around the cathedral proper are many monastic buildings that now serve as the university. In particular the cathedral treasury is well worth a visit because it contains some of the earliest Saxon church garments and other objects that have survived in Britain, including a fascinating portable altar used by St. Cuthbert. His processional cross and parts of his original oak coffin, which was carried by the faithful monks around the north of England when they fled the Vikings, can also be seen.

DURHAM CASTLE is a fine example of a Norman castle. It was modified by successive bishops and finally given to the university. The keep has been a student residence since 1840. The 15th-century kitchens and great hall may be visited. Inside are also two interesting chapels. In the beautiful 16th-century chapel, the misericords include scenes of nagging wives and pigs playing bagpipes. The older Norman chapel contains some grotesque ancient stone carvings.

ST. JOHN'S COLLEGE is both a teaching college and hall of residence with a strong evangelical tradition. Visitors are welcome, and accommodation is sometimes available in the summer months.

DURHAM UNIVERSITY ORIENTAL MUSEUM, located in an 18th-century house on the outskirts of the city on Darlington Rd., contains a wonderful collection of Asian art, many of which have religious significance.

EDINBURGH

Edinburgh's history is intimately linked to its famous castle. Indeed, until the 18th century, the town was a cluster of buildings clinging to the castle mount. Archaeological evidence suggests early human occupation of this superb defensive position, but the recorded history of the site does not begin until the building of the castle by Edwin, the 7th-century king of Northumbria, on the site of an earlier fortification. At that time it was called

Dun Eadain, which means "the fort on the hill." This name was changed to "Edwin's castle," which evolved into the modern name of Edinburgh. During the 11th century, a market developed under the protection of the castle walls, and King Malcolm strengthened the fortifications. His widow Queen Margaret died here in 1093 while the castle was under siege by an invading Norman army. In 1124, King David I made the castle his principal residence when he founded the nearby Abbey of Holyrood, or the Holy Cross. Robert the Bruce granted the town a royal charter in 1329, and in 1437 the town was enclosed in a protective wall. Today only a very small section of the town wall survives at the foot of Castle Rock. Work began on Holyrood Palace in 1500, and the Royal College of Surgeons was granted a charter in 1506. Scotland's first printing press was established in Edinburgh in 1508, and the Flodden Wall, some of which still survives, was built in 1513. In 1544 and 1547, Henry VIII of England stormed the city. Following the return of Mary Queen of Scots from France, Edinburgh became the scene of intrigue and a dynastic struggle that saw the young queen banished and her young son James VI placed on the throne. After the death of Queen Elizabeth I of England, he became James I of England in 1603. During the Reformation, Edinburgh was the stronghold of reforming Protestants led by John Knox (1513–72), the

minister of St. Giles' Church. Almost a century later, in 1638, the Solemn League and National Covenant was signed by Protestant nobles in Grayfriars. Later, over 100 of them were martyred in the Grassmarket. During the British civil war, Cromwell stormed the city in 1650. Following the restoration of the monarchy in England in 1661, Charles II rebuilt Holyrood Palace, which had been destroyed by Cromwell. In 1745 the Young Pretender, Bonnie Prince Charles, held court in Holyrood before marching south to England and defeat.

The 18th century saw the flowering of the Scottish Enlightenment, with men like the economist Adam Smith (1723–1790), the philosopher David Hume (1711–76), and the novelist Sir Walter Scott (1771–1832) in Edinburgh. This flowering of learning and the arts saw the building of the beautiful Georgian Edinburgh New Town that began in 1767. Edinburgh suffered little as a result of the Industrial Revolution or World War II, and in 1995 it was declared a World Heritage Site by UNESCO. More recently, in 1999, Edinburgh became the seat of the new Scottish Parliament.

PLACES TO VISIT

ST. GILES, High St., the High Kirk of Scotland, is often incorrectly called a "cathedral." Records show that a church existed here as early as 854. In 1120, this early building was replaced by a larger Norman structure. Richard II of England destroyed the building when he invaded Scotland in 1385. The church was rebuilt in the Gothic style, although some people think that its central piers may be of Norman origin. A few years later, in 1467, the church, which had been under the charge of the bishop of St. Andrews, was granted collegiate status, making it an independent congregation.

The church is named after St. Giles (d. 770), a French hermit. According to legend, Giles was crippled after the local king, Wamba, shot at a deer that Giles had befriended. The arrow missed the animal but hit the hermit, who was badly wounded and thereafter walked with a severe limp. Consequently, St. Giles became the patron saint of cripples and beggars. The cult of St. Giles became very popular in the late medieval period and spread throughout Europe to Scotland. The story of St. Giles and the deer is carved on the archway above the west door; it also appears in the north nave window, the south clerestory window, and in the Thistle Chapel. In 1454, shortly before his death, Sir William Preston donated what was believed to be a rare relic, a bone from the arm of St. Giles, to the church. The relic attracted a steady stream of pilgrims seeking miraculous healing. During the Reformation, the relic and a statue of St. Giles were thrown into Loch Nor, which was drained in the 18th century and is now known as the sunken gardens on Princess Street.

In the 16th century, John Knox became the minister of St. Giles and made it the center of the Scottish Reformation. He was responsible for the removal of 44 medieval altars and the remodeling of the church along Protestant lines. The 17th century saw two brief periods during which St. Giles became a cathedral under the Stuart kings.

During parts of the 18th and 19th centuries, the church housed as many as four different congregations at one time, while at other times parts of the building were rented out for secular use. It was restored as a church and national monument between 1872 and 1883 at the instigation of the publisher William Chambers (1800–83), the lord provost of Edinburgh, who paid for most of the work himself. The northeast chapel, which today is used for youth services, is dedicated to his memory.

The Albany Aisle is named after the duke of Albany (1340–1420), who built it in 1410 as an act of penance for his murder of the duke of Rothesay (15th century). This grim monument reminds the visitor that medieval Christians felt that they could get away with anything provided they made big enough donations to church. It is this type of religious manipulation of God that led to the Reformation.

The Preston Aisle at the back of the church is named after Sir William Preston (d. 1454), mentioned earlier. It was here in 1643 that the Solemn League and Covenant was signed, binding Scottish Protestant leaders to the cause of Oliver Cromwell and English Puritans in the Civil War. Today it houses the Royal Pew used by Queen Elizabeth II and the duke of Edinburgh when they visit the church.

The Chepman Aisle was donated by William Chepman (d. 1532), who set up Scotland's first printing press, thus making the spread of the Reformation in Scotland possible. Appropriately enough, the aisle contains an original copy of the Solemn League and Covenant signed at Grayfriars in 1638. There is also a monument to the duke of Montrose, who began his political career as one of the four nobles who drew up the National League and Covenant in 1638. In 1639 he began to have doubts about the wisdom of the League, and in 1640 he joined the king in his fight against Cromwell and the Covenanters. After numerous adventures, he fled to the Continent in 1646, only to return to Scotland in 1650, where he suffered utter defeat on the 27th of April. Subsequently he was arrested, tried, and hung for treason on May 21. After the Restoration, his remains were buried in St. Giles in 1661.

The Moray Aisle, or south transept, commemorates Lord James Stuart, earl of Moray (1531–70), who converted to Protestantism in 1556 and led Scottish Protestants in their revolt against the forces of his half-sister, the staunchly Roman Catholic Mary Queen of Scots (1542–87). After Mary fled to England in 1568, he became the regent ruling on behalf of Mary's infant son James VI of Scotland, I of England. He was buried here after his assassination in 1570 and is remembered by a monument erected in 1864. A stained-glass window depicts Moray's death and John Knox preaching at his funeral.

Look out for the small brass plaque opposite the window on the north side. It marks the spot from where the legendary Jenny Geddes, a local businesswoman, threw her kneeling stool at the preacher, who was reading from the Anglican *Book of Common Prayer* in 1637. Geddes, and her fellow Protestants, believed that the introduction of Anglican worship was the first step towards the restoration of Catholicism. This act of defiance led to the signing of the National League and Covenant by Protestant leaders the following year.

St. Eloi's Chapel, like St. Giles itself, is named after a French saint, Eloi (588–660), who became the patron saint of metalworkers. Notice the outline of a hammer, the symbol of the saint, in the floor. Today the chapel contains a memorial to the Protestant leader and Covenanter, the eighth earl of Argyll (1598–1661), who was executed after the restoration of the monarchy in 1661.

The Chapel of the Thistle, in the southeast corner of the church, was built in 1911 as the chapel of the Most

E

123

Ancient and Most Noble Order of the Thistle. This heraldic order was founded by James VII of Scotland, James II of England, in 1687 and is limited to 16 members. It is Scotland's most prestigious order. The names of its members are recorded in the chapel's antechamber.

Finally, notice the Burns memorial window that was installed near the west door in 1985. This window represents Scottish national pride in the great poet and can be seen either as an expression of civil religion, as evidence of the growing secularism of the church, or as recognition of the Christian spirit in many of Burns's poems.

St. Margaret's Chapel, located in the recesses of the castle, was probably built by the queen's son, David I, although it may well be a spot where the pious Margaret prayed. Although regarded by many, including Robert the Bruce, as a sacred spot, the chapel was also neglected and at times used for secular purposes. For example, during the 18th century, until 1845, it was used to store gunpowder. It was restored by Sir David Wilson (19th century) in 1853 as a result of the wave of national pride and interest in history launched by Sir Walter Scott a few decades earlier. This is the oldest building in Edinburgh, with some fine Norman stonework.

GRAYFRIARS CHURCH AND CHURCH-YARD is built on the site of a Franciscan priory. The present church was dedicated on Christmas Day, 1620. It became the place where the National

League and Covenant was signed on February 28, 1638, by nobles who used their own blood as ink. This second covenant renewed the original covenant, which was drawn up by John Knox to affirm the Reformed faith. The original covenant was signed by Scottish nobles in December 1557. Both covenants were superseded by the Solemn League and Covenant of 1643. On the north wall of the churchyard is a memorial to the many Covenanters who were martyred for their Protestant faith.

ST. ANDREW'S CHURCH, Royal Mile, was built between 1782 and 1785 by Andrew Fraser in a curious oval design. It is famous as a 19th-century evangelical stronghold and the scene of the secession movement led by the great preacher and church leader Thomas Chalmers (1780–1847). In 1843, 451 evangelical clergy resigned from the spiritually dead Church of Scotland to form their own Free Church.

JOHN KNOX HOUSE, High St., is the traditional home of the great Reformer John Knox (1514–72). Although the house was built in 1490, making it the oldest house in the city, most of today's building dates from the mid-16th century. Knox is believed to have lived and died here. An earlier occupant of the house was Mary Queen of Scots's goldsmith, James Mossman (16th century). The exhibition contains details about the lives of both men, although it concentrates on Knox.

HOLYROOD ABBEY, at the end of the Royal Mile, was originally founded as an abbey by David I in 1128 and rebuilt on a vast scale in the 13th century. English invaders sacked the abbey in 1544 and 1547. It was promptly rebuilt and by 1565 was regularly used as a royal chapel, although many of its buildings remained in ruins. Mary Queen of Scots and Lord Darnley were married here in 1565, and Charles I was crowned here in 1633. Charles II made the abbey church a royal chapel, which James VII of Scotland, James II of England, used for his newly founded Order of the Thistle.

The Norman arch, found behind the royal vault, is the only remaining structure from David I's original church. Most of the other ruins date back to the 13th century. David II, James II, James V, and Lord Darnley are all buried by the high altar. Their graves were desecrated by rioters in 1688. Subsequently, Queen Victoria ordered the collection of their remains and their reburial in the royal vault. It is also believed that Mary Queen of Scots had her secretary David Rizzio buried here after his brutal murder on March 9, 1566, but the site of his grave is unknown.

HOLYROOD PALACE. Built during the 15th century in the abbey grounds, Holyrood Palace became the preferred royal residence of Kings James I, II, and III, all of whom were married in the abbey church. The palace was destroyed by the English in the 16th century and rebuilt by the Stuart kings. Only the northeast tower survives from the original building. It was here in 1561 that the Roman Catholic Mary Queen of Scots attempted to dispute the truth of Christianity with John Knox. Here too Mary's husband, Lord Darnley, plotted the murder of Mary's secretary Rizzio, who was stabbed to death before Mary's eyes. After Mary's son James VI of Scotland, James I of England, accepted the English throne, the palace lost much of its importance. Cromwell lived here during his invasion of Scotland in 1650 and repaired parts of the palace that had been destroyed by a fire. Major restorations were carried out by Charles II between 1671 and 1680, creating what is essentially the present complex of buildings. The Young Pretender held court here in 1745, and the refugee Comte d'Artois, who became Charles X (1757–1836) of France, lived here from 1830–32. Both Queen Victoria (1819–1901) and her son Edward VII (1841–1910) spent short visits living in the palace.

The state apartments and picture gallery are among the more interesting parts of the palace and well worth seeing because of their rich associations with Scottish history. Note particularly the painting by Jacob de Wet (1610–71), *The Finding of Moses*. Its importance lies in the fact that the Scottish royal house claimed to be descendants of the Egyptian pharaoh's daughter, conveniently called "Scota," who was said to have rescued Moses from the Nile. This painting, hanging as it does with portraits of Scottish kings, was intended to remind the viewer of the antiquity and biblical origins of Scottish royalty.

St. Margaret's Well and St. Anthony's Chapel, Holyrood Park, are now romantic ruins of what was once a minor pilgrimage site associated with the pious queen. Before the Reformation, water from the well was believed to have curative properties, particularly for healing eye infections.

Edinburgh Castle, perched on a jagged rock dominating the landscape of the city, is Britain's most famous castle. Built by King Malcolm, it was held against the English by his wife Queen Margaret in 1093. Margaret died during the siege. Her body was lowered on ropes down the walls and cliff before being secretly transported to Dunfermline Priory, where she was buried. James VI of Scotland, James I of England, was born here in 1566. During the Napoleonic wars, French prisoners were kept in the dungeons, where they left a collection of graffiti.

The castle is entered from the esplanade, or ceremonial courtyard, which is the scene of the famous annual Military Tattoo during the Edinburgh Festival. Here there are memorials both to the Covenanters, who were executed for their faith, and to supposed witches, who were burnt here during the late Middle Ages. These grim monuments remind us of the intolerance of past gen-

erations and the advantages religious freedom bestows on all today. It was also on the esplanade that the earl of Stirling (1567–1640) received a royal charter to begin the colonization of Nova Scotia in 1625.

Across the moat at the entrance to the castle proper are statues of Bruce and Wallace. Above the portcullis gate is the Argyle Tower, named after the Protestant duke of Argyle, who was imprisoned here after the restoration of the monarchy and executed in 1685.

Inside the castle are the United Services Museum that honors Scottish regiments, the Royal Scots Dragoon Guards Museum, and the Scottish National War Memorial. Although the pride of many Scots, these museums are grim reminders of the bloodthirsty history of British imperialism, which conquered two-thirds of the globe during the 18th and 19th centuries. Anyone interested in adventure is bound to find these exhibits exciting. But Christians have a duty to reflect on them from a biblical viewpoint and ask whether conquests that promoted the North Atlantic slave trade and opium wars are really something to be proud of. Of course, these museums depict Scottish military achievements without considering what the many overseas wars were really about.

In a vault below the great hall is Mons Meg, one of the largest cannons to be created in the 15th century. It was capable of firing a huge amount of grapeshot at advancing troops. It was cast in 1449 and is of great historical interest in terms of both its technology and use. Oliver Cromwell knew its power and appropriately called it "the great iron murderer."

The crown room houses the Royal Scottish regalia that were successfully hidden from Cromwell in 1651. He wanted to capture them and melt them down, as he had the English crown jewels, because he believed that they represented all that was wrong with the pomp and ceremony of monarchy. Consequently, they are the only complete set of pre-Restoration crown jewels in Britain and were only returned to Edinburgh and public view after the Restoration. Following the Union of Parliaments in 1707, they were deposited in a chest and literally forgotten. After a long search, Sir Walter Scott rediscovered them in 1818. The crown, which is made of Scottish gold decorated with 94 pearls and 10 diamonds, was last used in a coronation in 1651, when Charles II was crowned at Scone. The ceremonial sword was a gift from Pope Julius II to James IV in 1507.

Here too is the Stone of Scone, or Destiny, that was brought to Scotland by Irish missionaries in the 7th century. Kenneth McAlpine gave it to the Abbey of Scone, near Perth, in 838, where it was used in the coronation of Scottish kings. According to tradition, it was the stone used as a pillow by Jacob in the biblical story of Jacob's ladder (Genesis 28:10–17), and testified to the fact that the Scots kings were a chosen people with a direct link to Moses and ancient Israel. Edward I stole it in 1296 and installed it in Westminster Abbey, where it was used in the coronation of English kings and queens until it was returned to Scotland in 1996. Although most people think that the stone is genuine, some believe that Edward I was tricked and that the real stone lies buried in a secret chamber in the Abbey of Scone.

In the royal apartments one can see the small room where the ill-fated, Roman Catholic Mary Queen of Scots gave birth to James VI of Scotland, James I of England. According to legend, Mary had such a long and difficult labor that one of her attendants, the countess of Atholl, performed an act of sympathetic magic, or witchcraft, to transfer her pain to another of her attendants. Whatever the truth of this strange tale, it certainly played a role in encouraging Protestant dislike of their loose-living and religiously suspect queen. James IV originally built the great hall for ceremonial occasions. It was restored in 1892 to its original Renaissance splendor and now houses a fascinating display of armor. Centuries earlier Cromwell had used it as a barracks and hospital for his troops.

EDINBURGH NEW TOWN. The old town of Edinburgh clusters around the castle. In 1767 the Town Council, led by Lord Provost George Drummond, decided to extend the city by building an entirely new town. To accomplish this task, an architectural competition was organized that was won by the 23-year-old James Craig. He laid out a series of streets named after British royalty, such as George Street, Queen Street, etc. The overall effect was to create a classic example of Enlightenment architecture based on a grid pattern, symmetrical design following strict rules of proportion, and neoclassical features. Today the entire area is a conservation area. Princess Street is the best-known part of the New Town, although it was barely featured in the original plans. At the end of Princess Street are the famous SUNKEN GARDENS, which were once Loch Nor. Thomas De Quincey (1785–1859), the author of *Confessions of an Opium Eater* (1821) and an important figure in British Romanticism, is buried in St. Cuthebert's Church graveyard at the west end of the gardens.

THE GEORGIAN HOUSE, No. 7, Charlotte Square, stands in one of the finest examples of New Town architectural planning and is now a museum devoted to recapturing the spirit of the age. Actually, it was built as the home of John Lamont (1773–1829) and is furnished in the Regency style of the period. The upper floors are now the official residence of the moderator of the Church of Scotland.

SCOTTISH PARLIAMENT VISITOR'S CENTER, Committee Chambers on King George IV Bridge, is a fine but temporary exhibition, awaiting the reopening of the new Scottish Parliament in a new Holyrood building. It has some excellent displays of Scottish history, ancient documents, and information about unique aspects of Scottish government.

LADY STAIR'S HOUSE, THE NATIONAL WRITER'S MUSEUM, off Brodie's Close, was built in 1622. Here lived Lady Stair (d. 1731), a renowned beauty whose life inspired Sir Walter Scott's *Waverly* novels. The museum is dedicated to the works of Scott, Robert Louis Stevenson, and Robert Burns.

NATIONAL PORTRAIT GALLERY, Queen Street, contains a fascinating collection of portraits by various artists of such important Scottish personalities as the Covenanter general David Leslie (1602–82), who first served under Gustavus Adolphus (1594–1632), the gifted and humane Protestant leader in the Thirty Years' War. Curiously, although he initially supported the Covenanters, he opposed Cromwell and fought for the Royalists during the British Civil War. After the Restoration, he became Lord Newark. His opponent, the eighth earl of Argyll, may also be seen here, along with the rationalist philosopher David Hume; the Romantic writer Sir Walter Scott; and England's first socialist leader and founder of the Labor Party, Kier Hardie (1856–1915), who was an evangelical Christian.

NATIONAL GALLERY OF SCOTLAND, Princess St., contains the best collection of paintings outside of London, including 38 watercolors by Joseph Turner (1775–1851), who illustrated various books on Scottish history. Older works include the

Trinity Altarpiece of 1462, Lucas Cranach the Elder's (1472–1553) *Venus and Cupid*, and Raphael's (1483–1520) *The Holy Family by a Palm Tree*. In the 17th-century gallery the Flemish and Dutch collection contains a Rembrandt (1606–69) self-portrait, Anthony van Dyck's (1599–1641) *St. Sabastian,* and Paul Rubens's (1577–1640) *Feat of Herod.* An unexpected aspect of the museum is its excellent 19th-century British and North American collection, which contains Frederic Church's (1826–1900) *Niagara Falls.* Less well known are the many fine Scottish painters located in the lower floor gallery.

NATIONAL GALLERY OF MODERN ART, Belford Rd., contains many outstanding examples of works by most modern European artists, including Picasso (1881–1973), Klee (1879–1940), Miro (1893–1983), etc. Anyone wanting to understand our times ought to visit this gallery armed with a copy of Hans Rookmaaker's *Modern Art and the Death of a Culture* (1970).

THE MUSEUM OF SCOTTISH ANTIQUITIES, Chambers St., contains an excellent overview of Scottish history from prehistoric times. Of particular interest are the Roman and post-Roman periods, which contain many items relating to the early evangelization of Scotland and the Celtic Church.

NATIONAL LIBRARY OF SCOTLAND contains a wonderful collection of books, including many ancient illuminated manuscripts that are in the rich medieval Christian tradition.

CALTON GRAVEYARD, off Waterloo Place, contains the Lincoln Memorial dedicated to Scottish volunteers who died in the American Civil War. It was erected in 1893. The grave of the famous skeptical philosopher and conservative essayist and historian David Hume (1711–76) lies nearby.

ROSSLYN CHAPEL. Twelve miles east of Edinburgh lies the small town of Rosslyn with its superb Late Gothic chapel that is rich in legend and local myths. Originally planned as a huge collegiate church, building came to an abrupt halt after the death of the benefactor in 1484 after only the Lady Chapel, choir, and sections of the transepts had been completed. This seemingly unfortunate development probably preserved the chapel from destruction during the Reformation. Inside, the recently restored interior testifies to the artistic energy of the late Middle Ages and the skill of masons and stone carvers in creating a small masterpiece. Note the wonderful, yet grim, apprentice's column. According to legend, this superbly carved pillar was completed by an apprentice whose skill so outraged his master that in a fit of rage the craftsman slew his young disciple. Overhead, in the apex of the ceiling, is a carving of a head with a slash across the forehead said to represent the unfortunate apprentice. Opposite is another head of his jealous master.

ELY

Queen Ethelreda founded a Benedictine monastery here in 673 on a small island in the middle of a swampy area known as "the Fens." The name is derived from the number of eels found in the surrounding swamps. Danes sacked the abbey in 870, but it gradually regained its influence in the following centuries as one of the great Saxon Fen churches. Hereward the Wake (d. 1071), the last English lord to resist the Norman invasion, made this island his headquarters until it was stormed in 1071 by the Normans. They built a causeway across the Fens using bales of wool to form a floating foundation for a pontoon-type bridge. After the defeat of his troops, Hereward sought sanctuary in the abbey, but the monks eventually gave him up to avoid its desecration. He was executed outside the church door. To commemorate their defeat of the English, the Normans erected the cathedral that was dedicated in 1189 and could be seen for miles around, thus proclaiming Norman ascendancy. During the 16th century, the Scottish Benedictine monk Alexander Barkley (1474–1552) translated the *Life of St. George* into English from Latin. He also wrote *Ship of Fools of the World* (1509) and *Eclogues* (1515), which inspired the work of Edmund Spenser (1552–99). Today Ely is a quiet country town that has changed little over the years. During the 18th century it took on the Georgian look that predominates today.

PLACES TO VISIT

THE CATHEDRAL is located at the center of the town at its highest point. It is a wonder of medieval architecture due to its unique central octagon with its wooden lantern tower and dome, erected in 1322 after the original tower collapsed, destroying a large part of the church. It was rebuilt in a highly imaginative manner by Alan de Walsingham (d. 1364), who was the sacrist of the cathedral and designer of the octagon. His grave lies nearby in the nave. The beautiful painted ceiling is actually the work of a 19th-century restoration directed by Sir Gilbert Scott. The transept walls date from the late 11th century and are the oldest surviving part of the church. The north transept leads into St. Edmund's Chapel and contains a 12th-century mural of the saint's death as a martyr. There is also a fine museum of stained glass.

Alan de Walsingham built the Lady Chapel between 1321 and 1353. The chapel carvings give a glimpse of their original glory despite the fact that they were vandalized by troops during the British Civil War in 1647. Outside the cathedral proper are the ruins of the chapel of St. Ethelreda, the founder of the abbey. Until the Reformation, the chapel attracted pilgrims to view her relics.

OLIVER CROMWELL'S HOUSE, St. Mary's Street, was once the vicarage of St. Mary's Church. It is a half-timbered building containing a small museum relating to the life of the Lord Protector, who was a local landowner and collector of tithes.

FOUNTAINS ABBEY

F

Fountains Abbey was founded in 1132 by a group of 13 reforming Benedictine monks. They left York, where they belonged to the Abbey of St. Mary, to find peace in the Yorkshire dales. The monks joined the Cistercian movement three years after founding their new abbey. Over the next hundred years, Fountains Abbey became the largest and wealthiest Cistercian foundation in Britain. The abbey church was built between 1135 and 1137 and remodeled on a grander scale between 1220 and 1247. A final stage of development, which included the construction of the tower, took place shortly before the Reformation, between 1498 and 1526. The abbey was bought by Sir Richard Gresham after the Dissolution of the Monasteries in 1539 and used as a quarry for stone to build his home, Fountains Hall. In 1768 the abbey and its grounds were acquired by William Aislabie. In 1983 it became a National Trust property comprising of 680 acres, and in 1986 it was declared a World Heritage Site.

PLACES TO VISIT

Visitors arrive at the tourist information and car park, where a small admission charge is made for entry into the abbey grounds. A small path leads across a field from the information center and then downhill through a wooded glen into the abbey valley proper, where a series of magnificent ruins suddenly come into view. The unexpected vista of the abbey ruins is quite spectacular. Each area of monastery ruins is clearly identified by numerous signs telling the visitor what they are looking at.

THE MAIN ABBEY building presents the ghostly outline of a large church with its empty nave and high tower built by the reforming abbot, Marmaduke Huby (15th century), around 1500. Entering the nave, one realizes the simple majesty of the Cistercian ideal that even in ruins evokes a sense of wonder at the great goodness of God.

THE LAY BROTHERS DORMITORY is one of the best-preserved areas of the original abbey. Lay brothers, who were not ordained priests, were an innovation of the Cistercian order. They performed essential tasks which were forbidden to monks, such as managing the abbey's flocks and herds. This building is a splendid example of fan vaulting over 300 feet long. During the spring, this dormitory also served to store the bales of wool harvested from sheering the abbey's large herd of sheep. The wool provided the abbey with the main source of its vast wealth.

GUEST HOUSES. Today not much can be seen of the extensive guest house complex. What remains is clearly marked and reminds visitors of the seriousness with which the monks took hospitality as a Christian duty.

THE WARMING ROOM was the only heated room in a Cistercian monastery. Here monks, the abbot, and the occasional visitor could huddle together for warmth between November 1st and Easter each year; the rest of the time

they simply froze in accordance with their ascetic ideal.

THE CHAPTER HOUSE remains impressive despite its ruined state. Here the abbot held court and directed the affairs of the monastery.

THE CLOISTERS form a central area where monks once walked in prayer, reading or reciting Bible verses.

FOUNTAINS HALL is a 17th-century stately home built with stone from the abbey ruins. It lies beyond the abbey ruins and is a vivid reminder that in many ways the English Reformation degenerated into a land grab that allowed local gentry to grow rich at the expense of the Church.

STUDLEY ROYAL GARDENS also lie beyond the abbey proper and beyond Fountains Hall, making a pleasant walk through some exquisite water gardens designed in 1720 by John Aislabie, the local member of Parliament. From the gardens, visitors have many excellent views of the abbey. The decorative Greek-style temples scattered throughout the gardens are a reminder of the 18th-century fascination with things Greek and the allurement of ancient paganism during the early Enlightenment.

GLASGOW

According to legend, St. Ninian (360–432) established a small church on the site of Glasgow Cathedral in the 5th century. A hundred years later, St. Kentigern, also known as St. Mungo (518–603), rebuilt the church and founded the community that developed into the city of Glasgow.

The city's motto is "Let Glasgow flourish by the preaching of the Word," while its coat of arms represents various miracles attributed to the saint. The Scottish king William the Lion (1143–1214), the grandson of King David I (1080–1153), granted the city a royal charter in 1175. In 1300, William Wallace (1274–1305) defeated an English army on what is now the Upper High Street area of Bell o' Brea.

Glasgow University, the second oldest university in Scotland, was founded in 1451 and quickly established itself as a major center of European learning. In 1568, the army of Mary Queen of Scots was routed at Langside close to today's Queen's Park. During the Scottish Reformation, Archbishop of Glasgow James Beaton (1470–1539) fled to Paris, taking with him the cathedral archives and all of its portable treasures.

The Roman Catholic priest John Ogilvie (1569–1615) was captured, tried for treason, and hung. He is revered as a martyr by the Roman Catholic Church and was canonized in 1976. Cromwell's army occupied the city from 1650–51 during the British Civil War.

The city grew rapidly during the 18th century and became a major industrial center. It flourished through trade with North America, particularly in tobacco. The American Revolution was a disaster for Glasgow, bringing an end to its lucrative North American trade. Most merchants quickly developed new trade ties with the West Indies, and Glasgow became Britain's main port for the importation of sugar. In the 19th century, shipbuilding, cotton, and locomotive industries developed as the city rapidly grew, and Glasgow became one

G

JOHN OGILVIE (1580–1615) was the eldest son in a Scottish Calvinist family who converted to Catholicism and entered the Jesuit Order in Louvain at the age of 17. He was ordained in 1613, after which he returned to Scotland to minister to Catholic families in the Glasgow area. After a nine-month mission, he was betrayed and arrested by the government. There followed a long period of imprisonment involving dreadful torture in an attempt to force him to betray his Catholic parishioners. But Ogilvie remained silent, preferring the pain to betrayal. His legs were broken and crushed. He was also kept awake through being prodded with hot irons. In the end even his captors admitted his courage and piety. Nevertheless, he was condemned as a traitor and hanged. As an "act of mercy," he was spared being hung, drawn, and quartered out of respect for his endurance under severe torture. In the 17th century, he was declared "venerable," and he was canonized in 1976.

of the richest cities in Europe. From 1815 to 1823, the great Scottish Evangelical leader Thomas Chalmers (1780–1847) was a minister in Glasgow, first at the Tron Church and then at the new parish of St. John's. During this time he developed a system of parish visitation and relief for the poor.

After World War I, a period of severe economic decline began as old industries became obsolete. Rearmament revived the town's fortunes in the 1930s for a brief period. During World War II, Glasgow was heavily bombed. After the war, Glasgow's industrial decline continued. In the late 1980s and 1990s, the city began a renaissance, with new industry and a vast redevelopment program that saw the renovation of many of the city's ancient and quite beautiful buildings. Consequently, Glasgow was declared the city of European Culture in 1990 and won the United Kingdom award for art and architecture in 1999.

PLACES TO VISIT

GLASGOW CATHEDRAL OF ST. MUNGO was founded by David I (1080–1153) and Bishop Achaius in 1136 on the site of an earlier church said to date back to Saints Ninian (360–432) and Kentigern (518–630) centuries earlier. After a mere 50 years, the new church was destroyed by fire. Rebuilding under the direction of Bishop Jocelin began in 1197. Bishop de Bondington completed the crypt and choir and added the tower

between 1233 and 1258. Bishop Lauder added a spire and the chapter house between 1408 and 1425. The final stage of construction was begun by Bishop Cameron in 1425 and completed by Archbishop Blacader between 1483 and 1508.

An unusual feature of the cathedral is that it is built on a sloping hill that effectively creates two distinct levels. Thus the crypt forms a lower church, rather than some dark cellar, as crypts are usually seen today. Consequently, people speak about the "upper" and "lower" church.

The long, well proportioned, lofty nave is a fine example of Late Gothic architecture. Two narrow aisles flank the nave. The whole area is lit by beautiful stained-glass windows, most of which were installed during the 20th century. The choir is separated from the nave by the large, curtained, stone pulpit. From here the minister lambasted Oliver Cromwell as a sectarian during a two-hour sermon in 1650 while the pious Cromwell meekly received the rebuke. Legend has it that Cromwell avenged himself by inviting the minister for dinner and then having prayers said for over three hours before they finally ate.

The choir, which is three feet higher than the nave, is a good example of early English architecture. The rood screen before the choir has some fine carvings depicting the seven deadly sins. At the south end are four lancet windows, an unusual feature since lancet windows are usually grouped in threes or fives. In the southeast chapel Archbishop Law is buried.

The sacristy is a square room on the northeast side of the cathedral built by Bishop Cameron (d. 1446). Glasgow University was founded here in 1451.

The south transept (the north transept was never built), located halfway down, has a stairway descending to the lower church's Blacader Aisle, a vaulted crypt built by Archbishop Blacader (d. 1508) on the site of an ancient cemetery. According to legend, the cemetery was consecrated by St. Ninian in the 5th century when he buried the body of a pious hermit, Fergus. Its name means "dear green place." The crypt has a highly decorated ceiling with fine fan vaulting.

The lower church is built around the tomb of St. Kentigern/Mungo. Actually his remains were removed during the Middle Ages to an unknown location. This is the oldest part of the church and contains stones and carvings from Bishop Jocelin's original building. Note the sculpture of Bishop Wischart, who in 1306 absolved Robert the Bruce of the murder of John Comyn and two months later crowned him king of the Scots. Note also the modern *St. Kentigern Tapestry* (1979), which illustrates the life of the saint.

The chapter house, in the northeast corner of the lower church, was built by Bishop de Bondington in the 13th century and added to by later bishops. It is important because it contains the grave of nine Covenanters who were killed in 1645 for the profession of Presbyterian beliefs.

THE NECROPOLIS is a 19th-century neo-Romantic cemetery full of imitation Greek columns and temples. The rich and famous are buried here. There is an excellent view of the city from here and a fine monument to the Protestant Reformers capped by a statue of John Knox (1514–72).

ST. MUNGO MUSEUM OF RELIGIOUS LIFE AND ART, Cathedral Square. This fascinating museum has two sections. The main collection focuses on world religions, while a smaller collection deals with religion in Glasgow. Buddhist, Christian, Hindu, Islamic, Jewish, and Sikh art objects provide the visitor with fascinating insights into the ethos of all the major religions of the world. Among its many treasures is Salvador Dali's *Christ Upon the Cross,* which is a stunning surrealist painting that offers a heretical, perhaps Gnostic, view of Jesus suspended in front of a cross devoid of the cruel nails or any other visible restraints to keep him there.

PROVAND'S LORDSHIP, Cathedral Square opposite St. Mungo Museum, is one of the oldest houses in the city. It was built in 1471 and now serves as a museum. During its long history, this house was used as the bishop's residence and later as a regular inn. The exhibits depict the life of both the upper and lower classes and contain many original

G

pieces of period furniture. According to tradition, Mary Queen of Scots slept here while in Glasgow. Behind the house is the St. Nicholas Garden, laid out along the lines of a medieval herb garden.

ST. ANDREWS CHURCH, Turnbull St., is a good example of 18th-century British neoclassical architecture.

G

THE PEOPLE'S PALACE, Glasgow Green. Opened in 1898, the People's Palace is perhaps the world's oldest cultural history museum to depict the life of ordinary people from the founding of the city to the present. Among its many exhibits are some very interesting items relating to popular religion and the temperance movement.

GLASGOW ART GALLERY AND MUSEUM, Argyle St., Kelvingrove, contains one of the best collections of art in Britain due to hefty donations from wealthy industrialists. Among its many treasures are Sandro Botticelli's (1444–1510) *Annunciation*, Giorgio Giorgione's (1478–1510) *The Woman Taken in Adultery*, and Rembrandt van Rijn's (1606–69) famous *Man in Armor*. The east wing contains an excellent collection of works by Scottish artists, including Alexander Nasmyth's (1758–1840) portrait of *Robert Burns*.

TRANSPORT MUSEUM, 1 Bunhouse Rd., is a real mecca for train lovers and anyone interested in the way people traveled in the past. This museum helps put our world in perspective by reminding us that until relatively recently,

travel was arduous and often very dangerous.

HUNTERIAN MUSEUM, 82 Hillhead St., is the oldest museum in Scotland and is named after William Hunter (1718–83), who bequeathed his collection of paintings to the University of Glasgow. It contains many historical items, an excellent art collection containing many Scottish works, and paintings by the American artist James McNeill Whistler (1834–1903).

POLLOK HOUSE, 2060 Pollokshaws Rd., three miles south of Glasgow, is an 18th-century stately home built by the Maxwell family in 1750. It is in neoclassical style and contains Britain's best collection of Spanish paintings. Other works include William Blake's (1757–1827) *Sir Geoffrey Chaucer and the Nine and Twenty Pilgrims*.

THE BURRELL COLLECTION, Pollok Park, three miles south of Glasgow, is a purpose-built art gallery given to the city by the industrialist Sir William Burrell (1861–1958). The present building was opened in 1983. The exhibits are divided into several distinct areas, beginning with the ancient art collection that concentrates on Egyptian art. The Oriental collection is the largest in the gallery and contains many excellent examples of ceramic work as well as Japanese prints and Persian rugs. The medieval and post-medieval European collection was Sir William's favorite and contains many exquisite examples of Christian art, including over 150 tapestries. There are also over 600 examples of stained-glass windows from both religious and secular sources. Finally, there are three period galleries: Gothic, Elizabethan, and Baroque. Among the gallery's treasures is a self-portrait of the young Rembrandt and Auguste Rodin's (1840–1919) famous sculpture, *The Thinker*.

INTERNATIONAL CHRISTIAN COLLEGE, formally the Glasgow Bible College, 110 St. James Rd., is one of the oldest Bible colleges in Britain, with close links to the Moody Bible Institute in Chicago. Actually, the Bible Training Institute, or BTI, as it was affectionately called, was founded in the wake of D. L. Moody's (1837–99) Scottish campaign in 1882. From the beginning this college was unusual in its evangelical and interdenominational, or ecumenical, stance. Today it has an exchange program with Moody Bible Institute and offers accredited degrees.

GLASTONBURY

Glastonbury is a small country town six miles from the ancient cathedral city of Wells. Today the town is both an important historic Christian site and the center of British occultism. Its main claim to fame is its ruined abbey. The town is situated at the foot of a series of low hills, the chief of which is known as the Tor. Throughout the Middle Ages, Glastonbury was one of the major pilgrimage sites in Britain. It claimed a direct link to Jesus through Joseph of Arimathea and boasted that King Arthur was buried in its church.

During the Reformation its great abbey was dissolved and its relics dispersed and destroyed, resulting in a loss of interest in the area. However, during this century there has been a revival of interest in Glastonbury among religious people. Around 1900 a group of Roman Catholic monks opened a novitiate in the town and expressed their wish to buy the abbey ruins with the intention of rebuilding it. When a member of the Church of England outbid them for the ruins in 1907, they moved out of the area. The Sisters of Charity opened a convent in 1904, and since 1920 there has been an annual Roman Catholic pilgrimage. Since 1924 the Anglicans have held their own pilgrimage, and they also run a retreat house attached to the abbey grounds.

Other less orthodox groups have also been attracted to the area. These include the British Israelites, who opened a center for a short time during the 1920s and returned in 1970 to open their national conference center. Dion Fortune (1891–1946), an occult writer,

> **BRITISH ISRAELISM** is a form of fundamentalism originating in the 18th century. It claimed that the English people were the descendants of the ten "Lost Tribes" of Israel and therefore heirs to all the biblical promises to the Jewish people. Today the most common form of this belief is to be found in its Americanized version preached by Herbert W. Armstrong and his original Worldwide Church of God. British Israelite activities in Glastonbury occupy a house called Mount Avalon.

G

founded the Society of the Inner Light and opened a guesthouse that also served as a cultic center during the 1920s. She also built a small pagan temple that had a mosaic of the signs of the zodiac on its floor. Another woman, Christine Jagar, who had been a spiritualist medium, claimed to receive messages from a cosmic being, the Lord Mikall, during the late 1930s. She published six small books, the chief of which is entitled *The Winds of Truth,* and founded a small society known as the Group of Solar Teaching. This group still exists, and although the original medium has died, it continues to propagate her "revelations." Other groups like the "Druids" and the "Essenes" have also been active in Glastonbury, and their members still occasionally return to hold meetings and perform sacred rites.

Glastonbury is rich in literary associations. C. S. Lewis (1898–1963) used Glastonbury as the model for the small university town depicted in his book *That Hideous Strength* (1946). Similarly, J. R. R. Tolkien (1892–1973) used Glastonbury as the setting for the Shire in *The Hobbit* (1937).

PLACES TO VISIT

GLASTONBURY ABBEY. When the abbey was first founded is unknown. Its history goes back long before the Saxon occupation of Britain and is shrouded in legends. The original Celtic foundation became a Benedictine one around A.D. 943. St. Dunstan (909–88) reorganized an existing institution and introduced the Rule of St. Benedict (480–554). After the Norman invasion, successive abbots enlarged the abbey. At least three Saxon kings—Edmund I (922–46), Edgar (944–75), and Edmund Ironside (981–1016)—were buried in the abbey.

In 1184 the great church was destroyed in a fire, as were many other buildings. But they were quickly rebuilt. During the rebuilding process, a grave was discovered containing the remains of a man and woman, whom the monks claimed were King Arthur and Queen Guinevere (4th or 5th century). Their remains were reinterred before the high altar with great pomp at a royal ceremony and high Mass attended by King Edward I (1239–1307) in 1276.

During the 15th century, Abbot Bere excavated a crypt beneath the Lady

Chapel. The last abbot, Richard Whiting, was hanged by Henry VIII's church commissioners at the top of the Tor on November 15, 1539, and is regarded as a martyr by the Roman Catholic Church. After its subsequent dissolution, the abbey fell into ruin.

Early in 1907, the ruins were auctioned by their owners and bought by the bishop of Bath and Wells for the Church of England. The Bristol architect F. Bligh Bond (1864–1945) was employed to restore the ruins and to carry out excavation work. He did this from 1908 to 1921, when the Bishop of Wells fired him. It is popularly believed that Bond was dismissed as director of the excavations at Glastonbury Abbey because of his interest in the occult. Bond claimed to receive "revelations" from long dead monks through spiritualist mediums and his own automatic writing. Bond originally claimed that he was experimenting in psychology and the messages were the result of a Jungian "racial unconscious." He later seems to have come to believe that they came from departed "spirits." His later writings, in addition to the Glastonbury Festival, made Glastonbury into a center of English occultism.

The nave is a magnificent and evocative ruin, which gives some idea of the size of the original church, once the richest Benedictine abbey in England.

The abbot's kitchen is one of the best-preserved examples of a medieval monastery kitchen in England and the only building to have survived extensive destruction. Inside is a small museum related to the history of the abbey.

THE GLASTONBURY THORN. Near the main entrance to the abbey grounds is a gnarled thorn tree that has the

THE GLASTONBURY FESTIVAL MOVEMENT. During the 1920s an artistic center was organized by a group known as the Glastonbury Festival movement. Its leader was a minor composer, Rutland Boughton (1878–1960), who wrote an Arthurian opera on the model of Wagner's Ring cycle. The art festival gained support from Sir Edward Elgar (1857–1934), George Bernard Shaw (1856–1950), C. K. Chesterton (1874–1936), Charles Williams (1886–1945), and C. S. Lewis (1898–1963). Although supported by some Christians, the Festival marked the beginning of modern occultism in Glastonbury. In 1971, the Festival was revived as the Glastonbury Fair and has since developed into an annual music festival and cultural event. The original "Fayre" was organized in nearby Pilton by Andrew Kerr as a "spiritual" event that he described as a "fertility rite." Following the original event, the fair was taken over by the local farmer on whose land the fair was held. He turned it into an annual festival and commercial success.

unusual habit of flowering around December 25. This tree was grown from a cutting taken from the original tree that was located on Wearyall Hill to the west of the town and chopped down during the Reformation because it was believed to have miraculous qualities. According to tradition, the original tree took root when Joseph of Arimathea, who legend says came to Glastonbury after fleeing Jerusalem following the death of Christ, stuck his staff in the ground while he prayed. When Joseph completed his prayer, he discovered that the staff was blossoming and interpreted the event as a sign from God that this is where he must build a church. Legend also says that among Joseph's possessions was the chalice used at the Last Supper, the legendary Holy Grail.

THE SOMERSET RURAL LIFE MUSEUM, Bere Lane, which displays traditional crafts, is housed in the medieval abbey barn and is well worth a visit.

THE CHALICE WELL, Chalice Lane, is a spring situated at the foot of the Tor that has a daily outflow of 25,000 gallons of water. The well has two unusually shaped chambers built of large ancient stones. These chambers probably date from the 12th century, being constructed with stones salvaged from the abbey fire of 1184. The purpose of the well's inner chamber is unclear, but it may have been a sedimentation tank. There is, however, some evidence to suggest that the well and its chambers may be much older than the date assigned

and that it was once approached through a grove of yew trees. This evidence has given rise to speculation about the possible Druid origin of the well.

The well appears to have been originally called Chickwell, but sometime in the 12th century it became known as Chalice Well probably due to the growing popularity of the Arthurian legends and their association with Glastonbury through stories about Joseph of Arimathea. During the 16th and 18th centuries, claims were made about the "healing properties" of the well's water, and it enjoyed brief spells of popularity as a center for people seeking healing.

In 1959 the well and an adjacent house, known as Little St. Michael's, were bought by the Chalice Well Trust, an occult group of Theosophical origin formed by Major W. Tudor-Pole (1891–1946) to prevent the water from the well being used for industrial purposes. Originally, the Trust intended to open a guesthouse and religious center in Little St. Michael's, but these plans were never fully developed. After beginning the project, Major Tudor-Pole believed that he received a vision of the "Upper Room" used by Christ and his disciples for the Last Supper. As a result of this vision, the attic of Little St. Michael's was made into a shrine intended to be a duplication of Tudor-Pole's vision. This reconstruction of the "Upper Room" differs from the one used by Jesus for the Last Supper. It is set not for supper but for breakfast when Christ returns. During the 1980s, the Chalice Well Trust was incorporated into, some would say taken over by, the Scottish occult Findhorn Community, which now runs the well, its house, and its gardens.

From a Christian viewpoint the well remains important because it is a good example of the way medieval monks sought to locate their foundations near reliable water supplies and provides an insight into medieval construction. It is also important because of its links to the Arthurian legends and the quest for the Holy Grail that inspired so many Christians during the Middle Ages. The fact that a New Age community now owns it emphasizes the fact that Christians are often lax in preserving their rich historical heritage.

THE TOR is a conical-shaped hill, owned by the National Trust, that dominates the area. From its summit it is possible to see for miles in all directions. Because of its steep "unnatural" sides, a

THE GLASTONBURY LEGENDS. A number of medieval legends connected with Glastonbury and the surrounding area give the town its appeal as both a Christian and occult center. In the Middle Ages, these legends were used to attract pilgrims; today they attract tourists. There are two basic themes for the Glastonbury legends. The first concerns Joseph of Arimathea who, it is claimed, first brought Christianity to Britain and in doing so brought the Holy Grail to Glastonbury, where he settled. The second theme concerns King Arthur and the knights of the Round Table in their search for the Holy Grail.

To these basic themes many elaborations have been added and are constantly being created by occultists in the name of the New Age. These include stories about the Druids, Christ coming to Britain, and flying saucers. Perhaps the most amazing addition to the Glastonbury legends is the claim of Miss K. E. Maltwood (1865–1971) to have discovered the true meaning of the Grail stories. She interpreted the stories in terms of Jungian archetypes that she then identified with the signs of the zodiac. Having done this, she then claimed to have discovered these signs constructed in gigantic earthworks in and around Glastonbury. All this she believed she could prove with the aid of a 1" ordnance survey map and aerial photographs taken from a height of 30,000 feet. Among occultists the existence of this "Somerset zodiac" is taken as proved. More recently, the stories of the zodiac have been linked with flying saucer stories. These, together with the more historical legends, provide the drawing power for occult interest in Glastonbury.

belief has existed that the Tor is man-made. It is in fact an unusual but natural hill. The archaeologist Dr. C. A. R. Radford believes that the Tor once formed a part of a vast pre-Roman pagan cultic center. This idea has been developed by G. N. Russell, who has suggested that the terracing on the sides of the hill can best be explained as the remains of a three-dimensional maze once used in cultic initiation rites. These theories have been in circulation among occultists for many years and are seized upon by local occultists. In actual fact, the shape of the Tor is probably best explained by the practices of local farmers, who used the hill to graze sheep.

On the top of the Tor is the ruined tower of the ancient church of St. Michael. This church is attributed in local legend to the work of St. Patrick (385–461) in the 5th century. All that is certain about its history is that a church existed on the site in the 12th century. During the Reformation this church was destroyed, the tower alone left standing. This tower was restored to its present condition in 1804. The tower is square, with sides about twelve feet long and a height of about forty feet.

GLOUCESTER

Although there was a prehistoric settlement in the area, the modern town of Gloucester originated as a Roman river port and administrative center situated at the last ford on the Severn River and dominating the Welsh border area. The town, Glevum, was honored with the status *colonia;* there were only four in Britain, meaning that it was a retirement center for Roman soldiers who also served as an active reserve force throughout the Roman world. After the withdrawal of the Roman legions, Gloucester seems to have fared better than most Roman towns.

The Saxons captured Gloucester after the Battle of Dyrham in 577. In 900, Æthelfaed—the daughter of Alfred the Great and wife of Aethelred, earl of Mercia—founded a monastery here and shrine that held the relics of St. Oswald.

At the time of the Norman invasion, Gloucester was a flourishing town. William the Conqueror (1027–87), whose armies plundered England after the Norman invasion of 1066, liked the city, which became one of his favorite residences. A royal charter was issued in 1155, and King Henry III (1207–72) was crowned in the cathedral in 1216.

During the British Civil War, the city fathers sided with the Puritan cause. Gloucester became a Parliamentary stronghold and successfully withstood a long siege in 1643, when 35,000 Royalist troops were held at bay by a mere 1,500 Parliamentarians supported by the local townspeople. The city was relieved on September 5, marking a turning point in the Civil War that eventually led to the defeat of the king. Following the restoration of the monarchy in 1660, the citizens were punished for their republican sentiments by a vindictive king, who robbed the city of extensive land holdings in an act of vandalism rivaling anything Cromwell is accused of. He ordered the destruction of the city's ancient walls, which went back to Roman times.

The famous 18th-century evangelist George Whitefield (1714–70), who with John Wesley (1703–91) helped initiate the great 18th-century revival in Britain as well as the Great Awakening in America, was born in Gloucester. Another illustrious native was Sir Charles Wheatstone (1802–75), the inventor of the electric telegraph. The composer and poet Ivor Gurney (1890–1937) was also born here.

PLACES TO VISIT

GLOUCESTER CATHEDRAL, College Green, was built by Abbot Serlo, who was appointed by William I (1027–87) to bring the Saxon priests into conformity with Norman ways. Construction of the new Norman Abbey church, which was built on the site of an older Benedictine monastery, began in 1089 and was completed in 1100.

Edward II (1284–1327) was buried in Gloucester Cathedral after his murder because the abbots at both Bristol and Malmesbury Abbeys refused to accept his body, for they believed he was a practicing homosexual. Edward's supporters capitalized on his murder by circulating tales about his piety. His tomb soon became the center of a pilgrimage cult which brought pilgrims and great wealth to the cathedral shrine. Consequently, the abbey was renovated at great expense in the new Perpendicular, or Gothic, style.

The nave retains much of its original Norman character, although two new Gothic bays were added between 1421 and 1437. The transepts are a remarkable example of Norman architecture transformed into graceful Gothic by skillful masons. The cloisters are particularly well preserved, with wonderful fan vaulting that captures an ethos of prayer and study. The east window is the largest stained-glass window in England and was donated by a local lord in 1352.

The central tower was built in 1440. The enchanting Lady Chapel was built between 1457 and 1498 and was constructed to avoid blocking the light to the east window. Its unusual elongated shape is a superb example of Late Gothic. The east window has a Jesse tree depicting the genealogy of Jesus.

Among the many tombs in the church is that of Edward II in the north arcade of the presbytery. Notice the monument to Osric of Mercia, who is said to have founded the first abbey in 681. The tomb of William I's eldest son, Robert Curthose (d. 1134), is in the south choir.

ST. MARY-DE-CRYPT, Southgate St., is a small 12th-century church. It contains the tomb of Robert Raikes (1735–1811), the proprietor of the *Gloucester Journal* and a pioneer of the Sunday school movement and social reform. Together with the Rev. Robert Stock, he founded his first Sunday school in 1780 to teach literacy and spread the gospel among the poor. The movement caught on and quickly spread throughout the world. A statue of Raikes can be seen in the local park.

It was in St. Mary's too that George Whitefield (1714–70) was baptized and later preached his first sermon after his ordination in 1736. He entitled his sermon "The Necessity and Benefit of Religious Society." Afterwards the bishop received a complaint that White-field had driven 15 people mad by his preaching about God's judgment.

BELL INN, Westgate St., is the birthplace of George Whitefield. Today the inn is a restaurant.

THE BEATRIX POTTER MUSEUM, College Court, near the cathedral, contains an interesting collection illustrating the life and times of this ever-popular writer of children's fiction.

CITY MUSEUM AND ART GALLERY, Brunswick Rd., contains a fascinating collection that illustrates the history of Gloucester from Roman times to the present. It includes a rare bronze Roman mirror and a set of late Roman sculptures. Other museums in the town are the NATIONAL WATERWAYS MUSEUM, on Commercial Rd., the nearby GLOUCES-TERSHIRE REGIMENTAL MUSEUM, and the ADVERTISING MUSEUM.

IONA

Founded in 563 by St. Columba (521–97), Iona became the main base for the evangelization of southern Scotland and northern England and Ireland in the 6th century and a leading center for Christian scholarship throughout Europe. The name of the island is believed to be the result of a misreading of the Latin for yew tree that may have been confused with the name Jonah. Good pasture and shallow coastal seas teeming with fish made the island an ideal location for a monastic community. The original buildings are thought to have been made of wood, although in the 8th century, stone was imported for the manufacture of large crosses and, presumably, construction purposes. At the height of the early community's success, the island was dotted with over

1000 skillfully decorated stone crosses, of which only a few survive today. Scholars also suggest that such great art treasures as the *Book of Kells* were produced by the monks of Iona.

This dynamic Christian community was brought to a sudden and violent end early in the 9th century when Viking raiders plundered the abbey, slaughtering many of its monks. Most of the survivors fled to the relative safety of Kells in Ireland, where they attempted to continue their scholarly and academic work. After the initial Viking raid, it seems that a group of monks continued to live on the island, where they attempted to revive the community. But they were slaughtered in subsequent raids.

The monastery lay in ruins for at least two centuries before it was revived as a Benedictine foundation around 1200. Although the new Iona community played an important role in Christian life along the west coast of Scotland, it lacked the dynamism and influence of the earlier community. Even before the Reformation, the monastery lost its independence and fell into decay, although from time to time the suggestion was made that it ought to become the site of a cathedral for the Western Isles. This latter suggestion was favored by Charles I (1600–1649), although nothing came of the plan, and the buildings were left to gradually fall into ruins.

During the 17th century, several antiquarians expressed interest in Iona,

leaving behind careful accounts of the buildings and their layout. Then, late in the 18th century, a steady stream of travelers, including James Boswell (1740–95) and Dr. Samuel Johnson (1709–84), visited the island and were greatly impressed by its holiness. Later the composer Felix Mendelssohn-Bartholdy (1809–47) was equally impressed by the Christian ethos of the area. On the other hand, the island left the Romantic writer Sir Walter Scott (1771–1832) wondering why anyone ever visited it.

Repairs were carried out on the buildings between 1874 and 1876 by the Scottish architect Rowand Anderson on behalf of the eighth duke of Argyle, who owned the area. Later he handed over the ruined buildings of the main monastery complex to the Iona Cathedral Trust on condition that the Trust would carry out the necessary renovations to make the church once more usable. This project was completed between 1902 and 1910. In 1938, Dr. George MacLeod, Lord MacLeod of Furney, created the Iona Community as an order within the Church of Scotland. The community MacLeod founded carried out extensive restoration work as well as once more bringing a real Christian communal presence to the island. Restoration of all the main buildings was completed in 1965. In 1979 the entire island was sold by the tenth duke of Argyle's trustees to the Fraser Foundation, which gave the island to the Scottish nation to be administered by the National Trust of Scotland. Today there is a thriving Christian community on the island that continues restoration work and promotes Christian spirituality.

Anyone wishing to visit Iona must first cross over from the Scottish mainland to the island of Mull from either Oban to Craignure or from Lochaline to Fishnish. Then a drive across the island brings you to the car park and Iona ferry. Here visitors must proceed on foot since cars are not allowed on Iona. There are also regular coach tours from both Oban and Lochaline that may well prove more convenient and less expensive than taking a car onto Mull. On Iona, visitors can stay in the Iona community, provided they make arrangements long in advance. There is also a small hotel on the island.

PLACES TO VISIT

The ferry docks at IONA VILLAGE, where there are some quaint houses, gift shops, a café, and a small hotel. Just south of the village, on the east shore of the island, is MARTYR'S BAY, where the Vikings slaughtered 68 monks in 806. In 986 another group of Viking raiders murdered the abbot and 15 monks on the northeast beach of the island.

THE NUNNERY is the first really historic building you encounter walking north along the small country road towards the monastery center. It was built around 1200 for Augustinian canonesses by the local lord, Reginald of Somerled, who installed his sister, Beatrice, as the first prioress. The nunnery was dedicated to the Virgin Mary and was probably a sister house of an Irish priory, since the Augustinian order was popular in Ireland but relatively unknown in Scotland at that time. The nunnery was relatively small, with few nuns and only limited land holdings on the Isle of Mull. Its last prioresses belonged to the MacLean family, who acquired its lands after the Reformation. Today all one sees are the ruins of a small refectory, cloisters, and a chapel. Restoration of the ruins was undertaken in 1874 and again in 1923. Casual visitors can easily be misled into thinking that the smallness of the ruins means that they are relatively unimportant. Actually, this is one of the best-preserved examples of a small medieval nunnery in Britain because most other nunneries of this size were completely destroyed following the Reformation.

ST. RONAN'S CHURCH, a few yards north of the nunnery ruins, serves as the nunnery museum. During the Middle Ages, this small church served as the parish church of Iona. It was built in the late 12th century or early 13th century as a one-naved building without elaborate stonework or decoration.

MACLEAN'S CROSS. Close to the nunnery, by the parish church and manse, is the 15th-century MacLean Cross, which is a well-preserved example of Iona workmanship. On the far side is a carving of the Crucifixion. The cross is located at what was once the junction of the island's two main roads.

THE PARISH CHURCH was built in 1828 after the British Parliament in

1824 decreed that every community ought to have its own church to ensure the Christianization of the population and counter the growth of political radicalism. Consequently, it was known as a "Parliamentary Church." This is a simple stone building that is entirely practical. Forty-two such churches were built in the Scottish highlands to a standard design drawn up by the architect Thomas Telford (1757–1834). Telford was the son of a shepherd who apprenticed as a stone mason in Edinburgh and London before becoming one of the most innovative architects and engineers of the age.

CAIRN BLÀR BUIDHE. Sixty meters west from the St. Columba Hotel is a small earthen mound that is one of the few prehistoric sites on the island. It is believed to be a 2nd century B.C. burial mound.

ST. ORAN'S CHAPEL is most likely the oldest surviving building on the island. It is dedicated to St. Oran, also known as Odran (d. 563). The present building was erected by Lord Somerled in the 12th century and is clearly inspired by the Irish style of the time. It fell into disrepair after the Reformation, but was restored and reroofed in 1957.

Oran was one of the founding monks of the Iona community who died on the island shortly after their arrival. According to legend, Columba received a vision in which he saw Oran's soul ascending to heaven protected by angels, who warded off devils seeking to take him to hell. As a result of this vision, the community named their cemetery Reilig Odhráin in his honor. His feast day was the 27th of October.

Surrounding the chapel is the ancient burial ground **REILIG ODHRÁIN** named after the saint. According to tradition, over 27 kings and queens of Ireland, Norway, and Scotland were buried here.

Today only three early free-standing **HIGH CROSSES** remain on Iona out of over 1000 that existed here in the Middle Ages. Such crosses often displayed remarkable artistic skill and were very popular in northern Britain, Scotland, and Ireland during the 8th century. The surviving crosses are St. John's Cross, St. Martin's Cross, and St. Matthew's Cross, all of which are found west of the abbey. The remains of two other early crosses, the St. Oran's Cross and the stem of an unknown cross, can be seen in the nunnery museum. Due to weathering, the original St. John's Cross has been removed for repair. A good replica now stands in its stead. All of these crosses were constructed from large pieces of granite slotted together with mortice-and-tenon joints. The sides of the crosses are elaborately decorated with vines, ornamental circles, flowers, and scenes from the gospels. The west face of the St. Martin's Cross depicts Daniel in the lion's den, while the east face of the St. Matthew's Cross shows the temptation of Adam and Eve. In an age when books were expensive and rare, high stone crosses served to communicate the gospel to a largely illiterate population.

TÒRR AN ABA is a narrow rocky ridge near the present abbey, which according to legend was the site of St. Columba's cell. Although many people have cast doubts on the authenticity of this tradition, archaeologists found the outline of a small square building on the summit during excavations in 1957. Even more remarkable was that they were able to date charcoal remains to around the time of Columba, making the tradition plausible.

THE ABBEY was built by Reginald, the son of Somerled (d. 1164), in the early 13th century on the site of the earlier Celtic monastery. The Benedictine chapel is believed to be on the site of the original church built by Columba. Today the abbey is named after this church, which was dedicated to the Virgin Mary. Hence the name St. Mary's Abbey, but the original name appears to have been St. Columba's Monastery. Because at the time of its founding it was endowed with extensive lands on the islands of Canna, Coll, Mull, Colonsay, and Islay as well as on the Scottish mainland, the monastic community on Iona appears to have been relatively wealthy. The austere design and layout of the buildings suggest that Irish masons built it using designs they brought with them from Ireland. Building in the Irish style continued until 1250, when it came to an abrupt halt until the mid-15th century. During this

time, the community appears to have stagnated for at least 100 years. Then in 1450, Abbot Dominic (1421–65) initiated a series of reforms and new building projects, including a new choir and the tower.

St. Columba's Shrine stands north of the west door between the nave and the monastic buildings. Originally it was a separate building that over time was incorporated into the overall design. Scholars believe that the shrine was originally an oratory used for preaching to pilgrims who gathered by the high crosses. In the shrine is the outline of a burial chamber, which in all probability was the grave of Columba.

The nave was restored in 1910, and most of the upper part of the building dates from then, although the lower sections are 15th century. The north transept dates from between 1200 and 1220 and is a fine example of Benedictine architecture. On the west wall is the reconstructed night stair that was used by the monks to gain access to the church from their dormitory for night services. The oak screen at the front of the transept was donated by Queen Elizabeth II, in 1956. The south window, installed in 1965, is a modern design showing the life of St. Columba. Outside the south transept lies the foundations of a large late 13th-century transept that was never completed. The choir was restored by Thomas Ross between 1902 and 1905; he preserved most of the 15th century construction, which replaced an earlier 12th-century construction. Parts of the 12th-century building, however, are still to be seen on the north side.

The cloisters and monastic buildings complete the abbey complex. The earliest of these was constructed in the 13th century. Over the chapter house is a small room believed to be the site of the original library. It was restored in 1938. The dormitory and other working buildings were restored between 1950 and 1953. Today these buildings provide living quarters for the abbey staff and a limited number of visitors. To the south are two detached buildings. The first houses the Abbey Museum, which contains numerous fragments of ancient Christian carvings found throughout the island. It is one of the richest collections of early stone crosses and gravestones in Britain. Next is Michael Chapel, which was built in the late 12th century and restored in 1959.

ST. MARY'S CHAPEL is now a ruin on the southeast side of the abbey. It is believed to have been a pilgrim church during the Middle Ages.

ST. COLUMBA'S BAY. Those with the time and energy can take a long stroll to Port na Curaich harbor, which is where Columba is reputed to have landed on his first mission from Ireland. On the beach are cairns that are thought to be the work of medieval pilgrims.

IRONBRIDGE

Originally known as Coalbrookdale, the area became a mining center as early as 1638, when an iron smelter was built in the area. After 1715, it became a major industrial location, with a booming economy until 1900. It was here in the first quarter of the 18th century that cast iron was first manufactured, making possible the Industrial Revolution, which created the modern world between 1780 and 1830. Here the Quaker Abraham Darby (d. 1717) first succeeded in creating crude cast iron in 1709. The technological breakthrough he initiated led to the industrial development of the area under the direction of his son, Abraham Darby II (1711–63). In 1767, the first cast-iron railway lines, for horse-drawn trucks, were created. The first cast-iron bridge was built in 1779 to span the Severn Gorge, and the first steam locomotive was built here in 1802 to a design by the mining engineer Richard Trevithick (1771–1833). After a long period of prosperity, the area saw a long period of economic decline from the late 19th century, with its last factory, the tile works, closing in late 1979.

The significance of this area for Christians is that it brings alive the pioneering spirit of nonconformist Christians in Britain during the 19th century. Excluded from the universities and law, nonconformists, Baptists, Methodists, and Quakers turned to manufacturing and industrial enterprises, which in the process caused them to become pioneers of modern science and technology. Unfortunately, although the old Quaker graveyard, with the graves of the Darby family in it, is open to visitors, very little about the Christian heritage of the area is mentioned in the museums or their literature. Yet it was out of a sense of Christian calling that the whole complex originally developed.

The other important aspect of the museum complex is its vivid recreation of the drama of the Industrial Revolution, which in a mere 50 years, from 1780–1830, changed the world forever by creating in embryo all the things we take for granted today. Before the Industrial Revolution, very few things ever changed, and what did change was mainly fashion. Consequently, people looked back to the past as a golden age, remembering Roman civilization with awe and hoping that they might recreate its achievements. After the Industrial Revolution, the Romans suddenly became ignorant peasants, unaware of the wonders of science. And with the downgrading of the Roman world came the belief that the disciples of Jesus, who had converted the greatest civilization known to Western peoples, were also ignorant peasants who were too stupid to know that miracles cannot take place

and that dead men do not return to life. Thus, although grounded in a Christian base, the Industrial Revolution laid the groundwork for modern skepticism and unbelief in ways few recognize today, because we lack a sense of history and an understanding of the impact of technology in creating the modern world.

PLACES TO VISIT

A visit to the IRONBRIDGE MUSEUMS is a must for anyone wishing to understand the origins of the modern world. Founded in 1967, and first opened to the public in 1975, this World Heritage Site is one of the largest museum complexes in the world, covering several miles along the Ironbridge Gorge. The complex contains nine separate museum locations, the largest being a reconstructed Victorian town. Anyone visiting Ironbridge should allow at least a day to see all of the exhibits.

VISITOR'S CENTER AND IRON BRIDGE stand close to each other with magnificent views of the gorge. This is a good place to begin a tour because it allows visitors to orient themselves to the complex and see an introductory video about the area. The bridge was built to a design by Thomas Prichard and constructed by Abraham Darby III (d. 1789) at a cost of £6000. It was opened on New Year's Day 1781 as a wonder of the age.

COALBROOKDALE IRON MUSEUM provides an excellent overview of the history of iron. At its height, the iron works employed over 4,500 men and boys and produced in excess of 2000 tons of cast iron a week. Linked to the museum is the **GLYNWED GALLERY**, which exhibits industrial art, showing the many uses of cast iron. Nearby is the reconstructed **DARBY IRON FURNACE**, first built in 1709 and used until it was replaced by more modern techniques in 1818.

THE ROSEHILL AND DALE HOUSE are where the Darby family of Quaker iron masters lived, thought, and conceived the inventions that launched the Industrial Revolution. These restored buildings contain period furniture and a wealth of information about the people who in many ways created our modern world.

BLISTS HILL OPEN AIR MUSEUM, near the real village of Coalport, contains numerous Victorian buildings staffed by people in period dress.

THE TAR TUNNEL is located to the east of the Open Air Museum and is located in a shaft originally sunk to build an underground rail link to transport coal. While building the tunnel, workmen discovered a bitumen pool that was far more lucrative than the tunnel they were building. After the discovery, bitumen was exploited on a commercial scale. Today you can still see where it oozes from the ground.

COALPORT CHINA MUSEUM. A few miles further along the valley is one of the original industries of the area, which was once as prized for its china as for its cast iron. The museum combines social with industrial history in order to tell a fascinating story.

THE JAKEFIELD TILE MUSEUM brings to life another aspect of the area's many contributions to the modern world. Originally, the good quality local clay brought industry into the area, thus creating a need for coal. The development of mining led to the manufacture of cast iron, and everything followed in rapid succession.

KIDDERMINSTER

Although a historic town, there is little left of the old city to make this town worth a visit by most tourists. For Christians and history buffs, however, it is worth visiting if you happen to be in the area, because it was here that the great Puritan divine Richard Baxter (1615–91) ministered, until his expulsion from the pulpit following the Restoration in 1660.

PLACES TO VISIT

ST. MARY AND ALL SAINTS CHURCH, Church St. Built around

RICHARD BAXTER (1615–91) was an English Puritan divine whose work *The Saints' Everlasting Rest* (1650) is considered a spiritual classic. His *Reformed Pastor* (1656) was taken as a model for the ministry in Reformed churches, while his *Christian Directory* (1673) and *Doctrine of Family Duties* (1681) gave practical instruction on a host of subjects, including economic life within a household. Finally, with John Owen (1616–83), it was Baxter who popularized the term *nonconformist* to describe evangelical groups that rejected the formalism of the Church of England and sought greater religious freedom. His books *Judgement on Non Conformists* (1671) and *Non Conformist Plea for Peace* (1679) are classic statements of both religious and political liberty.

1500, this Gothic church was restored in 1895. Today it lies beyond the Ring Road and is reached by a messy pedestrian underpass. The Lady Chapel was once a separate church, which was later joined to the main building by a room that now serves as a vestry. The dark stained glass is Victorian and not particularly interesting. A large brass engraving commemorates Walter Cookesey (d. 1407), Sir John Phelip (d. 1415), and their wife, Matilda, who was Cookesey's widow before she married Phelip. They are depicted praying in full armor. The inscription tells visitors that Sir John died while on campaign in France with

Henry V (1387–1422) just three weeks before the Battle of Agincourt.

Richard Baxter became curate, that is assistant minister, here in 1641, and stayed on as vicar until he was ejected in 1660 along with all other Puritan ministers in the Church of England. On the north side of the nave is a pillar, in front of which stood Baxter's pulpit. On the back of the pillar is the inscription from Tyndale's Bible: "We preach not ourselves but Jesus Christe our Lorde. We are not as the moste parte are which choppe and change with the Word of God." This summed up the great preacher's dedication to his calling.

LANCASTER

Originally a Roman fort, Lancaster prospered throughout the Middle Ages, when the Duchy of Lancaster was created by Henry III (1207–72) for his son Edmund (1245–96) in 1265. In the 18th century, it became a center for trade with the West Indies and, like Bristol, dealt in slaves, which made its citizens very prosperous. Many of its fine Georgian buildings were built at that time on profits from the slave trade.

PLACES TO VISIT

PRIORY CHURCH was founded around 1090 as part of a monastic institution by monks from the Benedictine Abbey of Sées and was transferred to the Bridgettine Order of the Most Holy Savior in 1414. Part of the west wall is thought to be Saxon in origin. The doorway on the south porch is Norman, but the rest of the church was remodeled in the Gothic style sometime in the 12th century. The chancel stalls are a good example of medieval carving.

LANCASTER CASTLE was built on the site of an earlier 12th-century fort between 1407 and 1413 by John of Gaunt (1340–99), the son of Henry IV (1367–1413), to secure the northwest of England for the king. In the 18th century, it became a prison while its walls were rebuilt according to the original 14th-century plans. The shire hall has an impressive carved ceiling with heraldic designs. Since 1176 the great hall, which was part of the original building, has served as the county court. It was renovated in the 18th century in Georgian style.

ST. PETER'S CHURCH HEYSHAM stands below a rocky headland near a modern atomic power plant. It is a Saxon foundation that contains a fine Anglo-Norman stone tomb in its south aisle. The tomb is carved with Christian and pagan Norse symbols, presumably in an attempt to ensure that the deceased received the benefit of both religions at a time when a dying paganism was still strong enough to raise real doubts about the truth of Christianity. There is also the fragment of a Saxon stone cross in the churchyard. On the headland above the church are the ruins of St. Patrick's Chapel, built by Irish monks in the 8th century.

LANCASTER UNIVERSITY is located on top of a hill about five miles south of the town, with fine views of the surrounding countryside. Although a "new" university established in the early 1960s, Lancaster has quickly established an excellent reputation and is regularly ranked as one of the top academic institutions in Britain. Its religious studies department was founded in 1967 by Ninian Smart as the first of its kind in Britain and is one of the university's best departments. Unlike many North American religious studies departments which are either disguised theology departments or violently hostile to Christianity, the emphasis at Lancaster has been on the study of all religious traditions in a genuinely academic and nonpartisan manner.

L

LEICESTER

Leicester was founded in the 1st century as a Roman supply base, Ratae Coritanorum. It was also a garrison town dominating the Fosse Way, which was a Roman military road cutting through England from Lincoln to Cirencester. Leicester became the capital of the Christian kingdom of East Mercia in the 8th century. During the Middle Ages, a strong fortress was built here by the earls of Leicester, who often played a key role in deciding who would wear the crown. The most famous of these great lords was Simon de Montfort (1208–65), who led an alliance of nobles that forced King Henry III (1207–72) to convene the first true English Parliament in 1265. Today Leicester is one of the most thoroughly multicultural cities in England, with large Indian Hindu and Muslim populations alongside various other ethnic groups practicing a variety of religions. The city elected Britain's first Asian member of Parliament, Keith Vaz, in 1987 and holds a huge street festival over the first weekend in August.

PLACES TO VISIT

ST. NICHOLAS CHURCH, Guildhall Lane, is the oldest of the city churches and was built by the Saxons using bricks salvaged from Roman buildings and incorporating part of the old Roman baths. The present building dates from the 11th century and is in the Romanesque style. The tower was rebuilt in the 12th century and restored in 1906.

THE JEWRY WALL AND ARCHAEO-LOGICAL MUSEUM, adjacent to St. Nicholas Church, contains some excellent Roman remains, including a fine mosaic pavement. It also documents the role of Jews in the history of the city and is built on the site of the old Roman baths.

ST. MARTIN'S CATHEDRAL, Guildhall Lane, is an Early Gothic parish church consecrated as a cathedral in 1927. The north porch has a well-preserved medieval wooden roof.

ST. MARY DE CASTRO was described by Sir Nicholas Pevsner as "a pattern book" because it incorporates so many different architectural styles. The original building is Norman, built in 1107, but it has been renovated many times since.

LEICESTER ABBEY, St. Margaret's Way, was founded in 1132 by the Augustinian Order. Here Cardinal Wolsey (1475–1530) died in 1530 during his final dispute with King Henry VIII (1491–1547). Later the abbey was "dissolved" during the English Reformation. Its stones were used to build Cavendish House, which was the headquarters of King Charles I (1600–1649) before the Battle of Naseby in 1645, when his forces were defeated by Parliamentary troops led by Oliver Cromwell (1599–1658). Ironically, like the abbey, Cavendish House is also a ruin today.

THE JAIN CENTER, Oxford Street, is one of a handful of Jain temples in the Western world and well worth a visit by anyone wanting to understand Indian religious traditions.

BRITISH INTER-VARSITY, THE UCCF, UNIVERSITIES AND COLLEGES CHRISTIAN FELLOWSHIP, 38 De Montfort St., is one of the leading evangelical organizations in Britain. There is not much to see, although the folk are welcoming and will tell you what is happening in British colleges and universities. Inter-Varsity Press, which is also housed here, is somewhat different from its American counterpart and often publishes scholarly books that rarely reach the American market. It is therefore worth a visit by anyone interested in Christian scholarship.

LEICESTERSHIRE MUSEUM AND ART GALLERY, New Walk, contains Britain's largest collection of German expressionist paintings, as well as some excellent works by British artists.

BOSWORTH FIELD, near the town of Market Bosworth some 14 miles from Leicester, is the site of Richard III's (1452–85) defeat by Henry Tudor, Henry VII (1457–1509). There is a well-equipped visitor's center in the village as well as an ancient parish church

where Richard heard Mass before the battle. Richard III is the English king whose words "A horse, a horse, my kingdom for a horse" were immortalized by William Shakespeare in his famous play *Richard III*.

ST. MARY'S CHURCH, Lutterworth, a few miles from Leicester, is a Late Gothic church quite off the beaten track. It is important because John Wycliffe (1330–84) was the rector here from 1374 to 1384. During his time in Lutterworth, Wycliffe wrote some of his most important works. In 1415 Wycliffe's teachings were condemned by the Council of Constance, and in 1428 his remains were dug up from St. Mary's churchyard and publicly burnt. A monument to Wycliffe was erected in 1837 and stands at the east end of the south aisle.

The spire was destroyed in a storm in 1703 and rebuilt in 1761. Sir Gilbert Scott restored the church between 1867 and 1869. The church has a number of medieval murals that are very interesting. Over the chancel is a 15th-century depiction of Christ surrounded by his angels overseeing the resurrection of the dead. In the north aisle are three 14th-century paintings, which tell a story about three living and three dead figures with some smaller figures, who seem to be clergy, in the background. The people in the paintings are thought to be kings and queens. Since the paintings were restored in the 19th century, it is hard to know what is original and what was

L

155

added. This is particularly problematic, since in 1983 some additional figures, including three skeletons, were uncovered. Many people think the painting dates from Wycliffe's time and may represent his views on contemporary politicians and their ultimate fate. The fine Gothic pulpit is said to be the one from which Wycliffe preached, but scholars say the style comes from a later age.

LITCHFIELD

A Christian community was established here in the 7th century, and the present cathedral was erected in 1195 on the site of an older Norman church. Litchfield is famous as the birthplace of the great essayist and Christian apologist Dr. Samuel Johnson (1709–84) and as the place where the Quaker George Fox (1624–91) preached stark naked while calling its citizens to repentance. The present town was built in the 18th century and is a model of Georgian architecture.

PLACES TO VISIT

LITCHFIELD CATHEDRAL dominates the town and is rightly considered one of the finest medieval buildings in Britain. It is the only English cathedral with three spires. Although extensively damaged during the English Civil War when its central spire was demolished and many of the carvings on its west front were shot away, the cathedral was completely renovated and restored to its original glory in the 19th century. Approaching the main west front entrance, visitors see over 100 finely carved figures depicting biblical charac-

ters and a few English kings and queens. Although relatively small inside, the magnificent Gothic architecture creates a sense of space and soaring height. Three interior bays are early English in style; other parts of the church are a mature Gothic, dating from the 13th century. The Lady Chapel has a series of superb 16th-century stained-glass windows bought from the Belgian Cistercian abbey of Herenrode in 1802.

The chapter house contains the cathedral's greatest treasure, the rare 8th-century *Litchfield Gospels,* which are illuminated manuscripts illustrating the gospels of Matthew and Mark and fragments of Luke's gospel. A bust of Samuel Johnson (1709–84) stands in St. Michael's Chapel.

SAMUEL JOHNSON MUSEUM is found a short distance from the cathedral. It is the birthplace of Johnson and contains a fine collection of books, with other details about his life and work.

LITCHFIELD HERITAGE EXHIBITION, St. Mary's Church, opposite Dr. Samuel Johnson's house, contains fascinating exhibits illustrating the history of the town.

SAMUEL JOHNSON (1709–84) is England's best-known literary critic, lexicographer, and author of his famous dictionary. Less well known is the fact that Johnson was a keen student of the Bible and strong defender of Christianity against the rationalism of his 18th-century contemporaries.

THE EDWARD WIGHTMAN MEMORIAL stands in the market square near the larger statues of Johnson and his biographer James Boswell (1740–95). In 1612, Wightman was the last person to be burnt for heresy in England.

LINCOLN

A British Bronze Age settlement was conquered by the Romans in A.D. 47 and made into the colony Lindum Colonia, which was the headquarters of the Ninth Legion. The legion guarded the important communication links on the Fosse Way, a major Roman road. Later it became one of four Roman provincial capitals in Britain. After the withdrawal of the Roman legions in the 4th century, the town was occupied by Saxon mercenaries, who were originally brought to Britain as auxiliary troops in support of the legionnaires. Subsequently it became the capital of the Saxon kingdom of Lindsey. When the Saxons converted to Christianity through the preaching of an evangelist called Paulinius in the 7th century, Lincoln became an important evangelistic and liturgical center. William the Conqueror (1027–87) built a strong fort here to control the economically valuable surrounding area.

The city prospered from the wool trade with Flanders. In the late 14th century, the center of the wool trade shifted to nearby Boston, and Lincoln went into a long economic decline, only recovering in the 19th century when heavy industry was introduced to the area.

The castle was captured in 1140 by King Stephen (1097–1154) during the 12th-century English Civil War between his supporters and Queen Matilda, the Empress Maud (1102–67). Queen Eleanor of Castile, the wife of Edward I (1239–1307), died eight miles outside of Lincoln. Her body was then carried in state to London, and stone crosses, known as Eleanor Crosses, were erected at key points along the route to Westminster Abbey. Only three—in Geddington, Northampton, and Waltham—survive today.

Among Lincoln's more famous personalities are the composer William Byrd (1543–1623), whose church music

157

is some of the finest produced in England, and the artist Peter de Wint (1784–1849).

PLACES TO VISIT

LINCOLN CATHEDRAL, Castle Hill, stands at the center of the city, where it dominates the landscape. The Norman Bishop Remigius began construction in 1072 on the site of an older church. It was consecrated in 1092, but later destroyed by an earthquake in 1185. Rebuilding was undertaken by Hugh of Avalon, who was bishop from 1186–1200. Lincoln Cathedral is one of the most architecturally unified Early Gothic cathedrals in the whole of Britain. The west front is decorated with 11 statues of English kings over the main doorway and a carved stone frieze depicting biblical scenes. On the south side are the Judgment Porch, named after the carving over its door depicting scenes from the Last Judgment, and the Galilee Porch. There is also a gargoyle figure of the Devil and on the buttresses three stately figures thought to represent Edward I (1239–1307) and his two wives, Eleanor (d. 1290) and Margaret (1283–90).

The west front doorway leads into a seven-bayed nave, which is exceptionally wide for an English cathedral. It is lined with limestone and marble columns. In the south aisle's second bay is a rare font carved from Tournai marble. Two beautiful rose windows adorn the large northwest and southwest transepts. In the north transept is the 13th-century Dean's Eye, and in the south transept the 14th-century Bishop's Eye. Most of the other stained glass is Victorian in origin. Six beautiful chapels are to be found leading off from various parts of the main building.

Beyond the central tower, through two finely carved doorways, is the exquisite Gothic choir. On the south aisle is the shrine of Little St. Hugh, a child whose murdered body was found in 1225. The rumor quickly spread that he had been ritually sacrificed by local Jews, leading to a pogrom. The north aisle has a plaque commemorating William Byrd (1543–1623). Beyond the choir are the lesser or northeast and southeast transepts. The remarkable Trondheim Pillars in the east transept get their name from their similarity to those in the city of Trondheim in Norway.

The St. Hugh's Choir, behind the main altar, contains some excellent 14th-century carved misericords depicting scenes from the Bible alongside King Arthur, Alexander the Great, and other heroic figures. The chapel lies beyond the central tower. Its asymmetrical ribbed vault is the first purely decorative ceiling of its kind in Europe. Beyond it is the 13th-century Angel Choir. Completed in 1280, the choir gets its name from the 28 carved angels, which may be seen below its upper windows. On the first east pillar high above the ground is the so-called Lincoln Imp, a strange figure that has become the city's emblem. Below the imp is the shrine of St. Hugh.

A passage from the northeast transept leads to the beautiful medieval cloisters. The north walk was redesigned in neoclassical style by Christopher Wren (1632–1723) in 1674 and contains a library. The chapter house is historically important as the site of several early English parliaments during the reign of Edward I (1239–1307).

LINCOLN CASTLE is located a short distance to the west of the cathedral. It was one of eight major castles built by the rapacious William the Conqueror (1027–87) to secure his grip on the local population. Originally this important fortification consisted of a stone keep protected by a 20-foot deep moat and a wooded stockade that enclosed approximately 13 acres. It was built in 1068 after William demolished over 160 Saxon houses to clear the land for his use.

The earliest part of the castle is the 12th-century Lucy Tower, built on the site of the Norman keep. The east gate dates back to the 12th century, and the Cobb Hall back to the 13th. The castle gardens, about six acres, contain the fragment of an Eleanor Cross. After losing its military importance in the 18th century, the castle became a jail and administrative center. The 18th-century Victorian prison, with its gruesome chapel, gives visitors a vivid insight into the terrible conditions under which prisoners lived before the Quaker Elizabeth Fry (1780–1845) and other Christian reformers campaigned for their humane treatment on the basis of Christ's teachings in Matthew 25. In the older Georgian prison building, built between 1787 and 1791, visitors can see one of the four surviving copies of the *Magna Carta* (1214).

CHURCH OF ST. BENEDICT, High St., has a squat late Saxon tower and a 13th-century interior.

CHURCH OF ST. MARY-LE-WIGFORD, High St. On the outside of the Saxon tower is a Roman memorial stone with a later Christian inscription dating from Saxon times.

CHURCH OF ST. PETER AT GOWLS, High St., has a Saxon tower.

THE USHER GALLERY was donated to the town by James Ward Usher, a 19th-century entrepreneur whose wealth came from selling copies of the Lincoln Imp. It houses his magnificent collection of porcelain, a fine coin collection, and watercolors by Peter de Wint (1784–1848), as well as several other paintings by English artists such as Joseph William Turner (1775–1851).

LINCOLN HIGH BRIDGE is one of the very few medieval house bridges in England. Lining the bridge are a number of half-timbered houses.

THE JEW'S HOUSE, Steep Hill at the end of the High St., stands as a reminder that in the Middle Ages Lincoln was the home to a thriving Jewish community. This house, which dates from 1170, is believed to be the oldest domestic house in England. Part of its court was once used as a synagogue.

GAINSBOROUGH OLD HALL, 18 miles northwest, is one of the oldest and best preserved medieval manors in England. It was built between 1460 and 1480 by Sir Thomas Burgh and was visited by Richard III (1452–85) in 1483.

Here the Pilgrim fathers planned their flight to America. A permanent exhibition is devoted to their exploits. In the nearby town of Gainsborough, King Forkbeard of Denmark died in 1014 after invading England. The town also is the model for St. Ogg in George Eliot's *The Mill on the Floss*.

LONDON

Londinium was founded by the Romans in A.D. 43 on the site of a Celtic settlement. A supply base, it eventually became the capital of the Roman province. Twenty years later, Queen Boadicea (d. 60) destroyed the town, but her revolt was quickly suppressed and the city rebuilt. After the Norman invasion in 1066, William I (1027–87), the bastard duke of Normandy, had himself crowned king of England in both Winchester and London's Westminster Abbey. Subsequently, London replaced Winchester as the center of Norman and later Royal rule. To consolidate his hold on the local population, William built the White Tower, which became the central building in the Tower of London. The city prospered under its new lords. In the 16th century, London became a Protestant center, leading its citizens to favor Parliamentary rule against that of the king during the English Civil Wars. Consequently, they expelled the king's representatives

and strongly supported the Parliamentary cause.

London suffered little or no damage during the Civil Wars and remained essentially a medieval city that was deeply religious and strongly Protestant. Following the death of Oliver Cromwell (1599–1658), the restoration of the monarchy saw a vicious reaction during which the many London clergy were expelled from their churches and Puritans were persecuted. The Glorious Revolution of 1688 saw an easing of religious oppression and the gradual reawakening of popular piety, although the upper classes remained essentially decadent.

In 1665, the Great Plague wiped out a third of London's population and killed over 100,000 people from a population of around 500,000. A year later, in 1666, the Great Fire swept away over 13,000 houses and 90 churches, 80 percent of London's buildings. Most of the ruling classes fled to the country during these events, returning only after the tragedies had run their course. A building boom followed, but to the disappointment of Sir Christopher Wren (1632–1723), who submitted plans to the king for an entirely new and spacious city a week after the fire, much of the reconstruction was the work of speculators who rebuilt London's crowded and unsystematic medieval streets. Nevertheless, Wren was commissioned to rebuild St. Paul's, several other churches, and some public buildings.

The 18th century witnessed the birth of Methodism in London and a widespread revival of religion throughout England that continued well into the 19th century. In particular the so-called "Clapham Sect" led by William Wilberforce (1759–1833) and Henry Venn (1725–97) played an important role in reshaping English morals and society in a Christian direction. Slavery was abolished, workers given the right to form unions, and Parliament reformed largely as a result of the activities of Christian reformers based in London.

During the 19th century, a few significant public buildings, such as the Houses of Parliament and various government offices, were built as the city continued to expand. Squalid slums rapidly developed. In 1855, the government established the Metropolitan Board of Works with responsibility for sewage disposal. This act led to the creation of the County of London in 1888. Then in 1965 the Greater London Council was created. It was abolished in 1986 to be replaced by various new borough councils. Further reforms were initiated in the 1990s and continue until the present.

During the 19th century, the evangelical tradition flourished in London's numerous nonconformist churches. In particular, the preaching of Charles Haddon Spurgeon (1834–92) gave a powerful boost to Britain's small Baptist community, while the formation of the Salvation Army by William Booth (1829–1912) in 1861 took the gospel into the slums.

London suffered heavily from German air raids during World War II. Although postwar reconstruction offered an opportunity to rebuild the city, the scope for renewal was limited. The 1960s, 1980s, and 1990s saw major building booms and the demolition of older buildings to be replaced by either inspiring works of modern architecture or monstrosities of bad taste, depending on one's point of view.

After World War II, the London-based Inter-Varsity Fellowship, which moved to Leicester in the 1970s, played an important role in keeping the evangelical tradition alive, as did the preaching of the nonconformist David Martyn Lloyd-Jones (1899–1981) at the Westminster Chapel and Anglican John Stott (b. 1910) at All Souls Langham Place. More recently, the Icthyus Fellowship, which originated in London, and similar charismatic congregations, have

161

become a major force in English religious life.

An old English saying goes, "If you are tired of London, you are tired of life." This may not be exactly true, but it does sum up the vast cultural and historic richness of the British capital. London has over 100 churches and numerous other interesting places to visit. Most of these places are well worth seeing. But there are far too many to list every one and to talk about every site in this guide. Therefore, only those which are important in terms of our Christian heritage were selected. In commenting on them I have also distinguished between places that are rich in Christian tradition and others that are of national importance.

Finally, because there are so many places to see, I have loosely grouped them in terms of their geographic location.

PLACES TO VISIT

ST. ETHELREDA, Ely Place, Holborn, EC1, was built in the 13th century as the private chapel of the bishop of Ely. It was dedicated to the Saxon princess St. Ethelreda, who founded the monastery of Ely in 673. This two-story medieval chapel was bought in a public auction by the Roman Catholic Order the Fathers of Charity in 1874. They have carried out an extensive program of restoration, making it as authentic as possible in terms of its original design. Inside are large carved statues of 16th- and 17th-century English Roman Catholic mar-

tyrs, reminding the visitor that Catholics as well as Protestants died for their faith during the Reformation. The reliquary contains the hand of St. Ethelreda. Although this seems both ghoulish and bizarre to most Protestants, the preservation of such remains serves as a good reminder that Christian leaders of the past were real people who lived and died in the real world and are not fictional characters like so many mythological gods. In this sense the reliquary, which itself seems superstitious to Protestants, originated as a rebuke to pagan superstitions and ancient British fables about gods and heroes.

The windows are among the best examples of modern stained glass in England and depict the glory of Christ and life of St. Ethelreda. The church itself is referred to as "Ely House" in Shakespeare's plays *Richard II* and *Richard III*. John of Gaunt died here in 1399. More recently the church became known for its healing services and revival of the medieval blessing of St. Blaise (d. 316), which occurs on or near the saint's day, February 3. In this increasingly popular ritual, two crossed candles are held to the throat of individuals seeking God's blessing and healing. A relic of the saint, donated in 1917, can be seen in the church.

ST. BARTHOLOMEW THE GREAT, Smithfield, EC1, is another of London's oldest church buildings and the most complete Norman, or Romanesque, church in the capital. Formerly an

Augustinian priory founded by Rahere in 1123, it became a parish church at the Dissolution of the Monasteries, when it was substantially reduced in size. The graveyard is built on the site of the church's original, medieval nave. The tomb of Rahere, erected 300 years after his death, lies in the north side of the sanctuary. In the south choir aisle is a monument to Sir Walter Midmay (d. 1589), the founder of Emmanuel College, Cambridge, which he created to train clergy for the newly reformed Church of England. It became a center of Puritan scholarship and evangelical piety. One of its most famous graduates was John Harvard (1607–38), after whom Harvard University is named.

WESLEY'S CHAPEL AND WESLEY HOUSE MUSEUM, City Rd., Finsbury, EC1, is the cradle of British Methodism and was built by John Wesley (1703–91), who lived next door at 47 City Rd., for the last 12 years of his life. It was erected between 1777 and 1778. Wesley was converted by Moravian preaching in a small chapel on Aldergate Street in 1738, when in his unforgettable words, he felt his "heart strangely warmed." His brother Charles was converted around the same time in the home of a John Bray (18th century) at No. 13 Little Britain, EC1. Following their conversion, the Wesley brothers opened Foundry Chapel in the same district of London. Forty years later, the congregation moved to the new Wesley Chapel. The exterior was beautified in

1815, and extensive restorations took place in 1880. Nevertheless, the chapel remains essentially as it was in Wesley's day. It is a simple affair with five bays and neoclassical Doric and Corinthian columns. The stained-glass windows and numerous memorial plaques commemorate great Methodist leaders. The pews date from 1891.

The Museum of Methodism in the adjacent John Wesley House has an interesting display that documents the history of this important movement.

Slightly to the north of the chapel is the original Foundry Chapel, a rather dark low room that has the distinction of housing the organ on which Charles Wesley (1707–88) composed some of his most famous hymns. From this a doorway leads into the churchyard, where John Wesley is buried in a simple neoclassical tomb. The inscription on the tomb tells the story of Wesley's life and achievements. Outside the chapel are statues of John Wesley on horseback and Charles Wesley preaching.

Anyone wanting to visit Charles Wesley's tomb must go to the CHARLES WESLEY MEMORIAL GARDEN in Marylebone. Closer to the chapel, however, is BUNHILL FIELDS, on the other side of City Road, where several evangelical leaders, including John Bunyan (1628–88) and Isaac Watts (1674–1748), are buried. William Black (1757–1827), whose poetry and heretical ideas have inspired many people in the New Age movement, is also buried here. Adjoining the nonconformist cemetery is the **FRIEND'S BURIAL GROUND,** where George Fox (1624–91), the founder of the Quakers, is also buried.

MUSEUM OF THE ORDER OF ST. JOHN, St. John's Lane, EC1, provides a fascinating insight into the life and work of a medieval monastic order.

SMITHFIELD MARKET, EC1, is the site of a Protestant martyr's memorial commemorating the over 300 Protestants who were burnt at the stake here during the reign of Queen Mary (1516–58). More than anything else, the deaths of these men and women, which were recorded in *Foxe's Book of Martyrs,* created a strong grassroots Protestantism in England and gave birth to the Puritan movement.

ST. MARY-LE-BOW, Cheapside, EC2, was rebuilt by Sir Christopher Wren (1632–1723) at great expense following the Great Fire of London in 1666 and is a jewel of British Baroque or neoclassicism. Its steeple is a city landmark. The interior was badly damaged during the Second World War and rebuilt between 1956 and 1964 in a more modern style that departs from the original conception of Wren. The church has an 11th-century crypt with "arches and bows" that give the church its name. The famous church tower contains the "Bow Bells," a peel of 12 bells,

CHARLES WESLEY (1707–88) AND JOHN WESLEY (1703–91)

Today Charles Wesley is best remembered for his wonderful hymns. In fact, he was one of the most prolific hymn writers of all time, composing over 3000. His brother John is remembered as an evangelist and the main force behind Methodism. He too was a prolific writer. In addition to his very detailed journals, which still make good reading, he published sermons and theological tracts. Equally important are the practical works he produced to assist the poor who were joining the churches he founded. Among these works, which are largely forgotten today, were his *Primitive Physic* (1747), which gave good medical advice for its day, and his *Grammar* (1751), which was intended to help people learn to read and write. His tract *Early Rising* (1798) also left its mark on the movement by encouraging what sociologists now call "the Protestant ethic" of thrift and hard work. Finally, in *Thoughts on Slavery* (1773), he issues a blast against one of the pressing social evils of his day. All of this serves to remind us of the rich heritage of the Christian tradition and the ways in which Christians have shaped our ways of thinking and society for the better.

including the "Great Bow." Anyone claiming to be a Cockney must be born within range of the peel of these bells. In 1698 England's first missionary society, the Society for the Promotion of Christian Knowledge, or SPCK, was founded here. The church also contains the Jamestown Memorial and a statue of John Smith (d. 1631) commemorating the founding of Virginia.

ALL HALLOWS BY THE TOWER, Byward St., EC3, is one of the oldest churches in England, although most of the present building was erected in between 1948 and 1957 after the old church was devastated by German bombs during World War II. The church appears to go back to a 7th-century structure that was once part of Barking Abbey founded by St. Erkenwald, who was the bishop of London, in 675. One of its arches is made of Roman brick, indicating the church's antiquity. From the tower of this church the diarist Samuel Pepys (1633–1703) watched the Great Fire of London devastate the city in 1666. The church has a 14th-century barrel-vaulted crypt that contains fragments of two 11th-century stone crosses. Lancelot Andrewes

(1555–1626), later bishop of Winchester and an outstanding Anglican devotional writer, and William Penn (1644–1718), the founder of Pennsylvania, were both baptized here. John Quincy Adams (1735–1826), the sixth president of the United States of America, was married here in 1779.

ST. HELEN, Great St. Helen's, Bishopsgate, EC3, is one of the few large medieval parish churches to have survived the Great Fire of 1666. Originally a Benedictine nunnery, the church has two naves. Against the north wall stands the nuns' night stairs, which were used in the Middle Ages to allow easy access to the chapel for late and very early services. The stained glass is Victorian. Sir Thomas Gresham (d. 1579), an outstanding patron of scholarship and advocate of Protestantism, is buried here. He founded both the Royal Exchange and Gresham College. There is also the tomb of Richard Staper (d. 1608), who played an important role in the development of British trade with India in the 16th century.

ST. MAGNUS THE MARTYR, Lower Thames St., EC3, was rebuilt by Sir Christopher Wren (1632–1723) between

WILLIAM PENN (1644–1718) was an English Quaker who emigrated to America and founded Pennsylvania. He held unorthodox views about the Trinity, atonement, and justification, attacking Calvinism in his book *Sandy Foundation Shaken* (1668). His most famous book, *No Cross, No Crown* (1669), is considered a spiritual classic.

1671 and 1676 in a neoclassical or English Baroque style. It replaced a church built around 1066 that was later dedicated to St. Magnus, a missionary to the Orkney Islands who was martyred in 1116. In the 19th century, this church became a major center of Anglo-Catholicism, which sought to return the Church of England to a form of pre-Reformation worship, which, while not Roman Catholic, retained many medieval rites and liturgical practices. Miles Coverdale (1488–1568), an early translator of the Bible into English, whose work greatly advanced the cause of Protestantism in England, was rector here in the 16th century and reburied here in 1840. A memorial to him can be seen on the east wall to the right of the high altar.

ST. MARY AT HILL, EC3, was rebuilt by Sir Christopher Wren between 1670 and 1676, and again after a disastrous fire in 1988. This church contains some rare high box pews of a type popular in the 17th century. Wilson Carlisle (1847–1942), the founder of the Anglican evangelistic ministry the Church Army, was rector of the church from 1892–1926.

ST. OLAVE, Hart St., EC3, was built in 1450 and restored after World War II. This church is dedicated to Olaf, the first Christian king of Norway, who reigned from 1016–29 and became a martyr in 1030. In 1014 his army came to the rescue of King Aethelraed II (968–1016) of England, saving him from defeat at the hands of pagan Danes. This church reminds visitors of the complex history of Christian Europe and the interdependence of Christian kingdoms. Look out for the grave of the diarist Samuel Pepys (1633–1703).

BEVIS MARKS SYNAGOGUE, St. Mary Axe, EC3, is the oldest surviving Jewish synagogue in England. It was built in 1701 in the style of the Portuguese synagogue in Amsterdam. The central chandelier was donated by Dutch Jews shortly after its opening.

THE TOWER OF LONDON, Tower Hill, EC3, is a grim building which for centuries was the source of royal power. Today it is one of the most popular tourist spots in England. Visitors ought not to forget its bloody history. This is a place where hundreds of people, including many Christians, were held prisoners in grim conditions, often because they had displeased a wayward king or held a faith different from that of the monarch. Many prisoners were hung, drawn, and quartered while still alive. For the lucky few, usually of royal blood, a less painful beheading or hanging on Tower Green dispatched them to their Maker.

The Tower contains some fascinating historical resources, including suits of armor, cannons, swords, and a host of other military equipment. You can also see the British crown jewels in the JEWEL HOUSE.

Within the Tower complex are two churches. THE CHAPEL ROYAL OF ST.

JOHN THE EVANGELIST is part of the original White Tower, built by William I between 1077 and 1097. It is a plain two-story chapel fitting of an austere military ruler. The second church is CHAPEL ROYAL OF ST. PETER AD VINCULA. The name of the church means "St. Peter in chains." It was erected in the early 16th century as a chapel for royal prisoners and as their last resting place. As such it is associated with a host of individuals who were publicly executed on Tower Green adjacent to the church. Although some of the prisoners genuinely rebelled against the monarchy, many more were executed after mock trials simply because they had lost favor with the ruling monarch and were considered too powerful.

Here one finds monuments to Anne Boleyn (d. 1536), the second and pious Protestant wife of the bloodthirsty Henry VIII (1491–1547); Catherine Howard (1521–1542), his fifth wife; and his faithful Roman Catholic servant Sir Thomas More (1478–1535), who died after a rigged trial made famous by the play *A Man for All Seasons*. Essentially More died because he refused to acknowledge that the king was the "head of the Church" and would not justify Henry's divorce of his first wife, Catherine of Aragon (1485–1536). Subsequently, the pious More was recognized as a saint by the Roman Catholic Church. Thomas Cromwell (1485–1540), who ruthlessly dissolved English monasteries and seized their wealth, is also buried here. Like so many of Henry VIII's servants, he eventually displeased his cruel master and paid with his life on a trumped-up charge of treason like the one he had helped bring against the godly More.

ST. PAUL'S CATHEDRAL, EC4, stands on the site of an ancient British church founded in 604 and is either the fourth or fifth church to have been built here. The present building is in the British neoclassical (some call it Baroque) style of Sir Christopher Wren (1632–1723) and is considered the crowning achievement of his life. Old St. Paul's was devastated by the Great Fire of London in 1666, so Wren was commissioned to build a new and grander building worthy of the king. Building commenced on June 21, 1675, and was completed 33 years later when Wren's son laid the final stone, at the top of the great lantern, to his father's great joy. Wren is buried in the church. His epitaph, which he wrote in Latin, reads, "Whoever reads this, if you seek his monument, then look around you."

The glory of St. Paul's is its magnificent neoclassical dome that is a major London landmark. Although the dome is modeled after St. Peter's in Rome, Wren deliberately avoided creating a true hemisphere. Topping the dome is a Baroque-style lantern. The dome has two tiers, with a viewing gallery in the upper tier. The west end of the church

L

has two Baroque spires which counterbalance the dome.

Inside, the nave is dominated by a monument to the duke of Wellington (1769–1852). A statue of Lord Nelson (1758–1805), another hero of the Napoleonic Wars, stands in the south transept. Although great war leaders, neither Wellington nor Nelson was particularly humane; indeed, they treated the men who served under them with barbaric cruelty. Nor were they democrats, or noted for their Christian piety. Rather they were the defenders of a reactionary and corrupt aristocracy that often oppressed evangelical Christianity. In the crypt are many more monuments to Englishmen who died in numerous colonial and continental wars of conquest. These monuments serve to remind the visitor that in England religion and politics are closely interwoven with a civil religion that honors military heroes above religious reformers. At the back of the altar are the coats of arms of all the American States. They were placed there as an act of gratitude for America's participation in World War II.

One of the few monuments dedicated to a Christian figure is the statue of the poet and theologian John Donne (1572–1631), found in the south aisle. He was dean of St. Paul's from 1621–31. The south aisle also contains William Holman Hunt's (1827–1910) famous, if somewhat cultic, painting, *Christ, The Light of the World.*

ST. STEPHEN, Walbrook, EC4, is a medieval church rebuilt in the neoclassical, English Baroque style by Sir Christopher Wren (1632–1723) and regarded as one of his masterpieces. The 45-foot dome makes it a miniature St. Paul's. Captain John Smith (1580–1631) of Virginia is buried here, and there is a monument to Pocahontas (1595–1617), the Native American princess who saved his life. More recently, the church was the center of an ecclesiastical struggle when a churchwarden, Mr. Peter Palumbo, supported by the rector, sought to replace the existing communion table with a marble altar created by the artist Henry Moore (1898–1986). Apart from theological objections, of which there were many, the huge marble structure totally departed from Wren's design and in the eyes of many ruined the aesthetic appeal of the church. Initially, the church court ruled against the installation of the altar on the grounds that it departed from the concept of a communion table. But in 1987 the decision was reversed by the Court of Ecclesiastical Causes, allowing the installation of the altar.

ST. BRIDE, Fleet St., EC4, is named after the 6th-century Irish saint Bridget of Kildare. Originally designed by Sir Christopher Wren (1632–1723), it is the original "wedding cake" church, so named because its steeple is said to be the inspiration for modern wedding cakes. The church was badly damaged during World War II. The interior was "restored" between 1957 and 1959 in a style that departs from Wren's original plan. Prior to the restoration, the site was excavated, revealing that the site had been used for Christian worship in Roman times before becoming a major church in preconquest London. The results of these excavations are on display in the crypt. Famous members of St. Bride's congregation in the 18th century include John Milton (1608–74), Izaak Walton (1593–1683), Samuel Pepys (1633–1703), Edmund Burke (1729–97), and William Hogarth (1697–1764).

THE TEMPLE CHURCH, Inner Temple, EC4, is where Crusaders from 1091 to 1200 are buried. It was built as a round church because this is how they believed the Temple in Jerusalem was originally built. It is a curious place dedicated to a form of medieval Christianity that few appreciate today. Nevertheless, without the sacrifice these men made, there is little doubt that Muslim armies would have overrun Western Europe, preventing the further expansion of Christianity and oppressing local Christian populations as they did in the Middle East, North Africa, Turkey, and those areas of Europe which came under Muslim rule, such as Greece. Today, following the work of some 19th-century secular historians, it is popular to downplay the importance of the Crusades. But more recent histor-

ical research has shown that they were essentially defensive wars intended to protect Europe and Christian pilgrims.

DR. JOHNSON'S HOUSE MUSEUM, Gough Square, EC4, is dedicated to the life and work of Dr. Samuel Johnson (1709–84), the great Christian apologist and author of the famous *Dictionary of the English Language* (1755).

WESTMINSTER ABBEY, Broad Sanctuary, SW1, was rebuilt in the Romanesque style by the pious Edward the Confessor (1003–66) in the 11th century on the site of an earlier 8th-century church. Here the gloatingly triumphant William (1027–87), duke of Normandy and conqueror of Saxon England, was crowned on Christmas Day 1066. This arrogant act of defiance and impiety symbolically linked William to both Edward the Confessor and the Frankish King Charlemagne (742–814), who was crowned Holy Roman Emperor on Christmas Day 800. Since then all but two coronations of English monarchs have been held here. The oldest known portrait of an English monarch to have been painted while he posed for the painter stands in the main entrance. It is of Richard II (1367–1400), who was defeated by Henry VII (1457–1509) and subsequently, rightly or wrongly, vilified by William Shakespeare.

The transformation to a Gothic cathedral was begun in 1220, during the reign of Henry III (1207–72). He built the Lady Chapel as a grand memorial to Edward the Confessor (d. 1066), who was canonized by the pope in 1163. Henry was inspired by a visit to the French cathedrals of Amiens and Reims and ordered his architects to build Edward's shrine in the new French style we now know as the Gothic style. During Henry's lifetime, only the first bay of the nave was rebuilt in the Gothic style. It took 200 years before the remainder of the cathedral was completely rebuilt. In 1503 the Tudor King Henry VII (1457–1509) began the construction of a new chapel at the east end of the church. This was completed by his son Henry VIII (1491–1547) in 1519 and is widely regarded as a jewel of the Late Gothic style.

When Henry VIII (1491–1547) embarked on a policy of reform and dissolved the larger monasteries in 1540, the abbey lost its community of over 50 Benedictine monks, its extensive land holdings, and its treasure, but the building itself survived as a church. In 1560 Elizabeth I (1533–1603) saved the remaining buildings by turning them into the College of St. Peter, now known as Westminster School.

The interior fan vaulting is among the very best Gothic stonework in Europe. Inside are numerous royal tombs, including that of Henry VII. In the nave a plain tablet commemorates the great British war leader Sir Winston Churchill (1874–1965), while another remembers "the Unknown Solider." The tombs of English Prime Ministers Charles James Fox (1749–1806) and William Pitt the Younger (1759–1806) are nearby. On the north wall is the grave of the dramatist Benjamin Jonson (1572–1637).

In the south transept is an area known as the Poet's Corner, where Geoffrey Chaucer (1345–1400) is buried. It contains plaques commemorating famous British poets such as William Shakespeare (1564–1616), T. S. Eliot (1888–1965), William Wordsworth (1770–1850), Lord Byron (1788–1824), Lord Tennyson (1809–92), and even Percy Shelley (1792–1822), who was expelled from Oxford for atheism. The north choir aisle contains memorials to Henry Purcell (1659–95) and Edward Elgar (1857–1934) as well as Charles Darwin (1809–82). The north transept has a number of memorials to politicians, including Robert Peel (1788–1850), Lord Palmerston (1784–1865), and the great Christian statesman William Gladstone (1809–98).

Beyond the choir is the sanctuary where the coronation of British monarchs takes place. Henry II Chapel, where the king is buried, has some of the finest roof vaulting in the entire cathedral. From its walls hang the banners of the Knights of the Grand Cross and the Order of Bath, emphasizing the way British civil religious ceremonies are to be found at the heart of British Christianity.

The Chapel of Edward the Confessor contains the saint's shrine surrounded by the tombs of five British kings and three queens. This chapel was a center of medieval pilgrimage and is still venerated by many British Roman Catholics.

In the center of the chapel, before the stone screen, which dates from 1441, stands the coronation chair on which British kings and queens are crowned. Once again the mixture of pre-Christian beliefs about royalty are merged in beliefs and practices sanctified by a veneer of Christianity to create a powerful civil religion that serves as a focus for British nationalism and communal sentiments. The graves of Elizabeth I (1533–1603) and her sister Queen Mary I (1515–58) are found in the south aisle.

The chapter house is an octagonal chamber where traditionally the bishop met with his clergy to discuss important practical and theological issues. This is also where the English Parliament met until 1547. A graceful central pillar supporting a beautiful Gothic ceiling and some fine examples of medieval wall paintings make this area well worth a visit. Finally, don't miss the Jerusalem Chamber, where the final text of the King James Version (or, as the British call it, the Authorized Bible) received its final form from its 17th-century translators.

WESTMINSTER CATHEDRAL, Ashley Place, off Victoria St., SW1, is a fine Roman Catholic cathedral. Work on it began in 1895 and continues until today. It is constructed in the Byzantine style, which is unusual in England. Note the Stations of the Cross by the modern artist Erik Kiln. Although once on the fringe of English religious life, Roman Catholicism is increasingly one of the major religious forces in Britain as traditional nonconformist churches, such as the Methodists, have steadily declined since the 1960s.

WESTMINSTER CHAPEL, Buckingham Gate, SWI, is where Dr. David Martyn Lloyd-Jones preached throughout his career as a minister. Today the pastor is Dr. R. T. Kendall, who continues the rich evangelical and Puritan tradition of Lloyd-Jones.

Most people think that the HOUSES OF PARLIAMENT, THE PALACE OF WESTMINSTER, is an ancient building because

DR. DAVID MARTYN LLOYD-JONES (1899–1981) was a distinguished Welsh physician who became a Presbyterian minister in 1929. He was one of the great 20th-century preachers. His popular biblical expositions include *Studies in the Sermon on the Mount* (1959–60) and his multivolume *Lectures on Romans* (1955–68). His lectures on Puritan theology helped revitalize British and American evangelicalism by encouraging a revival of evangelical scholarship allied to pastoral concerns.

of its ornate Gothic appearance. In fact, the original Palace of Westminster was built by Edward the Confessor and was the London home of English kings for five centuries. Its role changed in the 16th century when Henry VIII moved his court to Whitehall. Following Henry VIII's death, the lower chamber of the British Parliament, the House of Commons, moved into St. Stephen's Chapel in the palace. This led to a slow transformation during which the Palace of Westminster became the Houses of Parliament. Although it survived the Great Fire of London in 1666, the old palace was destroyed in a fire in 1834 and rebuilt in the popular neo-Gothic style by the architect Sir Charles Barry (1795–1860). His assistant A. W. N. Pugin (1812–52) took charge of the interior, which contains over a thousand offices.

Visiting the Houses of Parliament is not easy. The best way is to write well in advance to a local member of Parliament or the House of Lords and ask if he or she will assist you. Otherwise public tours are heavily restricted and there are always very long lines. An interesting sight inside Parliament is the common hallway between the House of Commons and the House of Lords. On the insistence of Prince Albert, Queen Victoria's able husband, this hallway was decorated with murals depicting the Pilgrim fathers and other scenes from Christian history to remind legislators that the freedom of religion is the root from which our liberties have grown.

Westminster Hall is the oldest surviving part of the old palace. It has a wonderful hammer-beam roof with carved flying angels. The hall was built by William Rufus between 1097 and 1099 and given its roof by Richard I in 1395. The House of Commons was destroyed during World War II but rebuilt to its original design. It is the debating chamber of British members of Parliament elected from local constituencies to represent the people. The House of Lords was originally a hereditary chamber of the great lords of England. Gradually, throughout the 20th century, its powers were reduced, and "life peers" were introduced. These were people who were given the title *lord* for their own lifetime on the basis of some public service. Eventually, in 1999, the rights of hereditary lords as legislators were totally abolished, making the upper house a non-elected yet representative chamber consisting of people nominated to office by the reigning government in collaboration with all political parties and various pressure groups.

Outside of Parliament is a statue of the great British Christian legislator, the Lord Protector, Oliver Cromwell (1599–1658). Following the restoration of the monarchy in 1660, Cromwell's body was disinterred and his head stuck on a pike on the roof of Westminster Palace. It remained there for 20 years until the Glorious Revolution of 1689, when Charles II (1630–85) was forced to flee England after the Dutch Protestant King William of Orange (1650–1702) came to free England from his tyrannical rule. Only then was Cromwell reburied. Royalist propagandists like Lord Clarendon (1609–74) in the 17th century and Lord Macaulay (1800–1859) in the 19th century have done incalculable harm to the reputation of Cromwell and his Puritan followers, to such an extent that today the word "Puritan" is synonymous with killjoy. However, modern historians such as Christopher Hill have shown that in fact Cromwell's rule was relatively humane and that under Puritan rule not only were several new universities begun, but also primary schools were established for all children in England. These and other progressive acts which made England one of the most modern societies of the 17th century were reversed after the Restoration, and the Puritans were maligned during a wave of vicious persecution by the ruling class. Today, Cromwell is rightly recognized as one of the forerunners of Parliamentary democracy and civil liberty in Britain. He is also lauded as the person who allowed Jews to return to Britain in 1656, almost 400 years after they had been expelled by King Edward I in 1290.

Opposite Parliament there is also a statue erected in honor of the great Victorian conservative prime minister and social reformer Benjamin Disraeli (1804–81). A converted Jew, Disraeli was a devout Anglican who maintained a strong interest in biblical prophecy and Jewish issues. On his initiative, the British government gained control of the Suez Canal and eventually most of Egypt. Some people believe that he did this with an eye to eventually bringing Palestine under British control and hastening the creation of the State of Israel.

THE TATE GALLERY, Millbank, SW1, was opened in 1897 on the site of the former Millbank prison after a donation of £80,000 was provided by Sir Henry Tate (1819–99), who invented the sugar cube. Tate also provided a rich collection of artwork, as did the Duveen family and Sir Hugh Lane. In 1923, Samuel Courtauld financed the acquisition of numerous works by French painters. Built in the neoclassical style, the Tate was extended in 1979, but even today it can only display about one twelfth of all of its holdings at any one time. The gallery displays works by numerous artists including John Constable (1776–1837), Joseph Turner (1775–1851), Thomas Gainsborough (1727–88), William Hogarth (1697–1764), and William Blake (1757–1827). It also has some excellent paintings by Miro (1893–1983), Picasso (1881–1973), Matisse (1869–1954), and numerous other modern artists. Anyone wanting to see the development of modern thought and the ways in which artists reflect their times can do no better than visit the Tate.

TEMPLE OF MITHRAS, Queen Victoria St., E4, was discovered in 1954 during post-war rebuilding. It provides a rare example of Roman religious life and the practices of a cult that once rivaled Christianity.

ALL SOUL'S, Langham Place, W1, was for years the center of English evangelicalism in the Anglican church. The famous Bible expositor and preacher John Stott (1921–) ministered here from 1945–75. Almost singlehandedly, Stott kept evangelical religion alive in the capital and did much to revive evangelical scholarship in both Britain and North America.

ST. GEORGE, St. George St., Hanover Square, Mayfair, W1, was erected between 1721 and 1725 as a result of the 1711 Churches Act, which required the building of 50 new churches in London. It is built in the neoclassical style that later became popular among English nonconformists and American evangelicals. The east window contains some fine Flemish stained glass by the 16th-century artist Arnold of Nijmegen. George Frederick Handel was a parishioner here from 1724 to 1759 and advised on the installation of the church's organ. Percey Bysshe Shelley (1792–1822), Benjamin Disraeli (1804–81), Theodore Roosevelt (1858–1919), the novelist John Buchan (1875–1940), who became Lord Tweedsmuir and the governor general of Canada, and a host of other famous people were all married here.

ALL SAINTS, Margaret St., Marylebone, W1, is a three-bayed church built between 1850 and 1859 as part of the Tractarian, or High Church, movement's effort to evangelize London. Not particularly interesting as a building, the church has a strong musical tradition. It also hosts the evangelical think tank, the London Institute for Christian Studies, established by John Stott in 1970 largely as a result of prodding by Alan and Elaine Storkey. The Institute has produced some significant scholarly monographs on important issues usually neglected by Christian writers.

HANDEL'S HOUSE, Brook St., Mayfair, W1, is where *The Messiah* was written by George Frederick Handel (1685–1759), the great German composer who made England his home. It has recently been opened as a museum devoted to the composer's life and work.

THE WALLACE COLLECTION, Manchester Square, W1, is a little-known treasure tucked away in what was once the London mansion belonging to Sir Richard Wallace (1818–1870), the illegitimate son of the fourth marquess of Hertford (1800–1870). His widow bequeathed the collection to the nation in 1900. It houses one of the richest art collections in Britain in a remarkably compact space. The collection is particularly famous for its 18th-century French art that was originally collected by the fourth marquess of Hertford, who spent most of her life living in Paris. The art gives some unique insights into life in pre-Revolutionary France and was a favorite of Francis Schaeffer.

LONDON'S SEPHARDIC SYNAGOGUE, Lauderdale Rd., Maida Vale, W9, is a local landmark with a huge Arabesque dome and a very traditional appearance. Many of the worshipers are conservative, and some of them still wear formal top hats when attending services.

THE SPANISH AND PORTUGUESE SYNAGOGUE, 2 Ashworth Rd., W9, is where Benjamin Disraeli, who became a famous Victorian prime minister and favorite of Queen Victoria, was circumcised as a baby shortly before his father converted to Christianity after a dispute with the synagogue's leaders. Apart from his political career, Disraeli was a highly successful novelist who, although a conservative, exposed the plight of the poor and fought for social reform.

SALVATION ARMY MUSEUM, King's Cross, WC1, commemorates the work of that great agency known worldwide for its social concern and good works. The Salvation Army was founded in 1861 by William Booth (1829–1912). A GENERAL WILLIAM BOOTH MONUMENT can be seen on Mile End Rd., E1.

A small but fine JEWISH MUSEUM is located in Woburn House, Upper Woburn Place WC1. It contains ritual objects dating back to the Norman conquest and a Latin charter from the 13th century giving Jews the right to live in England. Its prize possession, though, is a 16th-century Holy Ark believed to be of Venetian origin. There is a sketch by Rembrandt van Rijn of Manasseh Ben Israel (1604–67), who was highly regarded by Oliver Cromwell, who appreciated Ben Israel's biblical scholarship and passionate belief in the end times.

L

THE SALVATION ARMY was an evangelical Christian movement founded in 19th-century Britain by William "General" Booth to work among the poor and oppressed. From the beginning, the evangelistic efforts of the Army concentrated on practical steps to improve the lot of the poor as well as proclaiming the gospel to them. A strong but nonmoralistic stance was taken against alcohol and other forms of drug abuse. The Army provided homes for the homeless and met other chronic social needs. Although a numerically small group, the Army has gained great respect throughout the world.

WILLIAM BOOTH (1829–1912) was a native of Nottingham and of Jewish parentage. He converted to Methodism in 1844 to become a Revivalist preacher. In 1861 he left the Methodists and with the help of his wife, who was also a powerful preacher, established his own Christian mission,which became the Salvation Army. His book *In Darkest England and the Way Out* (1890) drew a vivid picture of social evil and decay.

THE BRITISH MUSEUM, Great Russell St., WC1. The old Royal Library and a priceless collection of medieval manuscripts donated to the nation by Sir Robert Cotton (1571–1631) provided the basis for the British Museum. But it wasn't until the heirs of the wealthy London physician Sir Hans Sloane (1660–1753) added his valuable collection of art objects, antiquities, coins, and fossils that Parliament decided to remove the earlier donations from the vaults of the Palace of Westminster and establish a national exhibition known as the British Museum. This decision led to the purchase of Montague House in 1759 on the proceeds of public lotteries that allowed for the acquisition of further collections from wealthy benefactors. The early exhibitions were totally unmarked public displays, leading the social critic William Cobbett (1763–1835) to dub the collection "the old curiosity shop." Eventually, in the 1850s Richard Westmacott was commissioned to build a new and more fitting building to house these national treasures. The result was the present British Museum, opened in 1857. The famous British Museum reading room is where Karl Marx (1818–83) wrote *Das Kapital* (3 Vols. 1867, 1885, and 1895) and other works that had such a profound and destructive influence in the 20th century. Today the British Library is no longer housed in the museum, but its famous reading room remains as an exhibit. The museum was the world's first public museum and is considered by many experts to contain the largest and best collection of ancient treasures on earth.

Of greatest interest to Christians is the section of the museum dealing with the Ancient Near East. For many years it was led by Sir Donald Wiseman, a well-known evangelical Christian. Here one finds numerous fascinating items that vividly illustrate the biblical story, including treasures from ancient Babylonia, Egypt, and, of course, Palestine itself. Most important of all is the precious Rosetta Stone, which is a large fragment of black marble containing inscriptions in three languages, including Greek and Egyptian hieroglyphs. It was discovered in 1799, enabling the French Egyptologist Jean-Francois Champollion (1790–1832) to decipher the hieroglyphs on the basis of the Greek inscription. His monumental effort unlocked the key to the hieroglyphs, enabling archaeologists to slowly decipher other ancient Egyptian inscriptions and eventually to read Egyptian documents.

The museum also houses the original copy of the Balfour Declaration, which the British Foreign Secretary Arthur Balfour (1848–1930) signed in 1917, leading to the establishment of a national homeland for Jews in Palestine. Lord Balfour was converted to a Zionist viewpoint by contact with the Jewish scholar and famous chemist, Dr. Chaim Weizmann

(1874–1952), who later became the leader of the World Jewish Federation.

The other great pride of the museum is the Elgin Marbles. These were the marble statues which once decorated the Parthenon in Athens. The Elgin Marbles capture the ethos of ancient paganism with its artistic sophistication and dynamism. Thus these marbles enable visitors to appreciate the world in which St. Paul preached the gospel and the importance of his work in Athens.

Carved around 447 B.C., the Elgin Marbles were slowly being destroyed and used to make building material when Lord Elgin (1766–1841), the British ambassador to the Turkish Court in Constantinople, bought them in 1816 and arranged their transportation to London. In recent years, the Greek government has demanded their return to Athens. But the British government has steadfastly refused to give them up, saying that they were legitimately acquired and paid for by Lord Elgin, who saved them from destruction. The Greeks counter by saying that while they appreciate Lord Elgin's efforts, they had no choice in the matter because at the time Greece was ruled by Turkish invaders who were systematically destroying Greek culture. Therefore, they argue that they have a moral right to the return of the Marbles to Athens.

The Egyptian rooms contain rare figures of Rameses I and Rameses II as well as a large mummy collection. In the Mesopotamian section one finds a section devoted to Ur of the Chaldees, from which Abraham set out on his journey to the Promised Land. The finds from Ur are of particular importance to biblical scholars because during most of the 19th century many archaeologists argued that Ur was a fictional city found only in the Bible. This led liberal theologians to revise their views of the Bible and argue that if Ur never existed, neither did Abraham. Unfortunately, many of these theories, based on faulty archaeological evidence, persist to this day, even though the evidence has shown them to be wrong.

The museum also contains a host of rich Greek and Roman finds, Celtic and old Germanic treasures, materials from China, India, and the Islamic world, as well as some excellent exhibits relating to the Americas. Although many of these exhibits have no direct Christian reference, they are invaluable for anyone wishing to understand non-Christian cultures.

SOMERSET HOUSE AND THE CAUTAULD GALLERIES, Woburn Square, WC1, was built between 1776 and 1786 to the design of Sir William Chambers, a founder of the Royal Society. The society was probably the most important scientific organization of the 18th century and was founded by a group of "natural philosophers," most of whom were strongly influenced by Puritanism. It is best known as the place where the General Registry of Births and Deaths was housed until 1973. Today it houses both an Inland Revenue Office and Britain's premier art school, the Cautauld Institute. The University of London's private art collection may be seen in the Cautauld Galleries, which displays works by Michelangelo (1475–1564), Rubens (1577–1640), and numerous modern painters. In particular the Fry Collection, donated by the artist Roger Fry (1866–1934), contains some outstanding examples of modern British art.

ST. MARTIN'S IN THE FIELD, St. Martin's Lane, Trafalgar Square, WC2, was built between 1721 and 1726 by the architect James Gibbs (1682–1754). His neoclassical design caught the imagination of the age and was copied by numerous architects in Britain and North America. The exterior, facing Trafalgar Square, has the appearance of a Greek temple, although it actually functions as a royal church, being the parish church of both St. James' Court and Buckingham Palace. Although the British Royal Family are not usually known for their piety, when St. Martin's was first built, King George I (1660–1727) served on the parish council as a churchwarden. Queen Elizabeth II (1926–) appears to take her faith very seriously, if her annual Christmas messages are any indication of her attitude towards religion. Elizabeth has no hesitation in talking about Jesus Christ and the importance of Christian-ity, even if other members of her family appear less enthusiastic.

Inside the church, the temple appearance is continued with gilded Corinthian columns. The wide nave and decorated ceiling with its gilded plasterwork give the visitor a sense of grandeur and space usually associated with the Gothic style. In the west gallery is the church's magnificent organ. Below in the northwest corner is a decorated font from 1698 and a painting of *St. Martin and the Beggar* by Francesco Soliona (17th century). The Royal Coat of Arms stands above the sanctuary arch.

St. Martin's is famous for its choir, excellent church music, a daily soup kitchen, and an extensive social work program among London's street people. In the 1920s and 1930s the Rev. David Sheppard was the minister here. He attempted to organize a pacifist movement around what was called the "peace pledge," which was against future wars. The movement floundered in the late 1930s. The warlike first duke of Marlborough (1650–1722), an ancestor of Sir Winston Churchill, is buried here. Nell Gwynne (1650–87), the famous mistress of Charles II, is also buried here. King Charles II (1630–85) was baptized on this site.

Nearby is the statue of nurse Edith Cavell (1865–1915), an English nurse who became the matron of the Medical Institute in Brussels. During World War I, she ran an underground railway that helped over 200 British prisoners of war escape from captivity to the safety of the Netherlands. Her activities were uncovered, and after a trial she was executed by the German army on the grounds that she was a spy. The British claimed that she merely helped wounded prisoners. She is remembered for her statement made just before her execution, "Patriotism is not enough," which in light of the fact that she was executed because she was a patriot is rather odd. Nevertheless, it made great propaganda in America, where Cavell was portrayed as a Belgian nurse who simply helped wounded British prisoners. This propaganda ultimately contributed to America entering World War I on the British side.

THE QUAKER MEETING HOUSE, St. Martin's Lane, WC2, is one of the oldest Quaker churches in the world. Its plain appearance and simple design stand in sharp contrast to nearby Anglican churches.

ST. CLEMENT DANES, the Strand, WC2, was originally built between 1680 and 1682 by Sir Christopher Wren (1632–1723). It was faithfully restored between 1955 and 1958 after being extensively damaged during the Blitz. Originally a parish church, the roots of which go back to preconquest, Danish London, it is now the main chapel of the Royal Air Force. Outside the church is a fine statue of the great 19th-century Christian statesman William Ewert Gladstone (1809–98).

In the east aisle is a statue of Dr. Samuel Johnson (1709–84), who lived in nearby Gough Square when in London and worshiped here. Hundreds of RAF squadron badges are set into the floor, books of remembrance, commemorating the dead of two World Wars, are displayed in glass cabinets along the aisles, and RAF flags hang from the galleries. In many ways the church is a nostalgic monument to national glory and a shrine for an ancestral warrior cult based on an essentially pagan civil religion overlaid by a veneer of Christianity.

ST. MARY OVERIE, SOUTHWARK CATHEDRAL, Broughton High St., SE1, was built in the 13th century as an Augustinian priory church. The choir dates from 1207 and is arguably the oldest example of Gothic architecture in London. The stone altar screen is a 16th-century creation. William Shakespeare's brother, Edmund, who was an actor, was buried here in 1607, as was Lancelot Andrewes in 1626. It is claimed that Shakespeare himself attended services in the church while working at the nearby Globe theater. The Harvard Chapel commemorates John Harvard (1607–38), after whom Harvard University is named. In the 19th century its east chapel was demolished to clear the area for the new London Bridge. A railway was also built dangerously close to its tower. Then, in 1905, it was elevated to the status of a cathedral and became the seat of a bishop.

METROPOLITAN TABERNACLE, Elephant and Castle, Southwark, is world famous as an imposing neoclassical church built between 1659 and 1861. It was built to seat 5000 people to accommodate the crowds who came to see the great Baptist preacher Charles Haddon Spurgeon (1834–92). The original building was destroyed in a fire in 1898 but rebuilt according to the original plans. It was destroyed again by German bombers during World War II. It was then rebuilt for a third time in the 1950s, on a smaller scale. Today it seats a mere 1,750 worshipers. Notice the way that the interior of the church draws the worshiper's attention to the pulpit and, of course, the preaching of the Word. This style, which is common in North America, is unusual in Britain, where most pulpits are off to one side, making the communion table or altar the focus of attention.

THE IMPERIAL WAR MUSEUM, Lambeth Rd., SE1, was opened during World War I in 1917 as a propaganda exercise. Although not usually thought of as a military nation, the British take great pride in their military exploits and almost alone among modern Europeans continue to present the image of a warrior race to themselves. No doubt much of this has to do with the heritage of the British Empire, which just over a century ago directly or indirectly controlled the destinies of almost two thirds of the world's population. Here you will see a moving recreation of the London Blitz and the horrors of trench warfare during World War I. Although the museum does not glorify war, it does create a sense of pride in British endurance and determination to win at all costs. This isn't a Christian heritage site by any means. But it is worth a visit because it is impossible to understand Britain and the British heritage worldwide, including many Third World reactions against missionaries and colonialism, without recognizing the military side of the British character.

THE MAYFLOWER INN, Rotherhite St., SE16, in Southwark is the place from which the Pilgrim fathers sailed to America. There is a plaque and small museum.

CENATAPH, Whitehall, SW1, is an empty tomb completely devoid of Christian or other religious symbolism. Nevertheless, the fact that it is empty is intended to symbolize the resurrection of each individual and hope for life after death. This neoclassical monument is the focus of Britain's intensely patriotic Remembrance Day ceremonies, which take place here on November 11. This date was the Armistice Day that brought to an end World War I, but Remembrance Day is intended to commemorate the dead in both World Wars.

ST. MARGARET, Parliament Square, SW1, was built between 1486 and 1523 on the site of an earlier parish church associated with a local monastery. This is the official parish church of Britain's House of Commons, making it one of the most fashionable churches in London. Today the inside has a neo-Gothic appearance due to 19th-century renovations by Gilbert Scott. A copy of Titian's (1487–1576) *Supper at Emmaus* graces the altar. The east window contains 16th-century Dutch stained glass that was given to Henry VII (1457–1509) by King Ferdinand of Spain to commemorate the marriage of his daughter Catherine of Aragon (1485–1536) to Prince Henry, later Henry VIII (1491–1547). William Caxton (1422–91), who set up England's first printing press, is buried here. It was his work that helped spread evangelical beliefs in the early 16th century and made the English Reformation possible. The poet John Milton (1608–74) was among the church's many famous congregants.

HOLY TRINITY, Brompton Rd., Brompton, SW7, is London's leading Anglican charismatic church. It developed the highly successful "Alpha Course," a curriculum which has been used worldwide to evangelize modern skeptics. The church building itself is a good example of the 19th-century neo-Gothic style.

THE LONDON ORATORY CHURCH OF THE IMMACULATE HEART OF MARY, Brompton Rd., SW7, is the second largest Roman Catholic Church in London. Its unique Italian Renaissance style is supplemented by a rich array of internal decorations, including many high-quality paintings. The statues of the 12 apostles were carved in Italy by Giuseppe Mazzuoli (1644–1725) between 1678 and 1694 for Siena

Cathedral. The altar of the Lady Chapel was rescued from destruction in an Italian church and brought to London; it dates from 1693. The Oratory itself is a living witness to the 19th-century Roman Catholic revival and evangelistic mission to England. It is staffed by a team of priests belonging to the Congregation of the Oratory, a Catholic order dedicated to urban mission founded by Philip Neri (1515–95) in the 16th century.

ST. GILES, Church St., Camberwell, was built between 1842 and 1844 and is one of Sir Gilbert Scott's neo-Gothic masterpieces and the crowning achievement of his early career. It replaced an older medieval church, which was destroyed in a fire in 1841. Although much of its 19th-century stained glass was destroyed during World War II, the stained glass in the east window of the Lady Chapel dates from 1844 and is the pride of the church. It was designed by John Ruskin (1819–1911) and his partner Edmund Oldfield in a 13th-century French style. The magnificent icon in the south transept was given to the church by a Greek Orthodox congregation, which worshiped here for a number of years before acquiring its own building. John Wesley's wife, Mary (d. 1781), and his great-nephew Samuel Sabastian Wesley (1766–1837), who was a well-known organist here from 1829–32, are buried in the graveyard.

The great anti-slavery crusader and evangelical reformer Sir Thomas

Foxwell Buxton (1786–1845) is commemorated in the BUXTON MEMORIAL FOUNTAIN, found in Victoria Tower Gardens, SW1.

FARADAY MUSEUM, Albermarle St., W1, is dedicated to the life and work of the great Christian scientist Michael Faraday (1791–1867), who revolutionized the study of chemistry. Unfortunately, very little is said about Faraday's deep personal commitment to Christ, which underlies all his work.

In the Victoria Embankment Gardens, WC2, you can see the WILLIAM TYNDALE MONUMENT, which commemorates the great English Bible translator and martyr Tyndale (1494–1536). He was tortured and then burnt at the stake in Antwerp for his efforts to bring the message of the Bible to ordinary Englishmen and women. Nearby is a monument to JOHN STUART MILL (1806–73), who was a great 19th-century social reformer and critic of evangelical Christianity.

CARLYLE'S HOUSE, Cheyne Row, SW3, provides visitors with an insight into the life and work of the Scottish essayist and leader of the British Romantic movement Thomas Carlyle (1795–1881), who moved here with his wife in 1834. The house itself was built in 1708 as a Georgian-style townhouse. Although Carlyle did much to introduce German Romanticism with its neoplatonic pantheism to Britain, he must also be remembered as the biographer of Oliver Cromwell. His editing of Cromwell's literary remains did much to rehabilitate Cromwell in English thought. The house provides fascinating insights into the thought of this complex man who helped shape the Victorian age and modern religious thought.

BADEN-POWELL MUSEUM, Queen's Gate, SW7. There is no doubt that Baden-Powell (1857–1941), the founder of the Boy Scouts, was a strange character. Nevertheless, his *Scouting for Boys* (1906) and the movement he created has, in its original form, strong Christian principles and an emphasis on service to God before all others. As such it differs markedly from similar move-

---

JOHN STUART MILL (1806–73) was a British philosopher, essayist, and political activist whose work still indirectly influences many academic disciplines, including sociology, political science, economics, and the philosophy of science. His best-known works are probably *On Liberty* (1859), *Utilitarianism* (1863), and *The Subjection of Women* (1871), while his neglected *System of Logic* (1843) has recently received renewed attention. Although he wrote little about religion, his posthumous *Three Essays on Religion* (1874) revealed a cautious but skeptical interest.

ments on the European continent that were clearly pantheistic in tone, such as the German *Wandervogel*. This museum is also well worth a visit by anyone interested in youth work.

HOLY TRINITY, North Side, Clapham Common, Clapham, was built between 1774 and 1776 to replace the older parish church of St. Mary. It was severely damaged during World War II and restored in the 1950s. The design is a simple form of the neoclassical style similar to many New England churches. Inside there is a gallery supported by low fluted Tuscan columns. The original box pews had their doors removed and were reduced in size in 1875 when the church's famous three-decker pulpit was moved from its central position to the north side of the church. From this pulpit John Venn (1759–1813) ministered to the famous "Clapham Sect" led by William Wilberforce (1759–1833). This influential group of evangelical reformers also included Zachary Macaulay (1768–1838) and John's brother, Henry Venn (1796–1873), the great missionary theorist and organizer. They fought for the abolition of slavery and various other forms of social justice. They are commemorated in the east window installed in 1950 and designed by the artist Lawrence Lee. A tablet naming all the members of the movement hangs on the south wall outside the church. Inside the church is a monument to John Venn, who was the church's rector from 1792–1813.

ST. ALFEGE, Church St., Greenwich, is named after the archbishop of Canterbury who was martyred on the site of the church by Viking invaders on April 19, 1012. He was later buried at Canterbury Cathedral. The present church was built between 1712 and 1718 in the new Baroque style and restored in the 1950s after it was bombed in 1941. The great Elizabethan composer of Christian music, Thomas Tallis (d. 1585), was the organist here in the 16th century, and the organ is said to be partially constructed from the one he used. Tallis is buried in the church and is depicted in the west window at the end of the south aisle. John Morton, a pre-Reformation archbishop of Canterbury, was rector here in the 15th century. Henry VIII was baptized here, as was General Gordon, the strange 19th-century evangelical adventurer. General Wolfe (1727–59), who conquered Quebec and seized the province from the French, is buried here.

ST. MARY, St. Marychurch St., Rotherhithe, is a neoclassical building rebuilt in 1714 and restored in 1876. The captain of the Pilgrim *Mayflower,* Christopher Jones, was buried here in 1624. He is commemorated by a plaque.

CHRIST CHURCH, Commercial St., and Fournier St., Spitalfields, was the center of settlement for French Huguenot refugees who fled to England after the Edict of Nantes was revoked in 1685. Designed by a student of Sir

L

Christopher Wren, the church is in the English Baroque style, with an Italianate portico and octagonal tower. In the adjacent graveyard are many tombstones of French Huguenot families. The church became a Methodist chapel in the 19th century and is today a mosque.

THE JOHN HENRY MEMORIAL stands on the river bank on the south side of the Thames. It is rather hard to find, but worth the trouble if you are really interested in history. John Henry was executed by Queen Elizabeth I for the crime of "voluntarism," the belief that everyone ought to be free to choose their own religion and practice it as they see fit. It is on this principle that the churches of the United States were built.

DICKENS'S HOUSE, Doughty St., WC1, is a fascinating museum devoted to the life and work of Charles Dickens (1812–70), whose novels stirred the conscience of Victorian England, leading to numerous social reforms that were strongly supported by evangelical Christians. Dickens is also largely responsible for the modern celebration of Christmas as a time of goodwill and helped stem a secularizing trend that was turning Christmas day into just another workday. Although not known for his overt piety, Dickens was a deeply religious man strongly influenced by the evangelical reformism of the Clapham Sect.

HOGARTH'S HOUSE, Hogarth Lane, W4. If Charles Dickens stirred the conscience of 19th-century Britain, the artist William Hogarth (1697–1764) did the same for the 17th century. His work vividly depicted and satirized the corruption of his day, making his work, which is informed by a sense of biblical justice, the source of the modern newspaper cartoon.

SCIENCE MUSEUM, Exhibition Rd., SW7. Although it is not very clearly mentioned, modern science arose in a distinctly Christian culture. Therefore, visitors to this museum need to be aware that almost without exception every scientist mentioned before the 19th century, such as Robert Boyle, and many in the 19th century, like Michael Faraday, were Christians. The museum itself is fascinating and gives numerous vivid insights into the creation of the modern world.

WILLIAM MORRIS GALLERY, Forest Rd., East 17. Popular for his flowery, natural, and romanticized designs, William Morris (1834–96) effected a small revolution in British art and popular philosophy that continues today through the environmental movement and various artistic expressions. Anyone wishing to understand 19th-century art and philosophy needs to take a close look at his work and ponder its theological significance.

BUCKINGHAM PALACE, the official London residence of the British monarch, was only opened to the public on a very limited scale in 1993 to help pay for repairs to Windsor Castle after the disastrous fire of 1992. Created for the duke of Buckingham in 1703, the palace was transferred to George III, who bought it as a wedding present for his wife in 1761. George IV commissioned extensive renovations that greatly increased its size, making it his principal residence in 1819. The guided tour includes visits to the throne room, drawing rooms, dining room, and picture gallery. All this is very interesting for history buffs, but has very little religious importance unless as a reminder of how attached the British are to the monarchy, which at times takes on a semisacred significance in British life. Although the present queen is outspoken in her Christian faith and takes her role as head of the Church of England very seriously, many members of the royal family appear more attracted to other religions.

SOHO. This café and nightclub area is of religious interest only because it was here that many Huguenots settled after the revocation of the Edict of Nantes in 1685. Today new waves of immigrants still settle in Soho, as can be seen from the many ethnic restaurants and shops.

VICTORIA AND ALBERT MUSEUM, Cromwell Rd. SW7, was opened in 1851 as an initiative of Prince Albert (1819–61), Queen Victoria's consort, in an attempt to foster a pride in manufacturing and scientific research among the British upper classes and inspire the imagination of students and workers.

The original concept was soon lost, and today the museum is famous for its collection of Raphael (1483–1520) cartoons that were drawn as designs for tapestries intended to grace the Sistine Chapel in Rome. There is also an excellent collection of Indian art, which is rich in religious materials, a fine Islamic gallery, and equally good Chinese and Japanese collections, which are invaluable for anyone wishing to understand these cultures and the role of religion in them. Medieval Christian art is also very well represented, as is Renaissance and more recent British art from the 18th to 20th centuries. John Constable's (1776–1837) famous painting of Salisbury Cathedral is on display here, as are various Rodin (1840–1917) statues.

SHERLOCK HOLMES MUSEUM, 239 Baker St., NW1, is devoted to the fictitious figure of the great Victorian detective Sherlock Holmes and his creator Sir Arthur Conan-Doyle (1859–1930). From a Christian viewpoint, the importance of the museum is the light it sheds on Conan-Doyle's life. Like many other Victorian writers, he was fascinated by spiritualism and the occult and in many ways participated in the movements that gave birth to the modern esoteric revival.

LONDON MOSQUE AND ISLAMIC CENTER, 14 Park Rd., NW8, testifies to the growing influence of Islam in British life. In addition to over a million Muslim immigrants, there are now over 100,000 British converts to Islam. It is a fine building that gives visitors a rare insight into Islam.

NATIONAL GALLERY, Trafalgar Square, WC2. Oliver Cromwell attempted to establish a national picture gallery in the 17th century, but his ideas were scrapped after the Restoration in 1660. Later, the British Parliament debated the need for a national gallery for almost a century, from the 1720s to 1820s, before finally deciding to create this national treasure in 1824 with the purchase of 38 paintings from the banker John Julius Angerstein (1735–1823), including works by Rembrandt, van Dyck, and Raphael. The new gallery, however, wasn't opened until 1838. William Wilkes designed the gallery in a bold neoclassical style. The gallery owns over 2000 priceless paintings and is one of the best public collections in the world.

The gallery is superbly equipped to help visitors. Free audio tours, using small tape recorders, are available upon request. There are also regular free guided tours. The micro-gallery in the newly added Sainsbury Wing allows you to preview the collection on computer and even print out your own personalized tour showing you where to go to see the pictures that interest you.

The Salisbury Wing houses one of the gallery's most precious items, the Leonardo da Vinci (1452–1519) cartoon of *The Virgin and Child with St. Anne and John the Baptist,* which is protected by its own dimly lit room and a bullet-proof

glass cabinet. His *Virgin of the Rocks* can be seen outside the cartoon room. You can also see the world-famous *Wilton Diptych*, one of the earliest works of English art. A portable altarpiece, it was painted for King Richard II by an unknown artist. In contrast to this purely religious work of medieval spirituality, Paolo Uccello's (1396–1475) *Battle of San Romano* can be seen in room 55. It illustrates the growing fascination with heroic themes that led to the Renaissance, and its style shows a growing awareness of perspective. The Renaissance's preoccupation with classical mythology is well illustrated in room 58, where you can see paintings like Botticelli's (1455–1510) *Venus.* Jan van Eyck's (d. 1441) *The Marriage of Arnolfini* is in room 56 with other Dutch works. Here again we see a transition from religious and mythic scenes to the everyday and secular pursuits.

The high Renaissance is well represented by numerous works housed in the west wing. Here you can see Paolo Veronese's (1528–88) moving *The Family of Darius Before Alexander,* which commemorates the conquest of Persia by Alexander the Great. Raphael's (1483–1520) *Pope Julius II* reminds us of the pomp and ceremony, power and politics, of the age leading up to the Reformation. The north wing contains a large collection of Dutch works, including ones by people like Vermeer and Rembrandt van Rijn (1606–69). One Rembrandt self-portrait, found in room

27, was painted when the artist was 33. Another shows him at 63. The contrast between them and the honesty with which Rembrandt portrayed himself is remarkable. Christian art historian Hans Rookmaaker argued in his book *Modern Art and the Death of a Culture* that paintings like these represent the flowering of truly Christian art. Have a good look and see if you can understand why he thought this and ask yourself whether you agree. In this wing you can also see works by Rubens and various other painters influenced by Spanish masters about whom Rookmaaker was not so enthusiastic. In room 30 you can see van Dyck's (1599–1641) famous portrait of *King Charles I.*

The gallery's east wing contains paintings from the 18th to 20th centuries and contains many of the most famous works of English painters in the 18th and 19th centuries, such as Joseph Turner's (1775–1851) *Fighting Temeraire,* which depicts one of the major warships from the Battle of Trafalgar being towed away to the scrapyard and in an uncanny way reminds us of the fleeting nature of worldly glory. William Hogarth's (1697–1764) satire *The Loveless Marriage* can be seen in room 35. Many of these pictures depict the lives of the ruling elite in England and on the continent during the periods we now call the Enlightenment and the Industrial Revolution. They provide vivid insights into the society that gave birth to both Methodism and the arrogant rationalism

that led to our present post-Christian age. Finally, this wing has a fine collection of van Goghs and various Impressionists works including paintings by Manet (1832–83) and Renoir (1841–1919).

Tucked away behind the main National Gallery is the smaller NATIONAL PORTRAIT GALLERY that visitors often miss. Here you will find a treasure trove of portraits, many of which depict great Christian leaders such as Oliver Cromwell and John and Charles Wesley. Royal portraits include Henry VIII, the ill-fated Charles I on his way to execution, and the decadent Charles II in a room full of his mistresses. Literary figures such as the pious Brontë sisters and great engineers like Isambard Kingdom Brunel and various scientists and soldiers are also portrayed here.

FREUD MUSEUM, 25 Maresfield Gardens, Hamstead, NW3, is devoted to the life of the psychologist Sigmund Freud (1856–1939). Although often portrayed as a pure scientist in search of truth, Freud was fiercely anti-Christian and clearly sought to undermine Christian faith. Anyone hoping to understand the modern anti-Christian movement should visit this museum for the insights it gives into Freud's life and work.

CROMWELL HOUSE, 104 Hilgate Hill, N6, is the London home of the great Puritan leader and statesman, Oliver Cromwell (1599–1658). It was built in 1637. A devout Christian who took the Bible very seriously, Cromwell was convinced that the Jews had a place in God's plan for the world. After he read the works of Manasseh Ben Israel (1604–56), he appears to have invited him to England. Ben Israel made a passionate plea for the readmission of Jews that was eventually published as *The Hope of Israel* (1650). When Cromwell was unable to convince a majority of his supporters that Jews ought to be welcomed back to England, he embarked on a compromise policy of unofficial settlement that gradually led to the reestablishment of the British Jewish community.

HIGHGATE CEMETERY, Swains Lane, N6, in what was once the village of Highgate on the outskirts of London, contains a variety of interesting tombstones and the graves of some very famous people. Buried here is the famous Victorian writer George Eliot, actually Marian Evans (1819–80), author of such classics as *Adam Bede* and *Middlemarch*. Eliot began life in an evangelical family but turned agnostic to become one of the most important critics of Christianity in Britain. She was responsible for the translation of both David Frederich Strauss's (1808–74) *Life of Jesus* (1835) and Ludwig Feuerbach's (1804–72) *The Essence of Christianity* (1840) into English, thus initiating in the English-speaking world both modern biblical criticism and the popularization of deprivation theories of

religion, which argue that only people who are in some way deprived turn to religion. Here too is the grave of Karl Marx (1818–83), who developed the work of Feuerbach and whose followers did so much to destroy Christianity and murder Christians in many lands.

NATIONAL MARITIME MUSEUM, Greenwich, is a unique museum devoted to the British navy that provides some vivid insights into the role of ships in transportation before the advent of aircraft. The museum documents the history of shipbuilding from Tudor times to the present and has exhibits dealing with naval warfare, pirates, various means of propulsion, as well as maritime archaeology. Although nothing is explicitly said about the 19th-century missionary movement, the exhibition helps visitors appreciate the courage of early modern missionaries who went overseas in what today seem very primitive ships.

HAMPTON COURT PALACE AND GARDENS, Richmond, KT12, were built between 1514 and 1529 by England's greatest medieval statesman and Roman Catholic primate, Cardinal Wolsey (1473–1530). The son of a tradesman, Wolsey raised himself to the highest office in the land to become its most powerful figure after the king. But his failure to secure a divorce for Henry VIII from Catherine of Aragon and his refusal to embrace Protestant doctrines, which would have made a divorce possible, led to his fall from power and early death.

Henry seized the palace after Wolsey's death to add it to a long list of properties appropriated by the monarchy as part of the English Reformation. The palace itself was redesigned by Sir Christopher Wren in the 17th century and is open to the public.

LONDON BIBLE COLLEGE (LBC), Green Lane, Northwood, Middlesex, HA6 2UW, is Britain's premier Bible college and a major theological seminary in the nonconformist tradition. In addition to residential and summer school courses, it offers a variety of courses by distance education. During the 1950s and 1960s LBC was one of the few evangelical academic institutions in Britain. Among its many well-known scholars was Donald Guthrie, whose introductions to the New Testament proved invaluable to thousands of students.

THE LONDON MUSEUM OF JEWISH LIFE is found in the Sternberg Center for Judaism, 89 East End Rd., N3. It testifies to the important role Jews have played in London society, including Prime Minister Benjamin Disraeli (1804–81), financier Nathan Rothschild (1777–1836) and his family, the poet Siegfried Sasson (1886–1967), and many others.

OAKHILL THEOLOGICAL COLLEGE, Chase Side, N14 4PS, is an evangelical Anglican theological college that has played a major role in the revival of evangelical religion in the Church of England. Among its best-known faculty members is the Christian sociologist Alan Storkey.

MANCHESTER

O riginally a Roman settlement, Manchester remained a village until the mid-18th century, when the development of trade with American cotton plantations led to rapid industrial growth and the building of some of England's worst slums. Several factors led to Manchester becoming the industrial capital of England. First, the building of the Bridgewater canal, which linked the cotton manufacturing plants with the coal mills of nearby Worsley and later Leigh. Second, the creation of Manchester-Liverpool railway, which was opened in 1830. And third, the construction of the Manchester ship canal in 1894. Today the canals are used for recreation, not trade, and the Manchester railway is an area of high unemployment and crime which is trying to reinvent itself after a devastating Irish Republican Army (IRA) bomb destroyed much of the city center in 1996. During the 19th century, Manchester was a center for Methodism and nonconformist churches with strong evangelical traditions. Today religious life in the city, particularly evangelical Christianity, is at an all-time low as cults and occult movements abound. It has the largest student population in the country and claims to be the gay capital of Britain.

The famous Peterloo Massacre took place in Manchester on August 16, 1819, when cavalry were unleashed on an unsuspecting crowd that had gathered to demand the repeal of the restrictive corn laws that limited free trade and kept prices high for farmers. Eleven people were killed in the attack and many others badly injured, sending shock waves throughout Britain. As the 19th century progressed, Manchester became the center of the free trade movement, with its city fathers strongly supporting modern capitalism. Friedrich Engels (1820–95), who worked in Manchester where his family owned cotton mills, reacted to this liberal capitalist ethos by embracing radical socialist doctrines. He worked closely with Karl

FRIEDRICH ENGELS (1820–95) was a German industrialist who became a patron, close friend, and collaborator to Karl Marx in founding Marxism. Engels contributed many ideas to the Marxist movement, including what was to become known as dialectical materialism. From 1842 he ran his family's factory in Manchester, England. While in Manchester he wrote *The Condition of the Working Class in England* (1845), supposedly based on his own experiences but actually written from outdated *Poor Law Reports*. This work is full of factual errors and deliberate attempts to exaggerate the true situation. As a militant atheist, he welcomed Darwin's theory of evolution as positive proof of his own antireligious views. Although condemning capitalist exploitation, Engels was actually a rapacious slum landlord. This little-known fact about Engels's life was revealed by the late Val Grieve of the law firm Crofton and Craven, which had acted for Engels and possessed letters from him demanding that they raise rents and otherwise exploit the tenants.

KARL MARX (1818–83) was a German Jewish philosopher. He was baptized as a child and appears to have been a Christian while at boarding school before rejecting all forms of religion as a university student. He became a newspaper editor and writer who is remembered as the founder of Marxism and modern Communism. After being expelled from Prussia for his revolutionary activities in 1849, he settled in England, where he did most of his writing. His most famous but little-read work is *Das Capital* (1867, 1885, and 1895, 3 vols.). Other writings include the slim but influential *Communist Manifesto* (1848).

Marx, who drew upon Engels's experience and used Manchester as a source for many of his examples of the evils of capitalism. In fact, there is no evidence that either Marx or Engels ever visited a slum dwelling or really knew members of the working class, whom they appear to have despised.

PLACES TO VISIT

MANCHESTER CATHEDRAL is built on the site of a monastic foundation established in 1421. It was elevated to the rank of cathedral in 1847 and contains an excellent choir screen that ranks among the best medieval wood carving in England. The misericords date from the late 15th century and are similar to those found in Beverly.

ST. MARY'S CHURCH, High St., Cheadle, was built in 1520 on the site of an earlier church going back at least to 1200. Fragments of an 11th-century preaching cross, discovered in 1874, can be seen inside the church. Although not very remarkable as historic churches go, this pleasant church is the home of one of the north of England's major evangelical congregations with a strong tradition of biblical preaching and evangelism. It is a spiritual oasis in an otherwise spiritually dead area.

JOHN RYLAND'S LIBRARY, 150 Deansgate, is housed in a superb neo-Gothic building donated to the city along with his collection of books and manuscripts by Enriqueta Ryland, the widow of John Ryland (d. 1888). On display are valuable Bibles and other precious manuscripts. Most important of all, the library houses the John Ryland's Fragment, which is the earliest known New Testament document. The fragment itself is a small scrap from the gospel of John dated at 120. During the 19th century, many German biblical critics argued that John's gospel was a very late creation and therefore unreliable. The Ryland's Fragment goes a long way to disproving such theories. The library also houses Britain's main collection of both Methodist and Plymouth Brethren books and manuscripts.

MUSEUM OF SCIENCE AND INDUSTRY, Lower Byrom St., is one of the best museums of industrial history in the world. In particular, it attempts to show the impact of industrial change on society. There is a working model of Robert Stephenson's (1803–59) steam engine, the *Planet*. The exhibits on gas works, electricity, and even sewers make this museum a must for anyone wishing to understand the great transition that took place at the end of the 18th century, which we now call the Industrial Revolution. It is this transition that more than anything else separates us from our ancestors as well as the world in which Jesus lived. Yet even today, few Christians understand the impact of industrialization or the challenges that the accompanying belief in modernity presents to Christian faith.

THE PUMPHOUSE PEOPLE'S MUSEUM, Bridge St., is devoted to working-class life in Manchester and vividly recaptures the ethos of 19th-century political radicalism

> **ANN LEE** (1736–84). Originally a Shaking Quaker, she left her husband in 1766 and assumed leadership of the local Shakers. Her cardinal doctrines were: confession as the door to the regenerate life, celibacy its rule and cross. "Mother Ann, the Word," she was called. Seven followers emigrated from England to New York in 1774, and the movement grew rapidly. She formulated the characteristic beliefs of the Shakers: celibacy, communism, pacifism, millennialism, elitism, and spiritual manifestations through barking, dancing, and shaking.

and Manchester's many reform movements. This too is a must for anyone interested in social history.

JEWISH MUSEUM, Cheetham Hill Road, is housed in a historic synagogue built by Spanish and Portuguese Jews in the Moorish style in 1874. The museum displays the history of Manchester's Jewish community, which is the largest and one of the most important in England outside of London.

MACCLESFIELD SILK MUSEUM is located some 19 miles south of Manchester in a large Georgian building that was once Macclesfield's thriving Methodist Sunday school. Nearby a working model of a silk mill can be seen at the **PARADISE MILL MUSEUM**. The Macclesfield silk industry developed during the 18th century as the British answer to French domination of silk production. Apart from its interest in terms of social and industrial history, these museums provide the background to the rise of the Shakers, who were to play an important role in American history. Mother Ann Lee, the founder of the Shakers, worked in Macclesfield silk mills, where she first joined the Quakers. Later "French Prophets," who presumably came on business from French silk towns, arrived, bringing with them new doctrines that Lee developed as the basis of her own cult.

NORTHUMBRIA

Because of its location in the far north of England and the isolation of many places of Christian interest, Northumbria, like Cumbria, is one of those areas best visited by car. Therefore, the present section provides details about a number of related sites, rather than dealing with one particular place as is usually done in this book.

For the 7th and 8th centuries, Northumbria experienced a brief but glorious flowering of Christian civilization during which it became the center of west European evangelization and learning. So important was this unexpected golden age in the midst of a pagan culture that many historians credit the monks of Northumbria with saving Christianity in the West. At the height of its civilization, evangelists were sent out all over Britain and Europe, the stunningly beautiful *Lindesfarne Gospels* were produced, Bede (672–735) wrote his histories and numerous Bible commentaries, and Alcuin (723–804) was recruited by Charlemagne (742–814) to educate his people in a mission that initiated the Carolingian renaissance. All of this intense Christian activity came to an abrupt end in 793 when Viking raiders suddenly appeared to shatter the peace and sack the center of Northumbrian Christianity at Lindesfarne. Within two years, all the other Northumbrian centers—including Hexham, Jarrow, and York—were devastated, and the Northumbrian golden age came to an end.

The turbulent history of Northumbrian Christianity, particularly its unexpected beginnings, provides an antidote to simplistic explanations of church growth and mission. Christianity arrived in Northumbria with Roman troops and traders. By the 5th century it appears that Christian communities were flourishing over a wide area. In 410, however, the Roman legions were withdrawn, leaving the security of the area to local auxiliaries. Shortly after the Romans left, a series of invasions by pagan Germanic tribes, known as the Angles and the Saxons, began to disrupt civilized life. By the late 6th century, Christianity seems to have disappeared from the entire area as pagan invaders displaced the indigenous population.

In 604 the pagan Saxon King Aethelfrith of Bernicia overran his equally pagan southern neighbor, Deira. Aethelfrith then united the two realms into one kingdom, Northumbria, that became the most important of the seven Anglo-Saxon realms in Britain. From the fortified town of Bamburgh in the north, he ruled his new kingdom, which stretched from the river Humber in the south to Edinburgh in the north and west to the Pennines. When Aethelfrith conquered Deira, he married Acha, the daughter of its last king, Aelle. The male heirs fled, taking refuge in the kingdom of Kent, where the process of Christianization was just beginning.

Eventually, probably in 616, Aethelfrith demanded that the king of East Anglia, Raedwald, who had granted protection to the eldest son of Aelle, Edwin, hand him over for execution. At first Raedwald seems to have agreed. But then he launched a surprise attack, killing Aethelfrith and scattering his army. Edwin now led a conquering army into Bernicia, which he united under his rule. Now it was the turn of Aethelfrith's family and nobles to flee and take refuge in Christian kingdoms in Scotland, with which they had previously been at war. Among these refugees were the king's sons Eanfrid and

Oswald, who seem to have spent a considerable part of their exile at the Scottish monastery of Iona.

In 625 Edwin, who was now king of Northumbria, proposed marriage to Ethelberga, the daughter of Ethelbert, king of Kent, at whose court he had lived as a refugee. According to Bede, her brother Eadbald told him, "It was not permissible for a Christian woman to marry a pagan husband." After receiving this rebuke, Edwin agreed to allow Ethelberga to practice her religion, permitted the evangelization of his kingdom, and promised to take instruction in the faith himself. Thus he allowed Ethelberga to bring Christian priests and attendants with her, to establish churches, and generally to promote the Christian cause. At the same time he took lessons in the faith from his wife's personal chaplain, Bishop Paulinius, who was consecrated bishop on July 21, 625, with the understanding that his task was to convert the Northumbrians.

Eventually after surviving various assassination plots by discontented pagans, King Edwin was baptized in York on April 12, 627, at the church of St. Peter, and plans were made to build York Cathedral. After his baptism, Edwin earnestly sought to spread Christianity among his people and surrounding tribes, often leading preaching missions himself. But in 633, after a reign of 17 years, his subject, King Cadwalla, who ruled a border kingdom in what is now Wales, rebelled against Edwin with the support of his pagan neighbor Penda, king of Mercia. Edwin and his army were slaughtered at the Battle of Hatfield near Doncaster, and the pagan Mercians overran Northumbria.

According to Bede, severe persecution of both Christians and Saxons followed, during which time churches were plundered and burnt and their clergy massacred. Bede describes this as genocidal war, during which time British forces under Cadwalla exterminated many of the hated Saxons. Bishop Paulinus and Queen Ethelberga escaped by sea to Kent, where they were protected by King Eadbald. Chaos ruled.

About a year later, order was restored, and once again Northumbria was divided into the kingdoms of Deira, ruled by Edwin's nephew Osric, and Bernicia, ruled by Aethelfrith's son Eanfrid, who returned from exile in Scotland. After a short while both Osric and Eanfrid were murdered by Cadwalla, who made Northumbria a province of his own realm.

Following the death of Eanfrid, his brother Oswald, who had been converted while in exile, claimed the Northumbrian throne. He led a small force against Cadwalla's far larger army, which he defeated in 634 at the Battle of Denisesburn, or Hefenfelth, modern Heavenfield, four miles north of Hexham. Bede tells us that before the battle, Oswald erected a cross and commanded his entire army to pray for victory. Thus treacherous Cadwalla was killed and Oswald assumed the crown of a united Northumbria. Once established as king, Oswald, in 635, invited the abbot of Iona to send monks to establish a monastery and evangelistic center on the island of Lindisfarne close to his capital, Bamburgh. To fulfill this task, the Iona community commissioned one of its leading scholars, the saintly Aidan. Oswald now established Northumbria as the leading power in Britain.

Seven years later, in 642, Oswald was himself killed at the Battle of Maserfelth by a combined Welsh and Mercian force under Northumbria's old enemy Penda. Oswald was succeeded by his brother Oswiu, who like Edwin married a Christian princess from Kent. After various dynastic intrigues, Oswiu managed to arrange the marriage of his son to the daughter of the pagan Penda. This was followed by the conversion of Penda's son Peada, who then married Oswiu's daughter in 653. These dynastic ties did not protect Northumbria from Penda's wrath, because three years later he once again launched an invasion. Oswiu did all he could to avoid war and then turned to God for protection. He promised God that if he was victorious, he would establish twelve new monasteries. Oswiu then took the initiative, surprising Penda's army with a small and greatly outnumbered force. His forces soundly defeated Penda's somewhere on a river bank near the modern city of Leeds. During the battle,

Penda was killed, and with his death the power of paganism was broken. Subsequently, the English church enjoyed a period of relative peace that lasted until the Viking invasion and destruction of Lindesfarne in 793.

PLACES TO VISIT

LINDESFARNE, known today as Holy Island, is off the Northumbrian coast seven miles past the village of Belford, along a clearly marked tidal causeway. Visitors must check the tide tables before attempting to visit the islands. According to legend, when King Oswald asked the monks of Iona to send missionaries to Northumbria, they sent an evangelistic team that quickly returned to Iona saying that the Northumbrians were too barbarous to receive the gospel. At this St. Aidan (d. 651) spoke up, saying that perhaps the missionaries had used the wrong methods. As a result of this comment, he was sent to become the apostle of the Northumbrians himself. Aidan's mission was remarkably successful. After building the monastery on Iona, he undertook many evangelistic journeys throughout the kingdom. He also regularly sailed over to the nearby Farne Islands for prayer and meditation. A few inscribed stones from Aidan's monastery are on display in the island museum. After the Viking attack, the monks fled, carrying with them various treasures and the body of St. Cuthbert (635–87), who was eventually interred in Durham

N

Cathedral. A monastic community seems to have been reestablished after the initial Viking raid, but by 875 the island was totally abandoned. The present LINDESFARNE PRIORY is a truly magnificent ruin, with a dramatic rainbow arch over the nave. It was built of red sandstone as a Benedictine foundation by the Norman bishop of Durham, William of St. Calais, who, inspired by local legends, began construction in 1093. The church was rather small and clearly designed as a replica of Durham Cathedral. The ruins of a number of monastic buildings are also open to the public, and there is an excellent visitor's center and museum.

To the west of the priory is the 13th-century parish church of ST. MARY with a fine chancel and fortified appearance that fits this very unruly region. Further west still lie the ruins of LINDESFARNE CASTLE, which were renovated in 1909 as a holiday home by an English publisher.

Although the ruins of Lindesfarne Priory are well worth seeing, it is the ethos of the island that impresses most people. Even secular historians describe it as "the most holy place in England." The unmarked grave of St. Aidan is also somewhere on the island.

BAMBURGH CASTLE, seven miles south of Holy Island, on the B1342, contains an 11th-century Norman keep. The castle itself was renovated in the late 19th century and is now open to the public. Originally Bamburgh was the capital of Saxon Northumbria, from where Oswald introduced Christianity to his pagan followers, but little remains from those far-off days. During the War of the Roses, it was the first castle in England to be bombarded by artillery. Inside is an excellent collection of art and many items of military interest. Thomas Malory (1405–71), who wrote the first recorded story of King Arthur, believed that Bamburgh was the castle of the legendary knight, Lancelot of the Lake.

The Bamburgh parish church has a 13th-century choir, although other parts of the building are much older. It is dedicated to St. Aidan, who died here as he leaned against the church doorpost. Below the chancel is a vaulted crypt, which is the oldest part of the church.

BEDE'S WORLD, the Museum of Early Northumbria, Jarrow, is located ten miles from Newcastle-upon-Tyne. Follow the A19 to the A185, near the entrance to the Tyne tunnel, and turn south towards South Shields. Bede's World is the first turn on the left. It can be reached by both bus and metro service.

This innovative museum complex is dedicated to the life and times of the Venerable Bede (672–735), who was a monk of Jarrow and the earliest historian of England. This is an outstanding exhibition that brings alive the past in a remarkably vivid way. It is located on the site of Bede's 7th-century monastery.

The main museum is housed in an 18th-century Georgian House, Jarrow

Hall, and devoted to the "Golden Age of Northumbria." The new museum is a purpose-built structure designed to display exhibits about Northumbria before Bede and the life of Bede himself.

St. Paul's Church, founded around 673, was originally part of the monastery complex. It was sacked by the Vikings in 794 and rebuilt by the Normans in 1074. Both the chancel and tower are part of the original Saxon building.

Gyrwe, Anglo-Saxon Farm, is an 11-acre complex that recreates rural life as it was in the 7th century, with rare breeds of domestic animals, ancient plows, and even cereals and vegetables that Bede would recognize. Several period buildings equipped with traditional tools are open to visitors.

HEXHAM, 25 miles west of Newcastle, on the A69, 35 miles northwest of Durham on the A68, is a bustling market town. A settlement existed in this area long before the arrival of the Romans, but the present town goes back to Saxon times and was originally called Hextoldesham after a local stream, the Hextol, now known as Cockshaw burn.

The Normans shortened the town's name to Hexham, which in some early documents is written Exam. Today most of the town's buildings are early Victorian.

HEXHAM PRIORY was founded by Bishop Wilfrid of Hexham in 674 and completed in 680, at the urging of Queen Ethelreda of Northumberland. The original church was described by Wilfrid's biographer, Eddius Stephanus of Ripon, as "the greatest and most magnificent church north of the Alps." Whether this grand claim was the truth or an exaggeration we have no way of knowing, since Wilfrid's church was sacked by the Vikings in 875 when they completely destroyed it along with the town. Wilfrid's church was raised to the rank of a cathedral in 681. It was ruled by a total of twelve bishops, until the last one fled Viking raiders around 821. The church was rebuilt on the site of Wilfrid's original building in 1180 by Augustinian monks in the Early Gothic, or transitional, style. Today the crypt and possibly the west front are all that remain of the original church. Another feature of the church is that it was built

THE VENERABLE BEDE (672–735) was the first historian of England and an important medieval Bible commentator and theologian. He entered the monastery of Wearmouth as a child and came to Jarrow several years later. It was here that he spent most of his adult life, apart from a few short visits to centers like York. At that time Jarrow had one of the best libraries in England, if not Europe, which enabled Bede to write his *Ecclesiastical History of England* and numerous Bible commentaries.

as, and until the Reformation remained, a monastic church that has seen very few alterations since its completion in the 12th century.

Near the entrance, in the south transept, is the tombstone of Flavinius. A Roman officer of the crack cavalry regiment *ala Petriana*, he is shown in full battle dress engaged in conflict with an uncivilized enemy. The inscriptions on the tombstone make it clear that this was a pre-Christian burial. It is just one of a number of pieces of Roman carving that was incorporated into the walls of the church when its builders used local stone from Roman ruins. The passageway between the south transept and the chapter house also contains two pagan Roman altars. One of the altars contains a dedication by the second in command of the Sixth Legion to the god Maponus, who was popular in northern England during Roman times.

The nave also houses the remains of several ancient Saxon crosses and Christian tombstones discovered during restoration work in 1908. Note the night stairs, which were used by the monks to link their dormitory to the church. At the Reformation most night staircases were destroyed, making these an interesting and very rare reminder of medieval religious life. The rood screen is a fine example of 16th-century religious artwork. The crypt, where the church's relics were held, was the center of pilgrimage in both Saxon and medieval times. Notice the Roman inscriptions on the ceiling and other carvings.

The early Saxon stone chair, the Frith stool, or "peace chair," is said to be the throne of Bishop Wilfrid, although many modern writers think it is an 8th-century creation. The chair is made from one piece of stone modeled on the stone chairs found in churches in Rome and Ravenna. The significance of the chair is that it marked the central point of sanctuary in Saxon times. Four stone crosses were erected a mile from the church in each direction, creating a sacred space or sanctuary. Any fugitive who entered this enclosed area was protected from prose-

WILFRID OF HEXHAM (634–700), builder of Hexham Abbey, was one of the most influential and controversial churchmen of the 7th century. He is principally remembered for his work in convening the Synod of Whitby in 664, which brought the northern churches into a loose conformity with Roman Catholicism and led to their accepting the Catholic dating of Easter. Bede takes an ambiguous stance towards Wilfrid, whom he appears to praise as a great hero of the Church while at the same time pointing out his vanity and many weaknesses.

cution as long as they remained within it. The location of these crosses are known, although the crosses themselves were destroyed centuries ago. The church also has a fine Saxon baptismal font and a rare Saxon chalice. Some of its excellent carved choir stalls date from 1425. Close to the high altar is a 14th-century painting depicting the *Dance of Death*.

HEAVENSFIELD, four miles north of Hexham on the B6318, is the site of the ancient battle between the greatly outnumbered Christian armies of Oswald and those of the pagan king Cadwalla of Gwynedd in what is now north Wales. The battleground is identified by a roadside cross and an interpretive panel recounting the story of the battle. A hundred yards away is the church of St. Oswald, built in 1737. The cross and the church are separated by Hadrian's Wall, making this the only known battlefield on the wall itself. Oswald's victory marked the death knell of paganism in England.

HADRIAN'S WALL. Hexham is the ideal place from which to visit Britain's most famous wall and the Roman antiquity which was declared a World Heritage Site in 1987. The wall is 73 miles long and stretches from Wallsend near Newcastle to the Solway Firth, near Carlisle. It was built at the command of the Roman Emperor Hadrian (76–138) in 122. Historians believe that the original height was 15 feet. In places it is nine feet wide, but at times the width is

reduced to six feet. Every mile the Romans built an observation turret, or mile castle, and every seven miles there was a fort. The total garrison of the forts was 10,000 men. North of the wall is a deep ditch 27 feet wide, adding to the defensive nature of the wall. Behind the wall was another ditch and military road. Beyond the wall were a series of forward observations posts that added to its defenses. Hadrian's Wall was the main frontier of the Western Empire in Britain from 122 to 409.

CHESTERS, the Roman fortress of Cilurnum, is five miles northeast of Hexham. It has been extensively excavated and is the best-preserved example of a Roman cavalry fort in the whole of Europe. Built to protect a key bridge over the Tyne, it covers six acres and originally housed a garrison of 500 cavalry.

CORBRIDGE ROMAN MUSEUM is three miles northeast of Chesters. Apart from military exhibits, it contains numerous stone carvings, including the famous Corbridge Lion.

HOUSESTEAD, eight miles northwest of Hexham, on the peak of a hill. Here are the remains of the major infantry fort of Vercovicium, which was a regional headquarters. Apart from the military buildings, the remains of a large civilian settlement have also been excavated.

VINDOLANDA lies another seven miles southwest of Housestead. It is a large fort and civilian complex located at the highest point on the wall.

GREENHEAD ROMAN ARMY MUSEUM is another seven miles west. It has an excellent collection of items related to the Roman army.

TEMPLE OF MITHRAS is a unique find that gives insight into the religious life of the legions. This pagan temple is found on a windswept moor ten miles north of Hexham just beyond the village of Chollerford.

NORWICH

Originally the site of a Saxon settlement on a ford crossing the Wensum River near its confluence with the Yarn, Norwich grew as a trading center that had close contacts with German-speaking lands. It was conquered by Danes and later by the Normans, who deposed the local ruler, King Harold's brother, and built a massive fortress to protect their newly acquired lands. In 1094, the town became a bishopric with the Norman Bishop Losinga destroying a large part of the Saxon town to build his new cathedral. In the 12th century, Norwich became the center of a large Jewish population attracted by its importance as a trading city. They were allowed to live in the town itself and were not restricted to a ghetto. The city was given a charter in 1194, which was renewed and extended in 1256. At that time the area enclosed by the city wall was as great as the area enclosed by the walls of London. The 14th century saw a flourishing wool trade with the Netherlands and the arrival of a large community of Flemish weavers, who settled in the city.

Due to its isolated position, surrounded by swampy land known as "the Fens," Norwich escaped extensive damage during England's various civil wars, although it was occupied by a peasant army in 1381 during the Peasants' Revolt. By the 18th century, Norwich was second only to London in wealth. Decline followed due to the rise of manufacturing in the north of England during the Industrial Revolution. But this economic decline meant that the city retained much of its medieval character until the inner city was heavily bombed during World War II. Today Norwich has more medieval churches than any other city in England, with 31 of its 56 medieval churches surviving, of which only ten are still in use as churches. Today Norwich, like so many other cities, is trying to recreate itself by becoming a center for Britain's new hi-tech industries.

The teachings of the early English Reformer John Wycliffe (1330–84) took hold among the weavers of Norwich and surrounding areas. Julian of Norwich (1342–1416) produced some of the most important mystical writings to appear in medieval England. Subsequently, the teachings of Martin Luther (1483–1546) quickly spread from the continent to Norwich, where they were well received by people whose ancestors had been influenced by Wycliffe. Later John Calvin's (1509–64) work received a ready reception, and the area became a Puritan stronghold. During the 17th and 18th centuries, Norwich became the center for the Quakers and later for Methodism. Today spiritual life in Norwich is at a low ebb. The city of Norwich boasts that it was the first city in England to appoint a woman as its lord mayor in 1925.

PLACES TO VISIT

NORWICH CATHEDRAL was founded in 1096 when the newly appointed Norman bishop drove the local Saxon population from their homes to clear the land for his new cathedral, which towered over them as a symbol of Saxon defeat and oppression. Even the facing stone on the cathedral was brought from Caen in France, as if to say that local stone was not good enough for Norman overlords. Perhaps these arrogant and callous acts, as well as Norwich's close commercial ties to Europe, help explain why numerous nonconformist and evangelical groups were so often welcomed here.

Since its unholy origins, the cathedral building has been plagued with disasters. In addition to various fires and its sacking during the Peasants' Revolt,

the spire fell down during a storm in 1362. The present spire was built in the 15th century and is the second tallest in England at 315 feet high. Only Salisbury spire, which is 404 feet, is higher.

The interior is in the heavy Romanesque style known in England as Norman, with thick pillars and a generally solid feel. The roof has a series of 15th-century bosses, which tell the story of redemption. These can only be clearly seen with the use of binoculars or with the mirror trolleys that are provided for this purpose. A similar set of bosses, illustrating the life of Christ and the book of Revelation, are to be found in the cathedral's cloisters. They are the only double-story monastic cloisters in England to have survived the Reformation.

Off the apse are a series of chapels built according to French designs that are quite uncommon in England. The 8th-century bishop's throne, which stands behind the high altar, is Saxon in origin and is believed to have been plundered from the Saxon Cathedral that once stood in Dunwich. The body of nurse Edith Cavell, executed by the Germans as a spy in 1915, was brought to Norwich in 1919 and is buried in the St. Luke Chapel. The vault has a rare painting dated 1275, while the five-paneled 14th-century altarpiece was made for Bishop Despenser in the 14th century. The misericords in the choir are also well worth seeing.

ST. PETER MANCROFT CHURCH is generally regarded as Norwich's finest

Gothic building. It has a beautiful hammer-beam roof and an east window containing 15th-century stained glass. Sir Thomas Browne (1605–82), whose *Religio Medici* (1642) was an important devotional and apologetic work, is buried in the chancel. His statue also appears outside the church. In the sacristy are some fine church ornaments and a rare 13th-century illustrated manuscript.

ST. JULIAN, St. Julian's Alley, is a tiny church containing the cell of Julian of Norwich (1342–1416), a nun from the nearby Benedictine convent at Carrow, which no longer exists. She moved here in 1373 after claiming to have received visions of Christ. The content of her various visions were recorded in her *Revelations of Divine Love* (1383). This is the first book in England known to have been written by a woman. This immensely popular work played an important role in reviving medieval English religion and, despite its deeply Roman Catholic orthodoxy, played a role in encouraging the acceptance of Protestant religion and the "born again" experience in later centuries.

ST. ANDREW'S CHURCH, Bridewell Alley, is a Gothic church built in 1506 with a hammer-beam roof. The church was used by Flemish weavers and became a center for Protestantism. John Robinson (1576–1625), who pastored the Pilgrim fathers, was a curate here before leaving the Church of England to found his own independent congregation.

ST. ANDREW'S AND BLACKFRIARS' HALL, Elm St. and St. George St., were built between 1440 and 1470 as the monastic church of the Blackfriars, who established a house in Norwich in 1226. St. Andrew's Hall is what remains of the church choir, while Blackfriars' Hall was the chancel. Together they form the only surviving Dominican church in England. After the monastery was dissolved during the Reformation, St. Andrew's Hall became an assizes (courthouse). Blackfriars' Hall became a Protestant church that was used by Norwich's Dutch congregation from the 16th to the 19th centuries. Today they are both used for concerts and similar functions. The former cloisters of this once great church is now the Norwich School of Art.

ST. PETER HUNGATE CHURCH was built in the 11th century and rebuilt in 1460. It has been preserved from destruction by its conversion into a very

JULIAN OF NORWICH (1342–1416) was an obscure English mystic and hermit possibly influenced by neo-Platonism. She claimed to have received 16 revelations from God on May 8–9, 1373. She wrote about these revelations 20 years later in *Revelations of Divine Love*, which extols divine love as the answer to all problems, especially the problem of evil.

interesting ecclesiastical museum containing numerous brasses, which people may "rub," or copy, for a fee. Among the treasures on view here is a rare copy of Wycliffe's translation of the Bible, dating from 1388.

ST. SIMON AND ST. JUDE CHURCH is a sad reminder of the decline of Christianity in England. This large Gothic church, like 20 other ancient places of worship in Norwich, has been preserved by the conversion of its interior into office space.

THE OCTAGONAL CHAPEL is a neoclassical structure built in 1766 to facilitate preaching for Norwich's main Presbyterian congregation. In 1820 the minister led his congregation out of Presbyterianism into the newly formed Unitarian movement.

NORWICH CASTLE still dominates the town, as was intended when it was first built by the Normans. They began construction as early as 1094 and completed it during the reign of Henry II in 1160. An unusual feature of the castle is its exterior stone decoration, which was carefully restored between 1833 and 1839. The keep is pure Norman, complete with battlements, a dungeon, and a deep well. The regimental museum is housed below the castle. An art gallery contains paintings by members of the 19th-century "Norfolk School," led by John Crome (1768–1821) and John Sell Cotman (1782–1842), who sought to develop Dutch-style landscape painting in England.

ORKNEY ISLANDS

P erched at the top of Scotland and only accessible by air or ferry, the Orkney Islands are well worth a visit for their historical heritage and strange northern beauty. The Orkney archipelago is made up of over 67 islands, although only 20 are inhabited, and visitors usually only go to the main island, known locally as "the mainland." The Orkneys were settled by Neolithic peoples in the 4th millennium B.C. These folk were followed by Iron Age tribes, who built fortified settlements and huge stone towers known as *brochs*. Orkney was converted to Christianity early in the Christian era, but much of this original Christian civilization was lost when the Vikings invaded in the 8th century. Until 1468, the Orkneys belonged to the crown of Denmark. Then they were given to King James III (1451–88) of Scotland as a dowry when he married a Danish princess. The isles are rich in sea life, birds, and seals.

PLACES TO VISIT

ST. MAGNUS CATHEDRAL, Kirkwall, on the southeast part of the mainland, was built by Earl Rogvald between 1137 and 1152 as a penance for the murder of his uncle, Earl Magnus Erlendson, by his father. Magnus was originally buried in Birnsay. Local people claimed to see a heavenly light over his grave, causing it to become a popular pilgrimage site.

The cathedral is a Romanesque red sandstone building, well proportioned although somewhat austere. The medieval shrine of St. Magnus, which contains his grave, is on the right of the organ screen.

During World War II, a number of islands along the shores of the Skara Brae, which was the main base for the British Navy, were linked together by the Churchill Barriers, which were earthworks that filled in the land between the islands to prevent attacks by German submarines. Italian prisoners of war were used for this task, and they lovingly built the ITALIAN CHAPEL from two prefabricated buildings known as Nissen huts and from whatever they could salvage as prisoners. It is now a tourist attraction and a place of pilgrimage for the Italians and their descendants.

THE EARL'S PALACE, Kirkwall, is now a museum of Orkney history from the Middle Ages. It was once a stylish Renaissance building built between 1600 and 1607 for Earl Patrick Stewart, who was executed for high treason in 1615.

THE BISHOP'S PALACE, Kirkwall, was built in the 12th century next to the cathedral. In 1263, King Haakon of Norway died here after the Battle of Largs. The present building dates from the 16th and 17th centuries and was renovated by Earl Patrick Stewart.

By contrast, the CORRIGALL FARM MUSEUM, Harray, provides insight into how ordinary people lived and it has a rich display of traditional crafts.

BROUGH OF BIRNSAY, west mainland, is reached by foot along a narrow causeway that is accessible only at low tide. Here one finds the remains of a group of houses and a 12th-century church, making this one of the earliest Christian sites on the island.

SKARA BRAE is an ancient prehistoric town site and one of the best-preserved Stone Age settlements in Europe. It appears to have been a thriving fishing and agricultural community for around 500 years, from about 3000–2500 B.C. Over the centuries it was buried in sand, which also preserved it from destruction, and only rediscovered after a severe storm in 1850. Visitors can enter seven of these ancient dwellings.

MAES HOWE is a huge Neolithic burial cairn dating from around 2700 B.C. and is one of the most important prehistoric monuments in the British Isles. The burial chamber is made from stone that was then surrounded and covered by a large mound of earth. In the 12th century, the Vikings entered the tomb and sacked it of whatever treasures there were. A record of this violation is found in carved Norse runes inside the burial chamber itself.

RING OF BRODGAR, close to Maes Howe, is an ancient stone circle standing between two lochs. Twenty-seven of the original 60 stones are still erect. There is a deep ditch around the circle that is entered by two causeways.

OXFORD

The earliest evidence of settlement in Oxford comes from the 8th century, when Saxons occupied the area. A nunnery, St. Frideswide, which is now Christ Church College, was built here around 780, but the town is not mentioned in written records until the *Anglo-Saxon Chronicle* of 912, when it is described as a thriving trading center and a seat of the royal court. The university is not mentioned in written records until the 12th century, although it is likely to have existed much earlier, and legend says King Alfred (849–99) founded it. During the 12th century, both the town and university grew rapidly, partially due to the expulsion of English students from Paris in 1167. The university gained recognition as a corporation, and in 1214 the papal delegate to England granted it legal privileges and immunity from the common laws of England. There are ongoing arguments about which is the earliest college, with University College (1249), Merton (1264), and Balliol (1265) all claiming that for one reason

or another they are the original college out of which the university grew.

The early English Reformer, John Wycliffe (1330–84), was a professor at Oxford. Famous students here included the Bible translator William Tyndale (1494–1536), Protestant martyrs Bishops Hugh Latimer (1485–1555) and Nicholas Ridley (1503–55), and Archbishop Thomas Cranmer (1489–1556).

During the English Civil War the town of Oxford supported the Parliamentarians, but the university supported the monarchy and delivered the town into Royalist hands. After his exclusion from London, King Charles I (1600–1649) made Oxford his capital. After the defeat of the king, the great Puritan theologian John Owen (1616–83) was made vice chancellor, which in England is the equivalent of president or rector of the university, a post he held until the restoration of the monarchy.

Until the 20th century, the town of Oxford was basically controlled by the university, which was able to prevent the development of industry. But in the

O

JOHN WYCLIFFE (1330–84) was an English precursor to the Protestant Reformation who was master of Balliol College, Oxford. His writings defended civil government from religious interference and attacked the papacy by promoting a return to biblical Christianity, especially through his attack on transubstantiation. He encouraged the first translation of the Bible into English, thus helping to create the Lollard movement. His works were destroyed on the orders of the Roman Catholic Church and only survived in Czechoslovakia, where they influenced John Huss (1372–1415). It is also possible that his writings had an indirect influence on Martin Luther (1483–1546).

WILLIAM TYNDALE (1494–1536) produced the first really popular and readily available translation of the New Testament in English. He began work translating the Old Testament but was betrayed, tried, and burnt at the stake in Antwerp before he completed his task. Of the original 18,000 copies of his New Testament, only two survive today.

1920s all that changed with the building of the Morris automobile plant in nearby Cowley, and industrial development began to change the character of the town. Today Oxford is a bustling industrial city that retains its earlier genteel atmosphere.

PLACES TO VISIT

CHRIST CHURCH CATHEDRAL, St. Aldates, is a Romanesque structure that was built between 1140 and 1180. It serves as the chapel for Christ Church College. It stands on the site of an earlier Saxon church that housed the shrine of St. Fridswide (d. 735). After the Dissolution of the Monasteries, the shrine was destroyed, only to be reconstructed later. It is located next to the Lady Chapel. Throughout the Middle Ages, this shrine was a center of pilgrimage and played an important role in the growth of the city.

Gilbert Scott redesigned the west front in 1870 in the neo-Gothic style. The round and octagonal pillars give an illusion of height, prefiguring later Gothic developments. The north aisle west window (1630) depicts Jonah and the destruction of Nineveh and has strong political overtones that reflect the disputes and preaching that led to the English Civil War. Several windows, including the west window in the south aisle, are by William Morris (1834–96). In the St. Lucy Chapel a 14th-century stained-glass window depicts the martyrdom of Thomas à Becket. It was defaced in the 17th century when some Puritan knocked out Becket's head, presumably because he thought it was idolatrous.

There are statues to the great Christian philosopher and apologist Bishop Berkeley (1685–1753) and Edward Pusey (1800–1882), a leader of the 19th-century Anglo-Catholic, or Tractarian, movement. In the Latin Chapel is the grave of Robert Burton (1577–1640), whose *Anatomy of Melancholy* is a popular devotional book with psychological overtones.

THE CHURCH OF ST. MARY THE VIRGIN, Radcliffe Square, High St., opposite Brasenose College, was built sometime in the 13th century and transformed into a Gothic building between 1463 and 1490. It has a high tower that is a well-known landmark and an Italianate Baroque porch that was built in 1637 by Archbishop Laud's chaplain, Dr. Owen Morgan. He also installed a statue of the Madonna, which was cited as evidence of Laud's Roman Catholic sympathies at his trial in 1644.

Since the 14th century St. Mary the Virgin has served as the university church, where invited "University Sermons" are preached each Sunday. The famous Bampton Lectures, originally set up to promote Christianity among the students through the presentation of topics of an apologetic nature, are also held here annually. Here in 1555–56, Archbishop Cranmer, Nicholas Ridley, and Hugh Latimer were subjected to a lengthy trial before being condemned as heretics and burnt at the stake in Broad Street. Here too Cranmer publicly repudiated his earlier recantation shortly before his martyrdom. On the north side of the nave is a pillar marking the spot where Cranmer sat during the trial. Two centuries later, the Wesley brothers John and Charles worshiped here as students. Later they preached here as university preachers, and John delivered all of his 44 sermons, which are the basis of Methodist ordination for lay preachers, in this church. Then in the 19th century, John Keble preached a famous sermon, known as the Assize Sermon, in which he criticized government policy towards the church in Ireland. This sermon is seen by many as the clarion call that launched the Tractarian or Oxford movement of Anglo-Catholicism within Anglicanism. John Henry Newman (1801–90), who became the acknowledged leader of the Tractarians, was the vicar from 1828–42. It was here that Newman preached his famous "The Parting of Friends" sermon, breaking his ties with the Oxford movement and Anglicanism in 1842 when he embraced Roman Catholicism. Sir William Jones (1746–94), who played an important role in creating European interest in Indian religions through his research and writing, is buried here.

ST. MICHAEL'S CHURCH, Cornmarket St., has an early preconquest tower that is the oldest in Oxford, as are the church's stained-glass windows. The late 13th-century windows depict the Madonna, St. Michael, St. Nicholas, and St. Edmund. The church stands at what was once the north gate of the city,

O

which was demolished in 1772. The nave was remodeled in the Gothic style in the 15th century.

THE CHURCH OF ST. JOHN THE EVANGELIST, Iffley Rd., was built in 1894 by the architect G. F. Bodley for the newly formed Cowley Fathers, an Anglican monastic Order inspired by Ango-Catholicism and the teachings of the Oxford movement. It now belongs to St. Stephen's House, a high church Anglican theological college.

BAPTIST CHURCH, Broad St., is one of the earliest Baptist churches in Britain and was founded in 1662 after the ejection of Puritan preachers from the Church of England. The present building dates from 1830.

MARTYR'S MEMORIAL, Broad St., was erected in the 19th century. It commemorates the death of the Reforming Bishops Nicholas Ridley and Hugh Latimer, who were burnt at the stake on this spot by the Roman Catholic zealot Queen Mary on October 16, 1555. A few months later, on March 21, 1556, Thomas Cranmer suffered the same fate.

CHRIST CHURCH COLLEGE, St. Aldates, is adjacent to the cathedral that was originally part of the college. It was founded by Cardinal Wolsey in 1525 as Cardinal College, and closed by Henry VIII following Wolsey's disgrace. Henry then refounded it in 1545 as Henry VIII College. Later, during the Reformation, it was once again closed, because it was a monastic institution for training clergy, and reopened as Christ Church

College. The college hall, which has a hammer-beam roof, is open to the public and contains portraits of fellows by various British artists. Members of the college have included numerous British prime ministers, including the 19th-century Christian politician William Gladstone(1809–98). Its other fellows include Sir Philip Sidney (1554–86), William Penn (1664–1718), John Locke (1632–1704), Albert Einstein (1879–1955), and John (1703–91) and Charles Wesley (1709–88). For a brief period, from 1651 to 1652, before he became vice chancellor, John Owen (1616–83) was the dean of the college. Bishop Berkeley (1685–1753) was also a graduate. He is usually known for his work as a Christian philosopher who strongly opposed Deism. What is not usually known is that Berkeley was also the founder of the Society for the Propagation of the Gospel, one of the earliest Protestant missionary societies.

QUEEN'S COLLEGE, Queens Lane, was founded in 1341 by Robert de Egglesfield, a royal chaplain to the wife of Edward III, who supported the venture. He endowed the college with sufficient funds to support a provost, 12 fellows, and 70 "poor scholars." These numbers were based on his reading of Luke 9 and 10 and intended to represent Jesus, his apostles, and the 70 Jesus sent out to spread the gospel. Between 1682 and 1765, the college buildings were remodeled in a unified Baroque style. Among its many distinguished fellows are the Puritan John Owen and the philosopher and social reformer Jeremy Bentham (1748–1832), who is the father of Utilitarianism.

PEMBROKE COLLEGE, Pembroke St., was founded relatively late (1624) and gets its name from the university's chancellor of that time, the earl of Pembroke. The buildings are pleasant but not exciting. Its most famous Christian graduate was the great 18th-century preacher and revivalist George Whitefield (1714–70). Other graduates include Dr. Samuel Johnson (1709–84); the jurist Sir William Blackstone (1732–80); John Lempriére (1497–1537), who produced a famous *Classical Dictionary;* James Smithson (1765–1829), who founded the Smithstonian Institute in Washington, D.C.; and William Fulbright (1905–95).

ORIEL COLLEGE, Oriel Square, was originally known as St. Mary's College when it was founded by Adam de Brome, the rector of St. Mary the Virgin and almoner to Edward II (1284–1327). It floundered and was refounded by Edward II in 1326, who renamed it King's College. The name *Oriel* comes from one of the buildings on the site acquired to build the college in 1329, which over the years attached itself to the institution. The Gothic front quad was built between 1619 and 1624, providing visitors with a good example of the Late Gothic style. Inside the college complex is a tennis court where King Charles II (1630–85) and Prince Rupert, the dashing Royalist cavalry officer, are supposed to have played tennis. Outstanding fellows include Sir Walter Raleigh (1554–1618); the great 18th-century Christian philosopher Bishop Butler (1692–1752), whose *Analogy of Religion* (1736) still provides a model for many evangelical apologetic works; Bishop Samuel Wilberforce (1805–73); Matthew Arnold (1822–88), who revolutionized English education while headmaster of Rugby School; and the adventurer and empire builder Cecil Rhodes (1853–1902). Most of the leading members of the Oxford movement were also graduates of Oriel, including John Keble (1792–1866), John Henry Newman (1801–90), and Edward Pusey (1800–1882).

CORPUS CHRISTI, Merton St., was founded in 1517 by Bishop Richard Foxe (1448–1528) who was a close associate of King Henry VII. It has some excellent fan vaulting and a hall with a hammer-beam roof. In the chapel, the altarpiece and east window are from the school of Rubens in Antwerp. On the outside wall of the quad is a famous pelican sundial that was installed in 1581. Its early graduates include Bishop Reginald Pole (1500–1558); the architect of Elizabethan Anglicanism, Richard Hooker (1554–1600); and General Oglethorp (1696–1785), who founded Georgia and Savannah as a utopian community in 1734 for freed debtors. John Wesley (1703–91) was the chaplain here.

RICHARD HOOKER (1554–1600) was a moderate English Anglican theologian who defended Episcopacy and attacked what he saw as the excesses of Puritan enthusiasm. His great work *Of the Laws of Ecclesiastical Polity* (1593–1662, 7 vols.) gave Anglicanism its basic form.

MERTON COLLEGE, Merton St., claims to be the oldest teaching college, even though both University College and Balliol College were actually established earlier. Walter de Merton founded it in 1264 for the education of secular rather than monastic clergy. By "secular," he meant clergy who would actually work in parish churches ministering to local congregations rather than those who lived in monasteries with little or no contact with the outside world. Later colleges took the governmental structure of Merton as their model. Its tower gateway was constructed between 1416 and 1465. The main hall was renovated by Sir Gilbert Scott in 1874, restoring it to what he saw as its original Gothic elegance. The chapel, the oldest in the university, is high Gothic and lacks a nave. Inside are numerous monuments to graduates. The choir windows contain 13th-century stained glass. The pride of the college is its excellent medieval library, constructed between 1373 and 1378. This was the first library ever to store books in the now usual upright position. Before that time books were kept on their sides in presses.

Graduates of Merton include John Wycliffe (1329–84) and T. S. Eliot (1888–1965), and J. R. R. Tolkien (1892–1973) was a fellow here.

BRASENOSE COLLEGE, Radcliffe Square, was also founded relatively late (1509) by William Smyth, bishop of Lincoln, and Sir Richard Sutton. The name of the college is something of an enigma, although the most popular suggestions are that it either refers to a brewery or comes from the name of a bronze lion's head door knocker of an earlier building that stood on this site. The library and chapel combine neoclassical and Gothic elements and were built between 1656 and 1666. Former students included John Foxe (1516–87) and William Golding (1911–), author of *The Lord of the Flies*. More recently, Archbishop Robert Runcie (1921–) studied here.

BODLEIAN LIBRARY, Radcliffe Square, which took 66 years to build and was first opened in 1488, is one of the world's great libraries. It was originally endowed by Humphrey, duke of Gloucester (1391–1447), but closed during the Reformation of Edward VI (1537–53). It was refounded in 1602 by Sir Thomas Bodley (1545–1613), who had been Queen Elizabeth's ambassador to the Netherlands, where Calvinism had taken root and education was highly valued. He donated his personal collection of over 2,500 books to form the library's core. Today the collection has over six million books and 150,000 rare manuscripts and is one of Britain's six copyright libraries, which means that publishers are supposed to provide it with a copy of every book they publish. Only two areas, the exhibition room and former divinity school, are open to the public. Cranmer, Ridley, and Latimer were "examined" in here before their formal trial in 1555. Guided tours of other areas of the library are available.

ALL SOULS COLLEGE, High St., was founded by the archbishop of Canterbury, Henry Chichele, in 1438 for advanced theological and legal studies. It was to have a resident warden and 60 scholars but no undergraduate students. In addition to their scholarly work, members of the college were expected to pray regularly for the souls of English soldiers killed in the Hundred Years' War with France who were, according to medieval Roman Catholic doctrine, languishing in purgatory. It was the only Oxford College with the status of what we now know as a "graduate school" until the founding of Nuffield College in 1937. The college's Codrington Library contains many valuable manuscripts, including many architectural drawings by Sir Christopher Wren (1632–1723), among which are his plans for the rebuilding of St. Paul's Cathedral in London. Fellows include

Wren himself, Jeremy Taylor (1613–67), and the jurist Sir William Blackstone (1723–80). More recently, T. E. Lawrence (1888–1935), known as Lawrence of Arabia, also studied here.

UNIVERSITY COLLEGE, High St., near All Souls, was founded by William of Durham in 1249, although legend says King Alfred (849–99) himself originally established it. Although the first college was built on this site in 1332, the present buildings are largely the work of 17th-century architects, with some significant 19th-century remodeling by Sir Gilbert Scott. Among its many graduates is the leader of 18th-century Deism, Lord Edward Herbert of Cherbury (1583–1649). In 1811 the poet Percy Bysshe Shelley (1792–1822) was expelled for atheism after publishing an anonymous pamphlet *The Necessity of Atheism,* which was soon traced back to him. After Shelley's tragic death in a boating accident in Italy in 1822, the college erected a Shelley memorial. It is a white marble monument with the dead Shelley being borne away by two winged lions. More recently politicians Harold Wilson (1916–95) and Bill Clinton (1946–) studied here, as did the social commentator and novelist V. S. Naipaul (1932–). From a Christian perspective, its best-known fellow is the great Christian apologist and writer C. S. Lewis (1898–1963).

The windows in the chapel depict the story of human history from the Creation to the time of Jesus. In the

O

quad is a statue of James II (1633–1701).

MAGDALEN COLLEGE, pronounced "Maudlen," High St., is generally regarded as Oxford's most majestic college. It was founded in 1458 by William of Waynflete (1398–1486), who eventually became the bishop of Winchester and lord chancellor, which in those days was the equivalent of a modern prime minister. The facade facing High Street is pure Gothic at its best, while the college's wall facing High Street is 13th century. According to tradition, Thomas Wolsey, later Cardinal Wolsey, was the college bursar who commissioned the building of its graceful tower, which was built between 1492 and 1505. The naveless chapel was remodeled by the Victorians. The quad's cloister buttresses are famous for their gargoyles. Among its many famous members are Cardinal Wolsey (1473–1530), Reginald Pole (1500–1558), John Foxe (1516–87), and Edward Gibbon (1737–94), who was expelled for converting to Roman Catholicism. Later Gibbon wrote his famous *Decline and Fall of the Roman Empire* and became a severe critic of Christianity. C. S. Lewis (1898–1963) studied here.

ST. EDMOND'S HALL, Queen's Lane, is the last surviving medieval college residence. It was built in 1220 and dedicated to St. Edmond of Abingdon, who taught at Oxford from 1195–1200 before becoming archbishop of Canterbury. Until 1937 it was administered by Queen's College, and only gained full independence in 1957. Its small chapel

LORD HERBERT OF CHERBURY (1583–1649) is recognized as one of the major intellectual sources of Deism. He rejected revelation and taught that religion is based on a belief in a god who should be worshiped through virtuous action. Humans are responsible to repent for sin and should believe in life after death. In attacking biblical revelation, Lord Herbert and fellow Deists strongly attacked the Old Testament and also the Jews, whom they saw as a depraved people. This attack on the Bible leads directly to modern anti-Semitism.

CLIVE STAPLES LEWIS (1898–1963) was a novelist, poet, literary critic, and Christian apologist. An Anglican layman, he taught at both the universities of Oxford and Cambridge. He is best known for his *Narnia Chronicles* (1950–1969, 7 vols.), *The Screwtape Letters* (1941), and *Mere Christianity* (1952). The story of his conversion is told in *Surprised by Joy* (1955) and the ponderous *The Pilgrim's Regress* (1933).

has stained glass by William Morris, and the Norman crypt, one of the oldest in Oxford, is open to the public.

BALLIOL COLLEGE, Banbury Rd., on the corner of Holywell St. and Broad St., was founded as a penance in 1282 by John de Balliol (whose son became king of Scotland) after he had insulted the bishop of Durham. None of its original buildings survived. The present college was built in the 19th century. John Wycliffe was the master of Balliol in 1364 and trained many of his students here, making the college the base from which the Lollard movement sprang. In the 18th century the economist Adam Smith (1723–90) studied here. A series of able 19th-century masters, the best known of whom is the philosopher Benjamin Jowett (1817–93), established the college's academic reputation as a center of excellence. The philosophers T. H. Green (1836–82) and poets Robert Southey (1774–1843) and Gerard Manley Hopkins (1844–89) worked here, as did the great Roman Catholic biblical scholar and apologist Ronald Knox (1888–1957) and the Catholic novelist Graham Greene (1904–91). Archbishop William Temple (1881–1944), known for his Christian Socialism and concern to make Christianity relevant in an industrial society, was also a student here. More negatively, Balliol produced the mythologist Andrew Lang (1844–1912), who popularized numerous ideas that fed into the 20th-century occult revival. Similarly, three other graduates,

the brothers Julian (1887–1975) and Aldous Huxley (1894–1963) and historian Arnold Toynbee (1889–1975), all contributed in their own way to the growth of alternate religions. It comes as little surprise to learn that Balliol is generally regarded as one of the more radical colleges in Oxford. Most recently the historian Christopher Hill served as its master. Although a Marxist, his books *The Century of Revolution, God's Englishman: Oliver Cromwell,* and *A Tinker and a Poor Man: The Life and Times of John Bunyan* treat Puritanism with great respect and have done a lot to restore its image as an important, scholarly, and humane movement.

TRINITY COLLEGE, Parkes Rd. and Holywell St., entered through iron gates facing Broad St., was founded by Sir Thomas Pope in 1555. It replaced and incorporated the monastic Durham College, which served students from the north of England and was supported by the Benedictine monasteries of Durham, which were suppressed at the Dissolution. The grounds are generally regarded as the best in Oxford. The chapel, which is decorated in the fussy Baroque style, contains some excellent Victorian stained glass. The old library, which is not open to the public, is almost all that remains of Durham College. Known for its conservatism and leanings towards Roman Catholicism, Trinity College includes such graduates as Lord Baltimore (1580–1632), who founded Maryland as a Roman Catholic colony in America;

O

Prime Minister William Pitt the Elder (1707–78); and Cardinal John Henry Newman (1801–90), the leader of the Tractarian movement.

NEW COLLEGE, New College Lane, was founded by William of Wykeham (1324–1404) in 1379 with its wonderful Gothic buildings being completed in 1386. Wykeham also founded Winchester College as a feeder school for his great institution in Oxford. The chapel was restored by Gilbert Scott in 1877. He "improved" on its original design with a new hammer-beam roof. Most of the stained glass in the ante-chapel, except the west window, is the original 14th-century glass. El Greco's (1541–1614) painting of *St. James* stands on the north side of the altar, and Epstein's sculpture *Lazarus* (1951) stands in the ante-chapel. The college hall, next to the chapel, is the oldest in Oxford. The fine cloisters and gardens are well worth seeing.

EXETER COLLEGE, Turl St., off Broad St., was founded in 1314 as a monastic institution by Walter de Stapeldon (1201–1326) and refounded in 1556 as a secular college by Sir William Petre following the Dissolution of the Monasteries. Most of the buildings are of 18th- or 19th-century origin. The chapel was built by Sir Gilbert Scott in 1857 and is one of his less successful works. Inside is a tapestry by two former students, William Morris and Edward Burne-Jones. The first earl of Shaftesbury developed his ideas of social reform here. J. R. R. Tolkien was a student here.

JESUS COLLEGE, Turl St., is the first post-Reformation college to be opened in Oxford by Queen Elizabeth I in 1571, although Hugh Price, of St. Davids in Wales, is regarded as its true founder. The chapel was extended in 1636, and its Gothic exterior was rebuilt in the 19th century. The chapel has a vaulted barrel roof. The hall contains portraits of Elizabeth I, Charles I, and Charles II. The godly Bishop Lancelot Andrewes (1555–1626) was a student here, as was the 18th-century dandy and master of ceremonies in Bath, Richard Nash (1674–1762), who was known as Beau Nash. Prime Minister Harold Wilson (1916–95), who was a professing Methodist, also studied here.

LINCOLN COLLEGE, Turl St., is said to be the most authentic of Oxford's medieval colleges. It was founded in 1427 by the bishop of Lincoln as an orthodox school where clergy were to be trained to combat Wycliffe's heresies. On the right of the hall, which has its original 15th-century roof, are the rooms where John and Charles Wesley founded the Holy Club, out of which Methodism eventually developed. Anyone who wants to see inside Wesley's rooms must ask the porter, who shows them to visitors. The chapel was built between 1629 and 1631 by Bishop Williams of Lincoln and has some excellent painted glass.

HERTFORD COLLEGE, Catte St., was founded as Hart Hall in 1282. It became Hertford College in 1740 but was absorbed by Magdalen Hall in 1822 only to be refounded as Hertford College in 1874. The buildings date from the late 16th century with 19th-century additions. The college's most famous pupil was the poet John Donne (1572–1631). The Bible translator William Tyndale (1494–1536) lived here when the college was still Hart Hall, as did the philosopher Thomas Hobbes (1588–1679).

WORCESTER COLLEGE, Beaumont St., was founded in 1714 by Sir Thomas Cooke on the site of the Benedictine Gloucester College that was suppressed at the Dissolution of the Monasteries. The main building is in the neoclassical style, although five older small houses survive from the former monastic buildings. The coat of arms of the Benedictine abbeys to which they once belonged can be seen over their doorways. Worcester has one of the largest and most beautiful gardens in Oxford surrounding a tranquil lake.

ST. JOHN'S COLLEGE was founded in 1555 by Sir Thomas White to replace the older Cistercian college of St. Bernard, which was disbanded at the Dissolution. The original college had been founded in 1437 by Archbishop Chichele. Three sides of its quad are part of the original college, which was a two-story building. A third story was added in the 17th century. Over the gateway one can still see a statue of St. Bernard. Inside is also a modern statue of John the Baptist (1936) by Eric Gill. Arch-

bishop Laud (1573–1645), who attempted to undo the English Reformation and defeat Puritanism, is its most famous graduate. The library contains a collection of materials related to Laud, but these may only be viewed by appointment. The Roman Catholic martyr Edmund Campion (1540–81) also studied here.

SOMERVILLE COLLEGE, Woodstock Rd., was founded for women in 1879 as a nondenominational institution; the only other women's college at the time was the Anglican LADY MARGARET HALL, Parks Rd., which was founded in 1878. Somerville is where the Christian novelist and apologist Dorothy Sayers (1893–1957) studied. Other famous graduates are prime minister of England Margaret Thatcher (1925–), prime minister of India Indira Gandhi (1917–84), and novelist Iris Murdoch (1919–99).

KEBLE COLLEGE, Keble Rd., was founded in 1870 as a memorial to the Tractarian leader John Keble (1792–1866) to provide poor students with a university education.

RUSKIN COLLEGE was founded in 1899 by American supporters who were inspired by the works of John Ruskin (1819–1900). It was intended to be a college where members of the English working class could obtain an education. Although famous in its own right, it is not officially part of Oxford University.

REGENT'S PARK COLLEGE, Pusey St., is a private Baptist hall and theological center linked to the university.

O

BLACKFRIARS, St. Giles, was established as a residence for Dominican monks studying at Oxford.

PUSEY HOUSE is a theological research center and since 1965 the home of **ST. CROSS COLLEGE,** a graduate school in the Anglo-Catholic tradition named after Edward Pusey (1800–1882), one of the founders of the Tractarian movement.

WYCLIFFE COLLEGE stands in the evangelical tradition to train Anglican clergymen. Like the other theological colleges, it is not formally part of Oxford University, with which it has a special relationship.

OXFORD CENTER FOR MISSION STUDIES, St. Philip and St. James Church, Woodstock Rd., was founded in the 1970s.

MANSFIELD COLLEGE, Mansfield Rd., was originally a theological college belonging to the Congregational Church. Today it serves as an undergraduate residence. It is particularly interesting because it represents the nonconformist tradition in Oxford. In its chapel there are a series of stained-glass windows by Sir Joshua Reynolds (1723–92) that point to the close links between Oxford nonconformity and the great tradition of Puritan education in North America. These windows depict the coats of arms of Harvard, Princeton, Yale, the University of Pennsylvania, and several other outstanding American institutions.

MANCHESTER COLLEGE, Mansfield Rd., is the main Unitarian College in Britain. Founded in Manchester in 1786, it came to Oxford in 1888.

THE LAMB AND FLAG INN, St. Giles, is an English pub. Here met the informal Christian writers group, the Inklings, which included Dorothy Sayers (1893–1957), C. S. Lewis (1898–1963), and J. R. R. Tolkien (1872–1973).

PITT-RIVERS MUSEUM OF ETHNOLOGY AND PRE-HISTORY, Keble Road, was founded in 1884 by the soldier anthropologist Augustus Henry Lane-Fox Pitt-Rivers (1827–1900). It is one of the world's great ethnological museums. Unfortunately, the museum has hand-written labels and a general sense of confusion. Nevertheless, the collection is superb and very informative for anyone wishing to understand the variety of human cultures.

ASHMOLEAN MUSEUM, Beaumont St., originated as the private collection of John Tradescant (d. 1638), who was King James I's gardener at Hatfield House. It was donated to the university by his widow and promptly nicknamed "Tradescant's Ark," reflecting the vast range and unorganized nature of the curios collected by Tradescant and his son. The museum's collection has grown considerably over the years but still remains somewhat unorganized and poorly labeled although incredibly diverse and rich. The museum claims to be the oldest public museum in the world.

The Egyptian collection is particularly interesting for the light it throws on biblical history. Note the 18th-century B.C. fresco of an Egyptian princess, which is the first known example of an artist depicting a round body on a flat surface. The Indian and Asian collections are also very good, and in the medieval room is a jewel belonging to the English Christian king and educator Alfred the Great (849–99).

In the Tradescant room, on the first floor, is Oliver Cromwell's (1599–1658) death mask and the lantern used by the Roman Catholic assassin Guy Fawkes (1570–1606) during his abortive attempt to blow up the Protestant Parliament in 1605. It also contains the famous Powhatan mantle, which is the earliest surviving example of clothing made by North American natives. Both the first and second floors display various works of art, including paintings by van Gogh, Monet, Renoir, and a host of other artists. Of particular interest is Gainsborough's (1727–88) *Descent from the Cross* and the strange visionary paintings of the 19th-century British artist Samuel Palmer (1805–81). The Pre-Raphaelite collection contains Holman Hunt's (1827–1910) *A Converted British Family Sheltering a Christian Missionary from Persecution by the Druids* and *Convent Thoughts* by Charles Collins.

MUSEUM OF THE HISTORY OF SCIENCE, Broad St., is housed in the original home of the Ashmolean Museum, and is one of the best collections of its kind in the world. Many of the founders of modern science, particularly those who worked in London and Oxford in the 17th century, were Christians. This collection contains a lot of information about the work of these scientists, who were motivated by their faith in an orderly universe. Unfortunately, the connection between the rise of science and Christianity is passed over rather quickly.

BOTANIC GARDENS, opposite Magdalen College, were founded in 1621 and are the oldest in Britain. They have a magnificent collection of rare plants.

PETERBOROUGH

Peterborough grew up as a village near a Saxon monastic community. The town and its religious community were sacked by Vikings in 870 but was soon rebuilt. In the 10th century a Benedictine abbey was built here. Unlike so many other Saxon churches, the abbey appears to have been undisturbed by the Norman conquest, but it was burnt down in 1116 and replaced by the present building. Today Peterborough is a center of the British computer industry. The city center is a pedestrian zone.

PLACES TO VISIT

PETERBOROUGH CATHEDRAL, built between 1117 and 1217, is a superb example of British Romanesque architecture that is remarkably simple and unified. It is viewed by art historians as one of the best examples of its kind in Europe. The roof paintings in the vault date from 1220. The west front was added in the 13th century and the porch in 1370; both are in the Gothic style. Henry VIII's wife, Catherine of Aragon (1485–1536), is buried in the north aisle. The crucifix which hangs over the nave was added in 1957 and is a good example of modern religious art in the Catholic tradition.

FEN BRONZE AGE CENTER, three miles east, is a small but very interesting museum, located in a modern industrial area where a Bronze Age settlement dated around 3000 B.C. was discovered. On display are finds from the founding of the settlement to Roman times. There is also a small working farm museum where old breeds of domestic animals like sheep and pigs can be seen.

PERTH

Perth was an ancient Scottish settlement which for centuries acted as Scotland's capital. In 1437, Sir Robert Graham assassinated King James I of Scotland while he was at prayer in the local Dominican friary. Graham fled north but was captured and executed in Stirling castle after severe torture. The town was a stronghold of Reformed thinking, and John Knox (1513–72) frequently preached here. During the 17th and 18th centuries it experienced a long economic decline. Today, however, it is a prosperous community.

PLACES TO VISIT

ST. JOHN'S KIRK, King Edward St., was founded in 1126 by the pious David I and rebuilt in the 15th century. The church was restored to its former glory between 1923 and 1928. John Knox preached his sermon "On Purging the Churches from Idolatry" here on May 11, 1559. The sermon aroused public sentiment to such an extent that, to Knox's horror, a mob sacked the town's four ancient monasteries, destroying many priceless works of art.

BLACK WATCH REGIMENTAL MUSEUM, Balhousie Castle, presents the dramatic history of what is arguably the most famous of all Scottish regiments, the Black Watch. Anyone interested in military history or mission history ought to visit here for the insights it gives into the expansion of the British Empire.

RIPON

Ripon is one of the great Christian foundations of northern England, being founded as a monastic community by Wilfrid of Hexham (634–700) in 672. According to legend, Ripon was granted a city charter by Alfred the Great in 886. Most of its history, however, is unremarkable, and Ripon remains a quiet but attractive small town.

PLACES TO VISIT

RIPON CATHEDRAL is a relatively small Romanesque building with a crypt that dates back to its original founding by Wilfrid in 672 on his return from a pilgrimage to Rome. This makes it one of the oldest places of continuous Christian worship in England. The original church was destroyed by Viking raiders in the 9th century, rebuilt, then destroyed again by the Normans. The present church was built by Archbishop Roger of York (1154–81). The twin-towered west front dates from the 13th century. The misericords were carved by the same craftsmen as those who worked on Beverly Cathedral and are magnificent examples of medieval skill and humor. Above the 13th-century font by the west door of the south aisle are some fine examples of 14th-century stained glass. They originally belonged to the great east window, which was used for target practice by Parliamentary troops during the English Civil War. Cromwell's army also defaced the choir screen, which was considered "idolatrous." The present carved figures, made during World War II, are replicas of the originals. In the Chapel of the Holy Spirit is a modern screen symbolizing the coming of the Holy Spirit at Pentecost.

THE MARKET SQUARE is a huge two-acre area where local markets are held each week. It is surrounded by interesting houses and shops, most of which date from the 17th or 18th centuries. The town hall was built in 1801 and has the city's motto on its frieze: "Except ye Lord Keep ye Cittie ye Wakeman Waketh in Vain." Inside are the four Ripon ox horns used by watchmen since the Middle Ages to signal the end of the day. One of them is blown at 9 P.M. every evening in keeping with the ancient practice which has never died out and has now become a tourist attraction. One of the horns, the Charter Horn, is believed to date from 886, and is said to have been presented to the city along with its charter by King Alfred himself. It is on display in the Town Hall.

RIEVAULX ABBEY is located on the north Yorkshire moors, in Ryedale, not too far from Ripon. This famous abbey, founded in 1132 by the Cistercians, was dissolved by Henry VIII and sold to local landowners, who stripped its roof of lead and used many of its stones to build walls and cattle sheds. The haunting, ruined nave dates from 1135, while the presbytery is 13th century. The shrine of the first abbot, who established the abbey as the motherhouse of the Cistercian Order in England, can still be seen in the west wall of the chapter house. The infirmary, chapel, kitchens, and warming room are all restored sufficiently to give visitors a good idea of the way a major medieval monastery, with over 150 monks and 500 lay brothers, worked. It was here that the great Cistercian scholar, Aelred of Rievaulx (1109–67), whose ancestors were married priests living in Hexham, wrote his famous treatise on *Spiritual Friendship.*

ROCHESTER

Rochester was built by the Romans as the port city of Durobivae on the river Medway and Watling Street. It was conquered by the Normans, who built a castle, and is best known as the setting for Charles Dickens's famous novels *The Pickwick Papers, Great Expectations,* and *The Mystery of Edwin Drood.* Dickens alternatively called Rochester the town of "Mudfog" and "Dullborough," reflecting his view of the town.

PLACES TO VISIT

ROCHESTER CATHEDRAL was founded as a military base by the Romans. In 1077 Bishop Gundulf (1024–1108) was appointed by William the Conqueror, who gave him the task of subduing southeast England. Later he became the archbishop of Canterbury. His original Norman church was renovated in the 12th and 13th centuries. The west front, particularly the main doorway, is an outstanding example of French carving and is in the Gothic style, as is the nave. The interior of the cathedral beyond the nave is essentially Romanesque. On the choir wall is a rare painting, *The Wheel of Fortune,* dating from the 13th century.

ROCHESTER CASTLE is a brooding Norman structure built by the Bishop Gundruf (who was also a secular ruler) to dominate the local population. Gundruf was also the architect of the Tower of London and Rochester Cathedral. The main castle keep was added by William de Corbeil when he was archbishop of Canterbury in 1127 and is a great example of Norman military building.

CHARLES DICKENS CENTER, Eastgate House, High St., is an excellent modern museum which gives vivid, if grim, insights into Victorian England

and the life and work of Dickens, who spent his youth in the Rochester area.

ROCHESTER MUSEUM, High St., is an excellent local museum that provides visitors with insights into social history. Exhibits include King John's (1167–1216) siege of the castle in 1215. There is also an interesting display showing conditions on 18th-century prison ships which were moored in the Medway.

CHATHAM DOCKYARD MUSEUM, two miles northeast, recreates the historic shipbuilding center established by Henry VII. Over 500 navel ships were built here, including Horatio Nelson's famous flagship, the *Victory*. The last ship to be built here was the *Okanagan* in 1966. In 1984 the Royal Navy closed its facilities, and the complex was gradually transformed into an outstanding maritime museum.

SALISBURY

Built on the site of an Iron Age fort, a settlement existed here long before the arrival of the Romans, who conquered the area and established a military garrison. After the withdrawal of the Roman legions, Saxons occupied the area. They were replaced by Norman overlords, who built a castle and cathedral on the site of the ancient fort known as Old Sarum. The first cathedral was built by Bishop Osmund (d. 1099) but was destroyed in a storm. In the early 12th century, it was rebuilt by Bishop Roger, who made the castle his palace. A period of civil unrest began in 1139 when Bishop Roger's fall from power led to a struggle for control of the area between supporters of the church and supporters of the king. A drop in the water table created problems for the inhabitants of both the castle and old town during the 13th century. Consequently, it was decided to move both the

town and the cathedral from their hilltop position into the valley. New Sarum, which eventually changed its name to Salisbury, was then built over the next 40 years some three miles south of the original town. It was granted a royal charter in 1227 and placed under Episcopal rule, a situation that lasted until 1611. The center of a relatively wealthy, yet suitably remote, farming area, Salisbury managed to miss most of the upheavals of English history and avoided serious bombing during World War II.

PLACES TO VISIT

SALISBURY CATHEDRAL is probably the best known of all English cathedrals due to the numerous reproductions of Gainsborough's famous painting of it. Its ornate west front and tall spire, 404 feet, which was added between 1280 and 1315 by Bishop Giles de Brideport, makes it an unforgettable sight. The interior is one of

S

the most unified Gothic buildings in England, although somewhat bare after Victorian renovations removed earlier decorations. What one sees, though, is the sheer wonder of Gothic stonework, with its fan vaulting and soaring pillars. On the south side are the tombs of Bishops Roger and Osmund, whose shrine became a center of medieval pilgrimage. William Longespée, the third earl of Salisbury (d. 1226) who with his wife founded Lacock Abbey, is buried in the same area. His tomb shows him in a coat of medieval armor. The west window contains medieval stained glass. The Trinity Chapel has a modern window dedicated to prisoners of conscience; it was made by the French artist Gabriel Loire (1904–96).

At the center of the crossing, which stands between the nave and transepts, an octagon is marked in the floor to outline the spire. During the 17th century, Sir Christopher Wren (1632–1723) was commissioned by the bishop to survey the state of the building because the spire appeared to be leaning. When he checked, he found that indeed it was 29.5 inches off center, due to the fact that the cathedral was built on boggy ground. A brass plaque marks the spot where Wren's plumb line rested after being lowered from the point of the spire. Because the spire was in danger of falling over, Wren made various devices, including tie rods, to stabilize the building. His work provided a much-needed respite but did not cure the problem. Today, as can be seen by the scaffolding

and other works, engineers are still attempting to find a more permanent solution and to provide the cathedral with a solid foundation.

The cloisters and chapter house were built in 1263 and are particularly impressive examples of Gothic vaulting. The chapter house is almost 60 feet in diameter, with its roof being supported by a narrow central column. On the outside of this octagonal structure are eight marble columns. Note the carved frieze depicting various stories from the Old Testament. One of the four surviving copies of the *Magna Carta* is owned by the cathedral library. It is not on display, and the library is closed to the public.

CHURCH OF ST. THOMAS is a Gothic church built in 1220. Its tower dates from 1390. Inside, above the chancel arch, is a painting of Christ in Majesty seated in the New Jerusalem that dates from 1475. The Lady Chapel contains some small 15th-century frescoes.

MOMPESSON HOUSE is one of several Georgian houses that grace the pleasant cathedral close. It was built in 1701 by Charles Mompesson and contains period furniture and a fine collection of drinking glasses.

THE SALISBURY AND SOUTH WILTSHIRE MUSEUM, in the King's House on the cathedral close, has some interesting items dealing with local history, plus an excellent collection of material relating to nearby Stonehenge. There is also a section dealing with Augustus Henry Lane-Fox Pitt-Rivers (1827–1900), who is regarded by many as the "father" of modern archaeology.

STONEHENGE is one of UNESCO's 380 World Heritage Sites. Beloved by New Agers, the site is usually associated with the Druids. However, the area was abandoned about 1400 B.C., long before the Druids, who were Celts, arrived in England.

Stonehenge is over 4000 years old and shows evidence of several stages in its construction, which began around 2800 B.C. The stones themselves were brought from the Valley of Pewsey. Archaeologists estimate that it took over 600 men to haul each stone and 200 to raise it to its upright position. During phase one of the building process, a deep round ditch, 300 feet in diameter, was built. The ditch was ringed by 56 holes, which presumably once held stones. These are the Aubrey holes, named after John Aubrey (1625–97), who first investigated them. An entranceway was cut through the northeast bank, which was marked by two upright stones on the inside. Within the enclosure four more stones were set, marking the four points of the compass.

Around 1900 B.C. a second phase of building began with the erection of a double stone ring known as the bluestones. Each of these massive, undressed stones weighs around four tons. They were brought on boats along the river Avon from the Presely Hills in southwest Wales, over 240 miles away. Dropped in an area known as the Avenue, they were then hauled over land to their present location.

A third building phase began around 1650 B.C. The undressed bluestone ring was replaced by tall tapered stones with mortised lintels held together by tongues and grooves in a horseshoe formation. These stones were made from sandstone hewn from the nearby Marlborough Downs. Finally, around 1550 B.C., another group of bluestones was brought from Wales, but this time they were carefully dressed before they too were placed in the horseshoe formation.

During the Middle Ages, local farmers used Stonehenge as a quarry and source of building material. Only in the 18th century did it really capture popular imagination, becoming a center of occult speculation. Today it is claimed by "Druids" and a host of other New Age and mystical groups who continually plea with its custodians for permission to hold religious ceremonies within its carefully controlled grounds.

At some point in Stonehenge's history, the outer ditch was filled in with earth and human ash. This fact leads to speculation that the area had been a temple complex where human sacrifice was performed. Another popular theory is that Stonehenge was a kind of ancient calculator used to predict eclipses and other astronomical events. But because we lack written records, it is unlikely that we will ever know the truth. All of these "mysteries," facts and fancies, are the subject of displays in the local visitor's center.

S

ST. ALBANS

St. Albans is not on the usual tourist route, nor is it one of the more scenic places in Britain. Nevertheless, its importance in Christian history cannot be overestimated. The Romans built a fort here in 43, on the south bank of the river, and founded the town of Verulamium six years later. It became the third largest Roman settlement in Britain. Sacked by Boadicea in 61, it was almost completely destroyed in a fire in 155.

Here a Roman soldier, Alban (d. 209), was beheaded on top of a small hill on the north bank of the river for sheltering Amphibalus, a Christian evangelist, through whom he had been converted. This is the first known Christian martyrdom in Britain. Later the soldier's grave became a pilgrimage site as miracles were attributed to it, and a church was built on the site. After the withdrawal of the Roman legions, the Roman town fell into ruins, while a new town was built around the church of St. Alban.

This church was destroyed by Saxon invaders who, after their conversion, also built a church on the site of Alban's martyrdom. In 793, King Offa of Mercia founded a Benedictine abbey dedicated to St. Alban. As they usually did, the Normans demolished the Saxon church in 1077 to make way for the present abbey, signaling their triumph over the local population by building what for many centuries was one of the largest churches in Europe. During the Middle Ages, this became one of the wealthiest monastic houses in Britain. Between 1154 and 1396, the abbot of St. Albans was the most important abbot in Britain, second only to the archbishop of Canterbury.

Henry VI's army was defeated at the Battle of Holywell Hill in 1455 when Henry was taken prisoner. In 1461, he was released after Queen Margaret's victory on nearby Bernard's Heath. The abbey was secularized at the Dissolution, when it became a parish church. During the 19th century, in 1877, it was elevated to the rank of cathedral. St. Albans suffered relatively heavy bombing during World War II, although many old buildings and the cathedral remained intact.

Apart from being the site of the first English martyr, St. Albans is also the birthplace of the only English pope, Adrian IV (1100–1159); he received his education in the cathedral school. The composer of church music Robert Fayrfax (d. 1521) was the organist in the abbey church from 1498 until his death in 1521. Sir Francis Bacon's (1561–1626) home was in nearby Gorhambury, where he is buried in St. Michael's Church. Finally, the great evangelical hymn writer and poet William Cowper was a patient here during his illness in 1764–65.

PLACES TO VISIT

ST. ALBAN'S CATHEDRAL was founded in 1077 by Paul of Caen, who was the abbot from 1077–88. Work was completed in 1116, when the abbey was dedicated. During the next two centuries, between 1235 and 1326, the already long nave was lengthened to its present size of over 300 feet. The extension work was done by builders who introduced early Gothic elements into the abbey's structure, thus destroying the unity of its Romanesque design. Nevertheless, the nave, which is the longest Romanesque nave in Britain, gives a sense of both space and permanence, as no doubt it was intended to do.

The pillars on the north side are the original Romanesque pillars. Five pillars on the south side, added during medieval repair work, are early Gothic. The tower remains pure Romanesque. The Lady Chapel was built between 1235 and 1326. The west front, which is frankly disappointing, was added by the Victorians in 1879, and the chapter house was built in 1982. Although not the most attractive of English cathedrals, the church contains some excellent medieval wall paintings and decorated roof panels. The carved Gothic nave screen is also very well done.

According to tradition, the center of the cathedral marks the spot where St. Alban met his death. The south aisle contains an 18th-century depiction of St. Alban's execution. St. Alban's Chapel, east of the presbytery, contains the shrine of the saint. It was vandalized during the Dissolution and for several centuries remained a heap of garbage. Repair work began in 1872, when over 2000 white marble fragments were gathered and identified. These were not restored until 1993, when the present shrine was reconstructed.

ST. MICHAEL'S CHURCH, St. Michael St., south of the river, was founded in 948 but remodeled by the Normans and later occupants. The pulpit is Jacobean. The church also contains the tomb and a statue of the famous natural philosopher and Christian thinker Sir Francis Bacon (1561–1626).

VERULAMIUM MUSEUM, St. Michael St., contains an impressive array of Roman remains, giving graphic insights into the city where Christianity first took root in Britain and the times when St. Alban lived. Among its many exhibits is an outstanding mosaic of the Roman sea god. To the northwest of the museum on the opposite side of the road is the ROMAN AMPHITHEATER in front of which there was a pagan temple. In all probability, Christians were tried here before their execution.

The HYPOCAUST, or Roman bath complex, is on the southwest side of the museum. Here one can see the sophistication of Roman buildings, complete with a central heating system.

225

FRANCIS BACON (1561–1626). English jurist and philosopher who championed empiricism, the use of induction, and experimental science. He is the author of *Essays, The Advancement of Learning* (1605), and *The New Atlantis* (1624). He was strongly influenced by Calvinism and Puritan ideas, although he never openly identified with the Puritan movement.

ST. ANDREWS

According to local legend, St. Andrews was founded by St. Regulus, who had been instructed in a dream to take the bones of St. Andrew to the farthest place on earth. So in the 4th century he set off from the Greek island of Patras. He was shipwrecked off the Scottish coast, coming ashore where the town stands today. Whatever truth, if any, lies behind this legend, it is certain that the town was a center for Christian evangelism at an early date. A preaching station and church were built here. In the 12th century, a cathedral was built around a shrine said to house five bones of St. Andrew. The town grew up around its church, which was a major pilgrimage site and the ecclesiastical capital of Scotland. St. Andrews University, Scotland's first university, was founded by Bishop Henry Wardlaw in 1410 with King James I of Scotland as its patron. It was to become one of the great universities of Europe and is often referred to as the "Oxbridge of the North."

During the Reformation the local bishop, Cardinal Beaton, was a Roman Catholic fanatic. He found George Wishart, a Protestant evangelist, guilty of heresy and watched him burnt at the stake in front of his castle in 1546. Three months later the bishop was assassinated, and a period of civil unrest followed. A mob sacked the cathedral in 1559, and it subsequently fell into ruins.

St. Andrews prospered throughout the Middle Ages until the 17th century because of its importance as a trading center with the states of the Baltic region. When the importance of the Baltic declined due to the development of trade with America in the 18th century, St. Andrews experienced a long period of economic decline. In recent years, the development of North Sea oil has helped St. Andrews. In addition, it has growing importance as a tourist center. Many avid golfers come to play the St. Andrews golf course, the oldest course in the world and the place where golf is said to have been invented.

PLACES TO VISIT

ST. ANDREWS CATHEDRAL was built between 1160 and 1318, with Robert the Bruce (1274–1329) attending its consecration. At the height of its power, the cathedral was the largest church in Scotland and the most powerful politically. Today, it is a picturesque ruin. The cathedral's destruction began on June 5, 1559, when John Knox himself visited St. Andrews to preach a rabble-rousing sermon inspired by the memory of the death of his friend John Wishart, who was burnt at the stake after a trial in the cathedral a few years earlier. Knox's sermon led to a mob attacking the cathedral and sacking it, a deed about which Knox uncharacteristically expressed no regret. St. Andrew's shrine was wrecked, the stained-glass windows smashed, and lead stripped from the cathedral roof, causing the building to quickly become a ruin. The various monastic buildings surrounding the cathedral were either turned to other uses or pulled down.

This situation continued until the 1820s when the Romantic movement took hold in Scotland. Largely through the influence of Sir Walter Scott's novels, people began to develop a strong interest and pride in their past. Since then a serious effort has been made to preserve and even partially rebuild the ruins, which today offer the visitor a glimpse into the sad fate of a once powerful and majestic church.

ST. ANDREWS UNIVERSITY, which is the oldest in Scotland, originally occupied the site of what is today the Old University Library. Three monastic colleges—St. Salvator (1450), St. Leonard's (1512), and St. Mary's (1538)—were founded before the Reformation, after which they were secularized and St. Mary's became the divinity school to train clergy for the newly Reformed Church of Scotland. The faculty of theology still resides in St. Mary's, although due to the phenomenal decline in the number of students seeking ordination in the Church of Scotland, it is becoming a department of Religious Studies where feminist theology is increasingly popular. Guided tours of the university, which is situated on beautiful grounds, are available all summer. The gardens of the quad are particularly beautiful.

THE CASTLE, like the cathedral, is now a romantic ruin. It occupies a superb strategic position, with steep cliffs falling to the sea on three sides and a deep moat on the fourth. From here local bishops, who were effectively princes, ruled the surrounding area throughout the Middle Ages. The castle was built in 1200 but fell into ruin in the 17th century, when changes in military technique and ideas about comfort made it no longer practical either as a fortification or as a palace. In 1546 Cardinal Beaton was assassinated here before his body was hung from the battlements and then dropped into a deep hole known as "the bottle dungeon."

THE BRITISH GOLF MUSEUM. The game of golf was played here at least as early as the 14th century. But it wasn't until 1754 that the Society of St.

S

Andrews Golfers was founded. Almost a century later, in 1834, it was granted the right to call itself the Royal and Ancient Society of St. Andrews Golfers. Today it is the sport's ruling body. When golf was really invented no one knows. But as early as 1457, King James II of Scotland sought to ban the game because too many people were skipping church in favor of playing golf—some things never change! This is a fun museum which is rich in social history.

ST. DAVID'S, TYDDEWI, WALES

Old-fashioned Roman Catholics who want to lessen their time in purgatory need to know that in the 12th century Pope Callixtus II declared that two pilgrimages to St. David's are equivalent to one pilgrimage to Rome. The only other pilgrimage site to share this distinction is Spain's Santiago de Compostella, which vividly illustrates the importance of St. David's in Christian history. On the other hand, Protestants will find it more interesting to learn that a Christian community has existed here since St. David (462–520) founded his monastery here around 506. His church was destroyed in a fire in 645 and again by Vikings in 1078. William the Conqueror visited the shrine shortly after his invasions of England in 1068. Peter de Leia (d. 1198), a monk from Florence and the third bishop appointed by the Norman kings, founded the present cathedral in 1180. The town flourished until the Reformation as one of Europe's major pilgrimage sites, after which it became a sleepy Welsh town which is dependent on tourism.

PLACES TO VISIT

ST. DAVID'S CATHEDRAL is one of the largest and certainly the most historic church in Wales. It is located in an enclosed area in a quiet valley by the river Alun and retains far more of its medieval ambiance than most British cathedrals. The church was built in the 12th century, although the tower fell down in 1220. Further damage was done by an earthquake in 1248, leaving the whole building on an unplanned slope, which gives it a unique aspect. The nave roof is 15th-century Irish oak that is beautifully crafted and decorated. There is an excellent rood screen. In the south aisle of the choir is the tomb of Giraldus Cambrensis (1146–1223), better known as Gerald of Wales, whose account of a journey through Wales still makes fascinating reading. Edmund

Tudor(1430–56), Henry VII's grandfather, is buried in front of the high altar. Edmund's body was moved here from its previous resting place in the Grayfriars monastery in Carmarthen at the Dissolution. The central shrine of St. David is on the north side of the presbytery, where it has been reconstructed after it was wrecked during the Reformation. St. David's remains and those of his personal confessor, a priest named Justinian, are preserved in an oak reliquary at the back of the Holy Trinity Chapel. During the Reformation, the priests of the monastery hid the relics of St. David in the wall of the chapel shortly before the Dissolution. They were rediscovered by workmen repairing the cathedral in 1886.

BISHOP'S PALACE, now a ruin, stands close to the cathedral in the same enclosed area, and was built in the 14th century by Bishop Gower (d. 1347). The remains of a wonderful rose window gives visitors an impression of the power and beauty which once resided here. A museum in the palace's vaults provides visitors with insights into the history and lives of the bishops of St. David's.

ST. DAVID'S CELTIC CROSS is located in the main market square of the town of St. David's.

ST. NON'S CHAPEL, one mile west of St. David's, stands close to where St. David (d. 589) was born. Today, the pre-Norman chapel, dedicated to his mother, is a romantic ruin on a windswept coast close to a small well and shrine where the saint was born one stormy night. Nearby is the harbor of Porth-Clais, where, according to tradition, St. David was baptized in the sea.

STIRLING

S
tirling's history is shrouded in the dim, distant past. In prehistoric times a settlement located here at a strategic point on the Firth of Forth. There is also some evidence that the castle rock was fortified by the Romans. But the first real evidence of fortification comes from the time of Alexander I of Scotland (1078–1124), even though legend says the castle was built here by the legendary King Arthur. A castle was built on an outcropping of rock that makes a superb defensive position, and the town grew up around it. In many ways, the history of the town is the history of its castle.

After the death of Alexander III (1241–86), Edward I (1239–1307) of England supported the claim of Alexander III's granddaughter, Margaret, maid of Norway (d. 1290), to the Scottish crown. When she died suddenly in 1290, Edward was called in to settle the dispute between three rival claimants and sided with John de Balliol (1249–1315), who in return for Edward's support pledged allegiance to the English king and was crowned king of Scotland in 1292. Shortly afterwards when war broke out between England and France in 1296, Balliol sided with the French, and a Scottish army invaded England. The Scots were defeated by Edward I, who invaded Scotland and stormed Stirling Castle, where he established an English garrison. A year later the Scots revolted against English rule under the leadership of William Wallace (1274–1305) and recaptured the castle after defeating the English at the Battle of Stirling Bridge. Edward I once more invaded Scotland and besieged Stirling Castle, which, defended by a mere 150 men, held out until 1304. During the siege, Edward I stripped the lead off every Scottish church from Perth to St. Andrews to provide ammunition for his catapults.

English rule was once more imposed on Scotland, but in 1307, Edward I died before completing his plans to subdue Scotland as he had subdued Wales. His son Edward II (1284–1327) failed to complete his father's plans for the conquest of the Scots and returned to England. The Scottish revolt slowly gained strength, and Stirling Castle was once more besieged in 1314. This time the governor came to an agreement with the besieging army that to avoid unnecessary bloodshed he would surrender if the castle was not relieved by the end of the summer. The siege caused Edward II to invade Scotland once more. His army was decisively defeated at the Battle of Bannockburn June 24, 1314, despite the fact that the Scots were outnumbered ten to one.

After freeing Scotland from English rule, Robert the Bruce (1274–1329) systematically dismantled Stirling Castle and all other English strongholds. The castle was rebuilt by the Stuarts in the 15th and 16th centuries, when it became a royal palace and seat of government. The Roman Catholic Mary Queen of Scots (1542–87) was crowned here when she was a baby only nine months old. She was then sent to France for her education. Her son James VI of Scotland, James I of England (1567–1625), also grew up in Stirling Castle. During the English Civil War, the Puritan General Monk (1608–70) captured the castle for Parliament. In 1746 the castle was besieged for the last time by Charles Stuart, the Young Pretender (1720–88), but he failed to capture it.

PLACES TO VISIT

CHURCH OF THE HOLY RUDE, Castle Wynd, once functioned as a royal cathedral. It was here that Mary of Guise (1515–60) assumed the role of regent for her infant daughter, Mary Queen of Scots, in 1544. Although she was initially tolerant, she increasingly favored the Roman Catholic cause, leading to a revolt of Scottish nobles in 1559. Her grandson, James VI, was baptized here in 1566, with the Scottish Reformer John Knox (1514–72) preaching the sermon. Built in 1414, this is a regal Gothic structure with a magnificent rare oak hammer-beam roof. An interesting feature of the architecture is that the church was deliberately built on a slope to allow the choir to be higher than the nave. Outside, you can see places where the square tower was hit by artillery shells from the Puritan General Monk's guns in 1651.

CAMBUSKENNETH ABBEY. Around one mile east of Stirling is the ruin of this once important Augustinian abbey built on the site where the legendary Kenneth Macalpine is supposed to have defeated pagan Picts in the 9th century. The abbey was founded by King David I (1080–1153) in 1140 and was the seat of the Scottish Parliament on several occasions, the most famous of which was the parliament called by Robert the Bruce in 1326 after he was proclaimed king of the Scots by the pope in 1323. Following the Reformation, the abbey was given to the earl of Mar, who used the buildings as a quarry to enable him to build a palace in Stirling. King James III (1451–88) and his wife, Margaret of Denmark (1457–86), are buried here.

DUNBLANE CATHEDRAL, four miles north of Stirling. Although Dunblane is best known today as the site of the terrible 1996 air disaster, the town has been a center of Christian evangelism and settlement since Celtic times. King David I (1080–1153) created a bishopric here in 1150 when he built a small but very beautiful Gothic cathedral that contains an interesting 13th-century hermit's cell and a 10th-century Celtic cross. There is also a small cathedral museum. Nearby is the famed Leighton Library, the largest private collection of books in Scotland. It contains many rare works and is open to the public.

STIRLING CASTLE dominates the landscape from a rocky crag overlooking the town. It is the Scottish equivalent of Windsor Castle and at least as impressive as its better known rival, Edinburgh Castle. It is a truly majestic fortress that was a popular residence of Scottish kings. Here the young James VI (1566–1625) was educated by the Scottish Reformer and humanist, George Buchanan (1506–82).

Most of the buildings in the castle, as is to be expected, are secular. The King's Old Buildings, with a plaque commemorating the commander who defended the castle against Edward I (1239–1307), date from the 13th century. They contain the famous Argyll and Sutherland Highlanders Regimental Museum, which gives vivid insights into warfare throughout the ages. The great hall is one of the most imposing medieval secular buildings in Scotland. The facade of the Royal Palace, which was built in 1540, contains some excellent carvings, including one of King James V (1512–42) dressed in peasant clothing. The Royal Chapel, built in 1594 by James VI for the baptism of his

S

sons, contains some excellent frescoes. Other sites are the Douglas Garden, which commemorates the murder of the eighth earl of Douglas (1425–52) by King James II (1430–60). Finally, the recently reconstructed kitchens provide visitors with an insight into the eating habits of medieval nobility. The castle also provides a superb view of Stirling's city walls, which are among the best preserved medieval fortifications in Britain.

Two miles north of Stirling on a crag overlooking a ford in the river is the **WALLACE MONUMENT**. It is built on the site where William Wallace (1274–1305) camped with his army awaiting the arrival of the English before the Battle of Stirling Bridge in 1297. It was erected in 1870 and reflects the influence of the Romantic movement launched by Sir Walter Scott (1771–1832) at the turn of the century. Today it is a shrine to Scottish nationalism as reflected in films like Mel Gibson's *Braveheart* (1996). Inside the museum you can see Wallace's large broadsword and a series of busts of other Scottish heroes.

BANNOCKBURN HERITAGE CENTER, two miles south of Stirling, is the battlefield where Robert the Bruce decisively defeated the English on June 24, 1314. This battle secured Scottish freedom from English overrule for almost 300 years. The visiting center is fascinating both as a historical site and for what it tells about contemporary nationalism and the myths it creates.

STRATFORD-UPON-AVON

Was William Shakespeare (1564–1616) a closet Roman Catholic, a Puritan sympathizer, a secret atheist, or a Wiccan? All of these and many other fanciful suggestions have been made about Stratford-upon-Avon's greatest son. Whatever conclusion is reached about the man himself, there can be no doubt that Shakespeare's numerous works are steeped in Christian symbolism and deeply religious themes. Therefore, even though we may not know very much about his personal beliefs, we can learn a lot from his plays and other writings about the human condition and our relationship to both God and other people. Stratford itself is a quaint country town dominated by the sometimes tacky Shakespeare industry.

The town itself was founded by King Richard I in 1196 and is built on a medieval grid pattern. It has a number of half-timbered houses, but without Shakespeare would be quite unremarkable.

PLACES TO VISIT

HOLY TRINITY CHURCH, Church St., is a striking example of Gothic architecture. The tower and transepts are Early Gothic, while the nave and aisle are later additions. William Shakespeare was baptized here on April 26, 1564. He died on April 23, 1616, and was buried here a few days later. His grave lies on the north side of the chancel. An unusual feature of the church is the tilt of the chancel, giving the church a shape that symbolizes the way Christ's head must have fallen when he was on the cross.

SHAKESPEARE HOUSE MUSEUM, Henley St., which was owned by the poet's father and is believed to be his birthplace, contains numerous items related to his life and work. Shakespeare's father is usually said to have been a butcher, although some people say he was a glover or even a merchant.

NASH HOUSE, Chapel St., was the home of Shakespeare's granddaughter Elizabeth Hall and her husband, Thomas Nash. It contains a local history museum.

In its gardens lie the ruins of Shakespeare's New Place, which he bought after his return from London in 1611. The house itself was torn down in 1759.

HALL'S CROFT, Church St., is a restored half-timbered house, with period furniture. It was the home of Susanna, Shakespeare's daughter, whose husband was the local doctor, John Hall. The exhibition contains some interesting insights into 17th-century medical practices and beliefs.

ANN HATHAWAY'S COTTAGE, one mile west of Stratford, is the small thatched farmhouse where Shakespeare's fiancée, whom he married in 1582, lived. The pleasant garden contains numerous shrubs and herbs.

ROYAL SHAKESPEARE COMPANY THEATERS. The Main House opened in 1932, and is a large modern theater. Behind it is the Swan, opened in 1986 as an Elizabethan theater-in-the-round, and the Other Place, opened in the 1990s, where modern plays are performed. Guided tours are available to view the backstage. Tickets to performances of Shakespeare's plays must be booked well in advance.

TINTERN ABBEY

Located in the picturesque Wye valley, six miles north of Chepstow, in Wales, the ruins of this 13th-century abbey became something of a cult center for British Romantics in the early 19th century. Today, it is a site of secular pilgrimage for thousands of tourists.

PLACES TO VISIT

TINTERN ABBEY. The 236-foot-long Gothic nave and choir of this ancient Cistercian abbey, founded by Walter de Clear in 1131, lack a roof and window glass; otherwise they are remarkably intact and impressive in their simplicity. The rule of Cistercian houses was silence and simple living, making the then remote Wye valley ideally suited for this retreat from the world. The abbey was dissolved in 1536, after which time its monastic buildings were plundered for their stone and other building materials. Today, all that can be seen of them is the outline of their foundations. The abbey's great drain, which formed the backbone of its complex sewage system, is clearly visible.

It was here that the troubled William Wordsworth (1770–1850) wandered as a young man, and the site is the subject of one of his most famous poems, "Lines Composed a Few Miles Above Tintern Abbey."

Other Romantics, like the painter Joseph Turner (1775–1851), found the abbey equally fascinating and inspiring. Apart from enjoying its innate beauty, anyone wanting to understand the Romantic movement and its more recent developments needs to visit Tintern.

WELLS

The quiet market town of Wells is technically a city, the smallest in Britain, because it is the seat of a bishop. Although there is little else to see other than a pleasant market place and numerous quaint houses, a visit to Wells is unforgettable because of the majesty of its 13th-century cathedral.

PLACES TO VISIT

WELLS CATHEDRAL was founded as the church of St. Andrews in 704 by King Ine of Wessey and elevated to the status of a cathedral in 909. The Normans pulled down the earlier church to build one of the most beautiful cathedrals in Europe. The magnificent west front, 150 feet high and 300 feet wide, contains over 300 13th-century sculp-

tures of saints and kings, many of which are life size. The display is crowned by a frieze of Jesus surrounded by his apostles and two six-winged cherubim. Originally brightly colored, today they are plain stone figures with a golden hue.

Once inside, the visitor is confronted by a fantastic arch that looks like a double "S" and is sometimes described as the scissor arch. It appears both in keeping with its Gothic surroundings and somehow far too modern. In fact, the arch was built as an emergency measure in 1338 by a brilliant architect intent on preventing the collapse of the central tower. In the north transept is a rare astronomical clock. Each capital and corbel in the transepts tells its own story from medieval life, including an old man with a toothache and another caught stealing. A flight of stairs approached through the door opposite the clock leads up to the splendid octagonal chapter house, where the clergy of the diocese once met with their bishop and higher clergy to discuss sacred and secular issues. In the 14th-century Lady Chapel one finds some exquisite stained glass. A breathtaking rose window lightens the main church,

and a Jesse window in the chancel illustrates the genealogy of Christ.

THE BISHOP'S PALACE, which is still the official residence of the bishop of Bath and Wells, stands beside the cathedral on its south side. It was built around 1300 with a protective moat and defensive wall. Today swans gracefully glide by in the picturesque moat. The public may enter the palace grounds through the drawbridge and enjoy the restful gardens inside.

WHITBY

Whitby was the site of a small Roman settlement, possibly a signal station given to St. Hida (d. 680), the abbess of Hartlepool, by her brother King Oswy of Northumbria to enable her to build a new abbey in 657. Seven years later it was chosen as the venue for one of the most important events in British Church history, the Synod of Whitby (664), which determined the future of Christianity in northern Europe. Prior to that time, both the Roman and Celtic rites existed throughout Britain, with the majority of churches following the indigenous Celtic rite. The Celts celebrated Easter several days later than the Roman Catholic Church, wore the tonsure differently, allowed married clergy, and put a greater emphasis on the role of hermits and monastic living. At the synod the majority of priests, and most

importantly the king of Northumbria and his nobles, were induced to adopt the Roman rite, thus bringing them within the Roman Catholic fold. This decision seems to have had an immediate effect among the higher clergy but only affected local churches very slowly. Thus Celtic ways seem to have continued in one form or another until at least the 10th century in many parts of northern Britain.

The town of Whitby, which is one of the most picturesque villages in England, grew up around a harbor on the banks of the river Esk. Above the town stood the abbey, which was sacked by Vikings in 867 and does not seem to have been rebuilt, although there are signs that some sort of community continued to exist in the area for some time after the Viking raid. The Normans refounded the abbey in 1078. The

W

subsequent history of Whitby is unexceptional. During the 18th century, Whitby became a center of the whaling trade. The town was bombarded by a German battle cruiser during World War I, making it one of the very few towns in England attacked by the Germans.

Captain James Cook (1728–79) was born a few miles outside of Whitby and served his apprenticeship in the town. The ships on which he made his voyages of exploration were built in the local dockyard, and a statue of him overlooks the town from the west cliff. Elizabeth Gaskell (1810–65) used the town as the setting for her novel *Sylvia's Lovers* (1863), renaming it "Monkshaven," while Bram Stoker (1847–1912) brought Count *Dracula* (1897) to Whitby during a storm, when the count's ship took refuge in the harbor and he fled to St. Mary's graveyard. Today the Dracula connection has made Whitby a center for the Gothic subculture, to the annoyance of most local people.

PLACES TO VISIT

WHITBY ABBEY. On the top of the cliff overlooking the town was a Saxon institution, known as a "double house" because it housed both men and women, which was completely razed by the Vikings. Today nothing remains of the original foundation, which was located a short distance from the present ruins. The current ruins stand at the top of a 200-foot cliff overlooking the sea and belong to the Norman abbey built between 1220 and 1320. The stone walls and surviving traceries show that the church was very well built, probably by the same craftsmen as those who built Rievaulx. It was destroyed after the Dissolution, when, like so many historic churches, it became the local quarry. In the 19th century, interest in the abbey revived, and today it is a well preserved part of England's heritage.

Caedmon (658–80), the first known poet in the English language, was one of the lay brothers in the abbey. According to tradition, he was in charge of St. Hilda's pigs. Nine lines of what was his great poem, the *Song of Creation,* have survived. Outside St. Mary's Church, a large cross commemorates his life and work.

ST. MARY'S CHURCH is reached after climbing 199 steps to the top of the cliff near the abbey ruins. It is a Romanesque building, modified in the 17th and 18th centuries, but left intact by the Victorians, who uncharacteristically made no changes to the interior. It contains quaint box pews and a triple-deck pulpit, giving visitors an insight into the way most churches looked after the Reformation and before the Victorians "improved" most other church interiors. Today the only internal illumination is still provided by either the windows or candles.

CAPTAIN COOK MEMORIAL MUSEUM, Grape Lane, tells the story of Captain James Cook (1728–79) who, between

1746 and 1749, was apprenticed to a local Quaker, John Walker. Cook later became famous as an explorer.

WHITBY MUSEUM, Pannett Park, has more about Captain Cook and Whitby's links to the sea as well as information on the abbey and other local history.

CAPTAIN COOK MUSEUM, Ormsby, 28 miles west, is a very good museum built near the house where Cook was born. It illustrates his naval career and numerous exploits. Anyone wishing to understand the Age of Discovery that gave birth to the modern missionary movement would do well to visit this informative exhibition.

WINCHESTER

Winchester was the site of an Iron Age hill fort and the early British settlement known as Gwent. The town itself, however, was founded by the Romans in 43 as Venta Bulgarum. The Saxon town of Wintanceaster was founded in 519, and the king of Wessex, Cenwall, Cenwalth, or Cenwalh (7th century), built a church here between 634 and 648. It was elevated to cathedral status in 662 with Birinus as its first bishop. Subsequently, Winchester became the capital of Wessex, and then in 829 the capital of the whole of England with the coronation of King Egbert (d. 839). Alfred the Great (849–99) made Winchester one of his garrison towns, known as a fortified borough, as part of his defense system aimed at repulsing Danish invasions. It was his capital, main military base, largest town, and the center of both his educational and evangelistic endeavors.

Recognizing its symbolic importance, William the Conqueror (1027–87) had himself crowned both in London's Wesminster Abbey and in Winchester Cathedral. To the southwest of the old city, he built one of his famed castles to subdue the local population. After 1070 he also built a new cathedral, symbolizing the spiritual dominance of the Normans over their Saxon subjects. William employed local monks to compile his famous *Doomsday Book,* cataloging the wealth of England. Henry III (1207–72) and Archbishop Stephen Langton (1150–1228) lifted the ban of excommunication on King John (1167–1216) in 1213 outside the doors of the cathedral. Later, in 1215, he sided with the barons against King John and signed the Magna Carta. This act led the pope to depose him, although he was reinstated in 1218.

During the 12th century William of Wykeham (1324–1404), who was bishop of Winchester from 1367–1404 and the chancellor of England (a post similar to that of the modern prime

W

minister), once more made Winchester a seat of learning when he founded Winchester College in 1382. It was intended to provide education to 70 poor scholars who would go on to study at New College, Oxford, which he founded in 1379. Another bishop of Winchester, William of Waynflete (1395–1486), who was also lord chancellor, followed his predecessor's example by founding Magdalen College, Oxford, in 1458. Despite the efforts of these and similar dynamic churchmen, Winchester slowly declined in importance as London increasingly dominated English trade and government and became the favored royal residence.

The Norman castle was destroyed during the English Civil War after a long siege, and the cathedral was badly damaged as victorious Parliamentarian troops looted the city. As a reward for its support of the Royalist cause, Charles II favored Winchester following the Restoration and employed Sir Christopher Wren (1632–1723) to build a palace for him in the city. This was never completed due to Charles's death. The later history of Winchester is fairly uneventful. Today it is a quiet country town with a famous cathedral, famous school (Winchester College), and extensive archaeological excavations. Both Izaak Walton (1593–1683), the author of *The Complete Angler* (1653), and Jane Austen (1775–1817), who died at 8 College Street, were residents of the town.

PLACES TO VISIT

WINCHESTER CATHEDRAL is an impressive Romanesque building. Founded by Bishop Walkelin in 1079 and consecrated in 1093, it was extended by Bishop Godfrey de Lucy between 1189–1204 in the Early Gothic style. The west front was built by Bishop Edington between 1346 and 1366, and the whole building was renovated by William of Wykeham (1324–1404), who created a beautiful Gothic nave, splendid windows, and a chantry. The Chapel of the Holy Sepulcher, off the north transept, still contains 13th-century wall paintings. The 13th-century Lady Chapel also has wall paintings and a fine seven-paned window. King Canute (995–1035) and various preconquest kings are buried behind the high altar. The grave of King Rufus (d. 1100), regarded as particularly "ungodly" in an ungodly age, can be seen under the tower in the presbytery. Officially he was killed in a hunting accident in the New Forest, although many historians believe that he was actually assassinated. The tomb of St. Swithun (800–862) lies in a Norman crypt that can only be visited in the summer months, if then. It is closed most of the year due to flooding. Originally, St. Swithun, a Saxon evangelist, was buried in the churchyard. When he was reinterred inside the cathedral's crypt on July 15, 961, against his express wishes, legend tells how it

W

rained for 40 days until the crypt was flooded. The crypt also contains a 14th-century statue of William of Wykeham (1324–1404). In the north aisle lies Jane Austen's (1775–1817) tomb. One of the first major women novelists and the daughter of a clergyman, her works, like *Pride and Prejudice,* are grounded in acute observation of human weakness and her deep, but unassuming, Christian faith.

In the cathedral library there are numerous ancient manuscripts and the famous 12th-century Winchester Bible, which is a richly bound illuminated manuscript. To the south of the cathedral proper are a few monastic buildings left over from the Middle Ages. These include the 14th-century deanery, which was originally the prior's residence, and the pilgrim's hall, which today houses part of the cathedral's choir school, and has the oldest known hammer-beam roof in England and possibly Europe.

HOSPITAL OF ST. CROSS. One mile south of the cathedral through peaceful meadows is the oldest charitable hospital in England. It was founded in 1136 by Bishop Henry de Blois. Cardinal Beaufort extended the buildings and added an almshouse in 1445. Anthony Trollope's (1815–82) novel *The Warden* (1855) is set here. It is based on the real life abuse of hospital funds by Francis North, the son of the bishop of Winchester and warden of the hospital.

CHAPEL OF ST. CROSS, within the hospital complex, was built in 1160 and represents the transitional style between late Romanesque and Early Gothic architecture. In its Lady Chapel is a superb 15th-century Flemish triptych, dated 1530.

THE CASTLE HALL is the only remaining part of the Norman castle, which was demolished by the victorious Parliamentarians in 1641. A large round oak table, 18 feet in diameter, hangs on its west wall. According to local tradition, this is the original Round Table belonging to King Arthur (5th century) and his knights. It is decorated with a list of the knight's names and a Tudor Rose, which gave the Tudor dynasty an excuse to claim decent from the most famous of all English kings. It was decorated in 1522 to impress the visiting Emperor Charles V (1500–1558). Unfortunately, the table is not mentioned in written records until the 14th century, making it highly unlikely that it ever belonged to the real Arthur, who seems to have been an English warlord in post-Roman Britain. On a more tragic note, it was here that Sir Walter Raleigh (1552–1618) was tried and heard his death sentence in 1603 on a trumped-up charge of treason. He was executed 14 years later after being held as a prisoner in the Tower of London. Judge Jeffreys, the hanging judge, held one of his Bloody Assizes here after Monmoth's Rebellion in 1685; he sentenced numerous men to a gruesome death.

WINCHESTER COLLEGE is the most famous of all English public (private)

W

schools. Contrary to its original founder's intent, which was to provide opportunities for poor people, it is the preserve of the most wealthy members of the English elite, known as "Wyke-hamists." The main gateway and court are 14th century. The chapel has some of the earliest examples of fan vaulting in England and also boasts original choir stalls and exquisitely carved misericords. The main school building, in red brick, was built between 1683 and 1687. A 16th-century portrait of the founder, William of Wykeham (1324–1404), hangs in the hall on the south side of the original 14th-century college buildings.

YORK

York originated as an ancient British settlement of the Brig-antian tribes. It was occupied by Roman legions under the leadership of Petillius Cerialis, the nephew of the Emperor Vespasian, who in 71 turned it into the capital of the north province of Britain and headquarters of the Ninth Legion. Emperor Hadrian (76–138) visited York in 121, while two other emperors, Septimius Severus (d. 211) and Constantius Chlorus (d. 306), both died in the city. Constantine the Great (724–337), the son of Constantius Chlorus, was proclaimed emperor in 306 in York. After the withdrawal of the legions in 407, York became the Saxon town of Eoforwic and eventually the capital of the pagan kingdom of Northumbria. The Northumbrian king, Edwin (585–633), converted to Christianity and was baptized in 627 by Bishop Paulinus. Subsequently, York became the center of the 8th-century renaissance of Christian scholarship. It was in York that Alcuin (735–804) trained and taught before being recruited by Charlemagne (742–814) to establish a system of schools throughout his domain in what are now parts of Germany and France.

The city was sacked by the Vikings in 866. They settled in the city, made it a major trading center, and named it Jorvik. The Normans conquered York in 1066, and William the Conqueror built two castles in the city indicating its strategic importance and the reluctance with which its citizens accepted Norman rule. As in so many other places, the Normans pulled down the existing cathedral, which they rebuilt. Throughout the Middle Ages until the 15th century, the city thrived on the Yorkshire wool trade, with over 40 churches and a population of around 10,000 by the year 1200.

The city walls and gates were built between the 12th and 14th centuries when York was the provincial capital of northern England. The Plantagenet dynasty favored York, with both Henry II and Edward II holding parliaments in the city, while Edward III was married in York Minster. The title of "duke of York" was now conferred on the monarch's eldest son.

As the city prospered, numerous religious houses were established in the area and various pilgrimage centers grew up around the minster. The medieval guilds that controlled York's lucrative wool trade supported these institutions. They also established the York Mystery Plays, which are still performed on a regular cycle every four years.

Following the end of the War of the Roses (1453–87) and the establishment of Tudor rule, the city's fortunes waned. General Fairfax (1612–71), a local man, defeated the Royalist army at the Battle of Marston Moor in 1644, leading the citizens of York to surrender their city to parliamentary forces. During the 18th century, the city experienced a building boom as many local landowners made York their city home. York was spared most of the ravages of the Industrial Revolution, although it did become the center of the Great North-Eastern Railway in the 19th century. The Christian chocolate manufacturing company, Rowntree, which is now owned by the Nestlé group, also built a factory here in the 19th century. York escaped serious bombing during World War II and is today a small country town rich in his-

tory. A "new" university was founded in York during the 1960s.

Margaret Clitherow (1556–86), canonized in 1970 as St. Margaret of York, lived in York in the 16th century, as did another Roman Catholic, the conspirator Guy Fawkes (1570–1606). He attempted to blow up the Protestant Parliament on November 5, 1605. His failed mission provided English children with their equivalent of Halloween, Guy Fawkes Night, when bonfires are lit and fireworks set off amid a party atmosphere. The poet W. H. Auden (1907–73) was born in York, while the famous 18th-century highway man, Dick Turpin (d. 1739), was hanged here in 1739.

PLACES TO VISIT

YORK MINSTER originated as a small wooden church erected for the baptism of King Edwin and his courtiers on Easter Day 627. Eventually, a grander stone chapel replaced the wooden building. It was dedicated to St. Peter to emphasize the close links between the English church and Rome following the Synod of Whitby in 664. This stone chapel was destroyed by the Normans following the conquest. Thomas of Bayeux oversaw the building of the first Norman church in 1080. The choir was rebuilt between 1154 and 1181 by Bishop Roger of Pont-l'Evêque. During his tenure as archbishop, from 1215–55, Walter de Gray replaced the south transept and began

Y

reconstruction of the north transept, a task which was completed in 1260, five years after his death. A new nave was built between 1291 and 1345, while the choir was replaced between 1360 and 1405. The magnificent west front was completed between 1430 and 1470 in the French Gothic style, and the chapter house added around 1300. The west tower was added in 1471 and the central tower in 1480. A serious fire damaged the choir in 1829, and another destroyed parts of the nave in 1840. In 1960 it was discovered that the central tower was in danger of imminent collapse. Therefore, extensive restoration work involving new concrete foundations was undertaken. In 1984 the minster was struck by lightning, and part of the south transept's roof was destroyed. Cynics joked that the angels had got the date wrong and that God intended to strike the church a week earlier during the installation ceremonies of Archbishop David Jenkins (1927–). Although skeptical to the point of questioning the Virgin Birth and other fundamental Christian doctrines, Jenkins, who is an able philosopher, is well liked by the clergy.

After the archbishop of Canterbury, the bishop of York is the most important Anglican cleric in Britain. The official title of the archbishop of Canterbury is "archbishop of all England," that of the archbishop of York, "archbishop of England." Although the cathedral has the title "Minster," which normally refers to the church in a monastery, York Cathedral was never a monastic institution. Therefore, it lacks cloisters and similar buildings intended for use by monks.

Following its numerous renovations, York Minster became the largest Gothic church north of the Alps and the biggest medieval church in England. It has a length of 534 feet and a breadth of 249 feet across the transepts. The height of the central vault is 90 feet, while the tower is 198 feet high.

The choir screen dates from the 15th century and contains statues of various English kings from William the Conqueror (1027–87) onwards. In the south transept is the tomb of the present building's creator, Walter de Gray (1215–55).

The minster's stained glass represents the largest collection of medieval glass in England and was created by a school of local craftsmen. Many believe that the minster's windows contain about half of all the surviving medieval stained glass in England. The oldest complete window is the five star or sisters window in the north transept, dating from 1255, although some of the glass in the second bay window of the north aisle is believed to date to 1155. In the south transept there is a 16th-century rose window created to celebrate the marriage of Henry Tudor, Henry VII of Lancaster (1457–1509), to Elizabeth of York (1466–1503), thus ending the destructive War of the Roses.

The west window was created for Archbishop William de Merton in 1339. Its heart-shaped upper tracery is known as the "heart of Yorkshire." The great east window was created between 1405 and 1408 by John Thornton, an artist from Coventry, and is the largest medieval stained-glass window in the world. It depicts the story of Creation, the Fall, Redemption, and Last Judgment. There is a Jesse window, depicting the family tree of Jesus, from 1310, and a window in the transept bay that illustrates the lives of saints Cuthbert (634–87) and William of York (d. 1154). A 400-year old astronomical clock can also be seen in the north transept, which is decorated with carvings of kings and knights.

The crypt is the oldest part of the church, with Romanesque columns and a musky smell. According to tradition, probably true, its baptismal font stands on the site where Edwin (585–633) was baptized. For a small fee you can also visit the Foundation Museum, created in 1967, which contains fascinating exhibits from Roman times to the most recent renovations. The Minster Treasury, beyond the museum, has an extensive collection of items, including the Horn of Ulf, presented to the minster by King Canute (994–1035) or one of his family in the 11th century. Outside the minster, opposite the south transept, is a Roman column, which stands on the site of the headquarters of the Ninth Legion.

ST. MICHAEL-LE-BELFREY is a Late Gothic church with some magnificent stained-glass windows. Guy Fawkes (1570–1606) was born nearby, in what is now Young's Hotel in Petergate, and was baptized in the church on April 6, 1570.

HOLY TRINITY, Goodramgate, is a 13th-century Gothic church with 17th-century box pews and an east window dating from 1470.

NATIONAL RAILWAY MUSEUM, Leeman Rd., is a modern pilgrimage site for railway enthusiasts and very well worth a visit by anyone interested in the revolution in transport that created the modern world. Here are 50 locomotives (the first of which was built in 1829), including the *Mallard,* which reached a speed of 129 mph, making it the fastest steam train in the world.

THE CITY WALLS are the original 14th-century walls, 2.5 miles long. They completely enclose the old city, making a very pleasant and interesting walk that gives visitors a vivid impression of medieval life. The Goodramgate contains a small museum devoted to the life of Richard III (1452–85), who was forever condemned by Shakespeare in his famous play. The museum raises the question of whether Shakespeare was indeed telling the truth or simply presenting Tudor propaganda.

YORK CASTLE MUSEUM contains a collection of items depicting local history, including a rare Viking helmet discovered during excavations.

Y

CLIFFORD'S TOWER is a site of pilgrimage for Jewish visitors. It was built between 1250 and 1275 on the site of an earlier wooden keep erected by William the Conqueror (1027–87). Here on Saturday, March 16, 1190, a Sabbath, over 150 Jews, led by Rabbi Yom To of Joigny, fled for protection against a raging mob that had been incited by rumors that the Jews had kidnapped several Christian children whom they planned to sacrifice as part of their Passover celebrations the following week. What happened next is unclear. Some accounts say that realizing there was no hope of escape and that death by starvation was inevitable, the community committed mass suicide. Other accounts suggest that the mob set fire to the tower, which was built of wood, killing its occupants. Still other accounts tell how the Jews were offered a safe conduct provided that they agreed to leave York, but when they left the safety of the tower they were butchered. Whatever really happened we will never know. What is certain is that the entire Jewish population of York died as the result of a pogrom and that their homes were looted by the mob.

Although this is an exceptionally evil event, the severe beating and murder of Jews was not uncommon in England or other parts of Europe during the Middle Ages. This type of action was often encouraged by popular preachers claiming to be acting in the name of Christ.

JORVIK VIKING CENTER, Coppergate. This modern multimedia show is hated by most guidebook writers who scorn it as a tacky reconstruction of Viking York. On the other hand, there is almost always a line to get in, and children love it.

THE SHAMBLES, off King's Square at the end of Goodramgate, is a section of medieval half-timbered houses and shops which is now a well-preserved and popular tourist attraction. Note the memorial shrine at No. 35 which commemorates Margaret Clitherow, who was lynched in 1586 for sheltering a Roman Catholic priest. She died a horrible death after being placed under planks that were then covered with piles of rocks until she was crushed to death. Her death reminds visitors that Protestants as well as Catholics were capable of the most brutal crimes in the name of religion.

YORK ARCHAEOLOGICAL CENTER is a well-thought-out exhibit that introduces visitors to the work of archaeologists. Children love getting their hands dirty while digging around and playing with bones. There are a variety of hands-on exhibits, including medieval locks, cobblers making shoes, and working spinning wheels.

ASSEMBLY ROOMS, Blake St., were built between 1732 and 1736 in the neoclassical style as the north's answer to the fashionable salons of London and the boom experienced by the Assembly Rooms in Bath. Today they house a pleasant café.

YORKSHIRE MUSEUM, Museum St., is located on the grounds of St. Mary's. There are exhibitions that change on a regular basis and a good permanent collection that outlines the history of Yorkshire and the city of York from Roman times to the present. Pride of place goes to the Middleham Jewel, which is said to be one of the best examples of medieval jewelry in England. There is also a reconstructed Roman kitchen and numerous items from the Viking age.

YORK ART GALLERY contains a good collection of paintings from as early as 1350 to the present. Its exhibits represent a broad cross section of both British and Continental art.

TREASURER'S HOUSE was the home of the treasurer of York Minster. Rebuilt in the 17th century, it was renovated 100 years later to create a grand Georgian house. It contains a good collection of period furniture, glass, pottery, and other items which give visitors an insight into the 18th century, the age of both Wesley and the Enlightenment.

SELBY ABBEY, 14 miles south. Encouraged by William the Conqueror, a Benedictine abbey was built here between 1066 and 1087. The church itself was begun in 1097 by Hugh de Lacy, the second abbot, with the Gothic nave being added in 1340. After the Dissolution, the church became a local parish church, saving it from destruction. A fire in 1906 resulted in extensive restoration work in 1909. Of particular interest are the famed Jesse tree east window and the coat of arms of the Washington family (which were the stars and stripes later incorporated into the American flag), which can be seen in the 14th-century window high above the south choir. There is also a Norman font with a richly carved 15th-century cover.

THE OLD RECTORY, 1 Rectory Road, Epworth, stands on the site of the birthplace of John (1703–91) and Charles Wesley (1707–88). Their father was the local Anglican clergyman known as a rector. This is the house in which they spent their childhood. It was erected in 1709 following a fire that destroyed the original rectory. It is now a guesthouse run by a Methodist trust.

BRONTË PARSONAGE MUSEUM, Haworth, Keighly, is found eight miles from the city of Bradford. Here one can see where the great women novelists, Charlotte (1816–55), Emily (1818–48), and Anne (1820–49) Brontë lived and worked. It is a fascinating exhibition devoted to the work of these great Christian writers.

Y

THE CHRISTIAN TRAVELERS GUIDES

> "In an era that often overlooks the significance of the past as such, and certainly the Christian past, Professor Hexham's well-crafted guides for heritage tourists truly fill a gap. Don't leave home without one!"

> —J. I. Packer, Author of *Knowing God*

By describing and interpreting the religious significance of people, places, and events in various countries, Irving Hexham illustrates the incredible impact Christianity has had on Western Civilization. Each guide is organized alphabetically according to the names of the cities and sites. The Christian Travelers Guides will help you deepen your faith by bringing to life the struggles and triumphs of great Christian leaders and common believers through the living witness of places where the saints once walked.

THE CHRISTIAN TRAVELERS GUIDE TO FRANCE
Irving Hexham, General Editor;
Written by Mark Konnert, Peter Barrs, and Carine Barrs

- Relive the experience of the Huguenots and the creators of such masterpieces as Chartes and Notre Dame.

  Softcover 0-310-22588-4

THE CHRISTIAN TRAVELERS GUIDE TO GERMANY
Irving Hexham, General Editor;
Written by Irving Hexham and Lothar Henry Kope

- Experience the church's struggle against Nazi paganism, ponder the sorrow of the Thirty Years' War, and see where the modern missionary movement was born.

  Softcover 0-310-22539-6

The Christian Travelers Guide to Great Britain

Irving Hexham, General Editor;
Written by Irving Hexham

- Come into contact with the Venerable Bede, who almost single-handedly preserved European civilization in an age of death and destruction, become a pilgrim with John Bunyan in his beloved Bedford, and see where John Wesley preached against slavery and converted thousands.

  Softcover 0-310-22552-3

The Christian Travelers Guide to Italy

Irving Hexham, General Editor;
Written by David Bershad and Carolina Mangone

- Experience a wealth of art and architecture stretching back to the early church and the age of martyrs, travel where Christians died in the arena, and see where great artists such as Michelangelo depicted unforgettable scenes of biblical truth.

  Softcover 0-310-22573-6

Pick up a copy today at your favorite bookstore!